Archaeology for Today and Tomorrow

Archaeology for Today and Tomorrow explores how cutting-edge archaeological theories have implications not only for how we study the past but also for how we think about and prepare for the future.

Ranging from how we understand migration or political leadership to how we think about violence or ecological crisis, the book argues that archaeology should embrace a "future-oriented" attitude. Behind the traditional archaeological gaze on the past is a unique and useful collection of skills, tools, and orientations for rethinking the present and future. Further, it asserts that archaeological theory is not only vital for how we conduct our work as archaeologists and how we create narratives about the past but also for how we think about the broader world in the present and, crucially, how we envision and shape the future. Each of the chapters in the book links theoretical approaches and global archaeological case studies to a specific contemporary issue. It examines such issues as human movement, violence, human and non-human relations, the Anthropocene, and fake news to showcase the critical contributions that archaeology, and archaeological theory, can make to shaping the world of tomorrow.

An ideal book for courses on archaeology in the modern world and public archaeology, it will also appeal to archaeology students and researchers in general and all those in related disciplines interested in areas of critical contemporary concern.

Craig N. Cipolla is Mellon Assistant Professor of Anthropology at Tufts University. Before moving to Massachusetts, he was Curator and Vettoretto Chair of North American Archaeology at the Royal Ontario Museum and Associate Professor of Anthropology at the University of Toronto. Author of *Becoming Brothertown*, *Archaeological Theory in the New Millennium* (with Oliver J. T. Harris, Routledge), and *Archaeological Theory in Dialogue* (with Rachel J. Crellin, Lindsay Montgomery, Oliver J. T. Harris, and Sophie Moore, Routledge), his research interests include collaborative Indigenous archaeology, historical archaeology, and archaeological theory. He currently directs the Mohegan Archaeological Field School in collaboration with the Mohegan Tribe of Connecticut.

Rachel J. Crellin is Associate Professor of Archaeology at the University of Leicester. She is the author of *Change and Archaeology* (2020, Routledge) and a co-author of *Archaeological Theory in Dialogue* (with Craig N. Cipolla, Lindsay Montgomery, Oliver J. T. Harris, and Sophie Moore, 2021, Routledge). Her research interests center on archaeological theory, especially posthumanist feminism and new materialism, Neolithic and Bronze Age Britain and Ireland, and metalwork wear analysis. She currently co-directs the *Round Mounds of the Isle of Man* fieldwork project and the Leverhulme-funded project *A New History of Bronze*.

Oliver J. T. Harris is Professor of Archaeology at the University of Leicester. He is the author of *Assembling Past Worlds* (Routledge) and the co-author of *Archaeological Theory in the New Millennium* (with Craig N. Cipolla, Routledge), *Archaeological Theory in Dialogue* (with Rachel J. Crellin, Craig N. Cipolla, Lindsay Montgomery, and Sophie Moore, Routledge), and *The Body in History* (with John Robb, CUP). He is interested in archaeological theory, the philosophy of Gilles Deleuze, and the Neolithic and Bronze Age of Britain and Ireland. He co-directs fieldwork on the Ardnamurchan Peninsula, western Scotland.

Archaeology for Today and Tomorrow

Craig N. Cipolla, Rachel J. Crellin
and Oliver J. T. Harris

Routledge
Taylor & Francis Group

LONDON AND NEW YORK

Designed cover image: Cover image from "Lapse" by Emmy Lingsheit.

First published 2024
by Routledge
4 Park Square, Milton Park, Abingdon, Oxon OX14 4RN

and by Routledge
605 Third Avenue, New York, NY 10158

Routledge is an imprint of the Taylor & Francis Group, an informa business

British Library Cataloguing-in-Publication Data
A catalogue record for this book is available from the British Library

ISBN: 978-1-032-15430-5 (hbk)
ISBN: 978-1-032-15431-2 (pbk)
ISBN: 978-1-003-24414-1 (ebk)

DOI: 10.4324/9781003244141

Typeset in Times New Roman
by Apex CoVantage, LLC

CNC: For Maya and Siany.

RJC: For the tomorrows of my nieces and nephew: Evie, Gabby, and Milo. And all my oddkin niblings—Rosa, Elena, and Kara; Samuel and Coral; Eric and Teddy; Fionn and Maeve; Thea and Jacob; Bea and Ernest; Wren and Runa; Zoe; Jesse; and Wyn.

OJTH: For the acceptable face of Stroud Labour Party— otherwise known as my Dad, Nick.

Contents

Acknowledgments   *ix*
Provocations   *xii*
List of figures   *xiv*
List of tables   *xvi*

1 Building an archaeology for today and
   tomorrow: an introduction   1

2 Archaeology and migration: more-than-human
   movements   17

3 Archaeology and capitalism: flows and desires   35

4 Leaders of the past, leaders in the future: rethinking
   power   53

5 Violence across the human/non-human divide:
   the virtual and the actual   71

6 All the world's a type: rethinking difference
   and taxonomy   89

7 How we know the past: truth as relational and
   emergent   109

8 The past as multiple: positive difference, ontological
   difference   127

9 Archaeology and the Anthropocene: futurity and affect   147

10 Building an archaeology for today and tomorrow: a conclusion   165

References cited   *180*
Index   *204*

Acknowledgments

Craig, Rachel, and Ollie would like to collectively thank all those who offered their expert comments and guidance along the way. Two anonymous peer-reviewers offered constructive feedback on our initial book proposal. Matt Gibbons, Manas Roy, and the rest of the team at Routledge provided generous support throughout the project. Funds from the University of Toronto and the Royal Ontario Museum were used to defray the cost of open access. Craig's work on the manuscript was also partially supported by a Mellon Bridge Professorship at Tufts University.

The book draws on case studies from around the world and through time, sometimes well beyond the expertise of the authors. Luckily, their colleagues offered invaluable support, taking the time to read through chapters and offer helpful feedback. This helped the authors improve the book immeasurably. The authors are grateful to the following colleagues for their support: Penny Bickle (Chapter 2), Brodhie Molloy (Chapter 3), Andrew Roddick (Chapter 4), Nathan Acebo (Chapter 5), Kiri Hagerman (Chapter 6), Zoë Crossland (Chapter 7), Stephen Mrozowski (Chapter 8), Eva Mol, Þóra Pétursdóttir, and attendees of the 2023 Material Worlds Masterclass (Chapter 9). All mistakes found within the book are, of course, the sole responsibility of the authors.

The beautiful cover image features the work of artist Emmy Lingsheit; the authors are grateful to her; the piece (titled *Lapse*) captures so many of the themes in the text. The book also benefits from an array of figures that accompany the text and a series of images that are placed before each chapter as provocations for the reader. We thank the following colleagues and friends for sharing their images with us and granting us copyright: Rachel Kiddey (Chapter 3), Noa Corcoran-Tadd (Chapter 4), Emma Dwyer and David Broshwer at MOLA (Chapter 4), Wiltshire Museum (Chapter 4), Nathan Acebo (Chapter 5), Pamela Graves (Chapter 5), Doug Bailey (Chapter 6), David Horan (Chapter 6), Kiri Hagerman (Chapter 6), Dana Lepofsky, Jennifer Carpenter, and Julia Jackley (Chapter 8), and Darryl Wilkinson (Chapter 8).

Craig, who forgets that co-authoring a book while changing jobs and moving internationally is never a good idea, is deeply indebted to many people and institutions. Without them, this book would not be possible. Without them, his many life changes could not happen. Without them, none of this would be very fun! For supporting his work on this book in various ways, Craig thanks his colleagues from the University of Toronto (St. George) Anthropology Department, the Royal Ontario Museum Anthropology Department, and, especially, the Tufts University Anthropology Department (Amahl Bishara, Alex Blanchette, Tatiana Chudakova, Sarah Luna, Zarin Machanda, Sarah Pinto, Nick Seaver, Cathy Stanton, Lauren Sullivan, Jamie Gorman, Akbota Suadabayeva). His thinking on the topics discussed in this book took shape from many conversations with his colleagues Nate Acebo, Anna Agbe-Davies, Amélie Allard, Zoë Crossland, Neal Ferris, Tiziana Gallo, Kat Hayes, Jay Levy, Diana Loren, Gavin Lucas, Lindsay Montgomery, Stephen Mrozowski, Robert Preucel, Stephen Silliman, Paulette Steeves, James Quinn, and many more, along with countless discussions with undergraduate and graduate students—both at the University of Toronto and at Tufts University. In everyday life, there is a whole other host of people to thank—for distracting him from work, for tolerating his constant archaeologizing, for making him laugh, and for much, much more: the Friday night Covid Zoom Trivia community (who got him through some very strange times), the Amesbury morning skate group, Bevilacquas, Browns, Cipollas, Fergusons, LeClairs, and Newtons. As always, Craig is grateful to his co-authors, Rachel and Ollie, for remaining open to new collaborative thinking and writing projects. He is happy, thankful, and sometimes a bit surprised that they keep including him in these efforts. Thinking together with them has been one of the more rewarding privileges of his short career. Finally, he offers special thanks to Pete, Siany, Maya, and Kelly for giving him endless love and support through book projects, through tenure cases, through successes, through failures.

Rachel always has an endless sea of people she wants to thank. She does her best thinking in collaboration with others. Therefore none of her ideas feel like they are truly singly authored: sometimes they come from dialogues, other times they come from reading, and often they come from the non-human world whilst walking Pebble along paths and cliffs, through fields and woods, and on beaches. She would like to thank her colleagues at the University of Leicester for their continuing support and, most especially, the wonderful collective that is the *Research Centre for Material Worlds Past and Present*, a place of inspiration, challenge, and collaboration. She would like to thank all the excellent colleagues she learns from and with: Jo Appleby, Seb Aycock, Huw Barton, Jo Brück, Neil Carlin, José Carvajal Lopez, Hannah Cobb, Noa Corcoran-Tadd, Brian Costello, Karina Croucher, Andrea Dolfini, Brandon Fathy, Marianne Hem Eriksen, Chris Fowler, Michelle Gamble, Mark Gillings, Jonny Graham, Nathan Gubbins, Mary Harlow, Rob Hedge, Holly Holmes, Simon James, Ben Jervis, Andy Jones, Kevin Kay, Matt Knight, Fenella Logan, Naoise Mac Sweeney, Lesley McFadyen, Andy Merrills, Eva Mol, Brodhie Molloy, Colleen Morgan, Lindsay Montgomery, Luíseach Nic Eoin, David Osborne, Þóra Pétursdóttir, Nikki Rollason, Andy Rogers, Amber Roy, Alice Samson, Sarah Scott, Irene Selsvold, Dan Stewart, Jeremy Taylor, Julian Thomas, Christina Tsoraki, and Marion Uckelmann. For distractions, context, and perspective, she thanks all the people that draw her away from work: particularly Cassia, Hannah, and Luíseach; the megathread; and everyone at Catmose Sports.

Rachel still cannot believe her luck that she gets to work with Craig and Ollie. They are the very best of co-authors: generous, kind, forgiving, challenging, collaborative, thoughtful, occasionally funny, and (most importantly) joyful. Thanks to Ellie, Maggie, Teddy, Cynthia, Kelly, Siany, Maya, and Pete for keeping Craig and Ollie whole. Huge thanks go to Rachel's family and friends on the Isle of Man, in London, and in Widnes for their constant love and support. Finally, to Dave and Pebble, for holding me together through the difficult bits and for their endless inspiration, good company, joy, and love.

Ollie is aware that his list will repeat a lot of the previous two, but repetition, as we know, is never the repetition of the same but always the repetition of difference. So thanks to everyone who makes the School of Archaeology and Ancient History at the University of Leicester, and especially the *Research Centre for Material Worlds Past and Present*, such a great place to work, including especially Jo Appleby, Huw Barton, Jose Carvajal Lopez, Brian Costello, Marianne Hem Eriksen, Brandon Fathy, Jonny Graham, Nathan Gubbins, Jan Haywood, Sarah Inskip, Ben Jervis, Kevin Kay, Andy Merrills, Brodhie Molloy, David Osborne, Andy Rogers, Alice Samson, Irene Selsvold, Dan Stewart, Jeremy Taylor, and Christina Tsoraki. Beyond Leicester, he remains indebted to the friendship and support of Hannah Cobb, Phil Richardson, and John Robb in particular, and to the wider intellectual guidance that friends across the UK and the world provide, especially Nate Acebo, Ben Alberti, Jess Beck, Brian Boyd, Zoë Crossland, Jeff Fleisher, Chris Fowler, Mark Gillings, Tim Flohr Sørensen, Art Joyce, Lesley McFadyen, Eva Mol, Colleen Morgan, Lindsay Montgomery, Paul Murtagh, Tim Pauketat, Þóra Pétursdóttir, Peter Rowley-Conwy, Julian Thomas and Darryl Wilkinson. Of particular relevance to this book, it is worth noting Ollie has learned a great deal about politics and society over the last eight years of sharing a reading group with friendly sociologists Bob Carter and Simon Dyson. It bears repeating, but writing collaborations are hard to find, and Ollie is very fortunate to find himself tagging along with people like Craig and Rachel, who are much cleverer than him if not, realistically, as funny. Beyond archaeology, the world would be a much quieter place without the more-than-human family that lives together on Howard Road in Leicester: Cynthia, Ellie, Maggie, and Teddy (which is both alphabetical and in order of appearance in his life). It would also be much less painful without the unspeakable exercise routines inflicted by Leicester Outdoor Fitness, which is compensated, just about, by everyone there being the loveliest group of friends you can possibly imagine. Last but not least, thanks to all the friends and family who make having a tomorrow something worth fighting for, but especially my Dad, Nick.

Provocations

Chapter 2   Sonoran Desert Hills. Image: Horálek, CC BY 4.0 license
             (https://creativecommons.org/licenses/by/4.0)   16
Chapter 3   Turbo Island, Bristol, 2011. Image: Neil Owen, CC 2.0
             license (https://creativecommons.org/licenses/by-sa/2.0)   34
Chapter 4   Bronze Age Knife Dagger (STHEAD.165, from Wilsford
             G56). Image: Oliver J. T. Harris, courtesy of Wiltshire
             Museum, Devises   52
Chapter 5   Fallen Christopher Columbus statue in St. Paul, Minnesota,
             June 10, 2020. Image: Tony Webster, CC BY 2.0 license
             (https://creativecommons.org/licenses/by/2.0)   70
Chapter 6   BucurestiMNIRc by Doug Bailey (Bailey et al. 2010, 91).
             Photograph copyright: Doug Bailey   88
Chapter 7   Fingerprint. Image: Metrónomo, CC BY-SA 4.0 license
             (https://creativecommons.org/licenses/by-sa/4.0)   108
Chapter 8   An Inkan Wak'a. Image: Darryl Wilkinson   126
Chapter 9   Ruins of Abandoned Building in Chernobyl After the 1986
             Nuclear Accident. Image: George Chernilevsky,
             Public domain   146
Chapter 10   Archaeology for Today and Tomorrow. Mash up by Rachel
             J. Crellin. Created from the following images: Sonoran
             Desert Hills. Image: Horálek, CC BY 4.0 license (https://
             creativecommons.org/licenses/by/4.0); Turbo Island,
             Bristol 2011. Image: Neil Owen, CC 2.0 license (https://
             creativecommons.org/licenses/by-sa/2.0); Fingerprint.
             Image: Metrónomo, CC BY-SA 4.0 license (https://
             creativecommons.org/licenses/by-sa/4.0); Anti-Capitalist
             Message. Image: Craig N. Cipolla; Monolith from
             Tiwanaku. Image: SodaCan CC by 4.0 license (https://
             creativecommons.org/licenses/by-sa/4.0); Empty pedestal.
             Image: Caitlin Hobbs CC 3.0 license (https://creativecom
             mons.org/licenses/by/3.0); Arrowheads. Image: Peter

Reavill, Birmingham Museums Trust via Creative
Commons 2.0 license (https://creativecommons.org/
licenses/by/2.0); Painting of Sky Woman by Ernest Smith
(Tonowanda Seneca Nation). Image: Ernest Smith, Public
domain; A rubber duck from a rubber duck race on the
river Liffey in Ireland in 2006 washed up on the shores
of the Isle of Man in 2022. Image: Kevin Rothwell, Duck
number 26845, Derbyhaven, Isle of Man, CC BY-SA 2.0
license (https://creativecommons.org/licenses/by-sa/2.0/)   164

Figures

1.1	NODAPL protest	2
1.2	Fieldwork underway in western Scotland	6
2.1	Vanuatu map	20
2.2	Map of North Atlantic. Arrow shows the direction of Norse expansion	22
2.3	The spread of the Linearbandkeramik; dark is the early phase, light is the later phase	24
2.4	Leonardo da Vinci's Vitruvian Man	27
3.1	Anti-capitalist message	36
3.2	Materials abandoned by mainstream capitalism (a pizza box) re-purposed to form a bed for a person experiencing homelessness	46
4.1	The northwest corner of the Akapana at Tiwanaku	57
4.2	Monolith from Tiwanaku	59
4.3	Plan of Andover Airfield	65
5.1	Iconoclasm to the faces and some of the hands of saints on the rood screen of Great Snoring parish church, Norfolk, England	77
5.2	Edward Colston statue on display in the M Shed Museum in Bristol	78
5.3	Empty pedestal. The empty plinth after the Colston statue was removed	79
5.4	The archaeological site of Puhú	83
6.1	A cabinet of curiosity, Natural History Museum of Ole Worm, Museum Wormiani Historia Engraving Museum Wormianum Published: 1655	90
6.2	The interior of the Pitt Rivers Museum, Oxford. Objects are organized by type and boxed into separate cabinets	90
6.3	Two barbed and tanged arrowheads—the one on the left is close to perfect, and the one on the right is lacking a barb	96
6.4	Teotihuacan, Mexico	100
6.5	Middle and Late Formative gynomorphic sexual attributes from Huixtoco (top row) and Axotlan (middle row), and Terminal Formative gynomorphs from Teotihuacan (bottom row.)	101

7.1   Donald Trump's inauguration   110
7.2   Emily Banfield records the beads of a jet necklace *in situ*   112
7.3   The Great Sphinx of Ghiza   121
8.1   Painting of Sky Woman by Ernest Smith (Tonowanda
       Seneca Nation)   135
8.2   Map of Northwest Coast showing key landscapes studied (black
       dots) collaboratively with three communities (grey dots)   140
8.3   A chief, his wife, and son who were turned to stone during the
       flooding of Hauyat   141
9.1   Healthcare workers die-in at the front of the Victoria Parliament,
       Melbourne, Australia. From Day 1 of Extinction Rebellion's
       Autumn Rebellion 2021   148
9.2   A rubber duck from a rubber duck race on the river Liffey in
       Ireland in 2006 washed up on the shores of the Isle of Man in 2022 151

Tables

1.1   Roadmap of key themes, theoretical tools, and case studies for
      each chapter   13

Chapter 1

Building an archaeology for today and tomorrow

An introduction

Introduction: water is life, but what does archaeology have to do with it?

In late 2016, conflicts over the Dakota Access Pipeline (hereafter DAPL), an underground oil pipeline on and around the Standing Rock Reservation in North Dakota, boiled over into violence (Estes 2019) (see Figure 1.1). Police and other state officials attacked water protectors[1] using a potentially deadly combination of pepper spray, water cannons, and police dogs. The broader tensions that led to these attacks extend back to the beginning of settler colonialism in North America; these specific conflicts in 2016 were aggressive reactions to the #noDAPL movement which, after months of peaceful protest, began to hinder the pipeline's construction. An Indigenous-led movement, #noDAPL stood against the $3.8 billion, 1,700-plus mile pipeline project in the name of environmental and social justice. This resistance movement was about maintaining access to clean water on the Standing Rock Reservation but concerned more than just that (Estes 2019; cf. Kiddey 2017). This local conflict was global in scope; it involved issues that affect all peoples' futures regarding the commodification of nature, colonialism, environmental crisis, and the vast social asymmetries of late capitalism. The DAPL is one example in a world teeming with crises—social, environmental, political, and more. Extinctions. Climate crisis. Migrants drowning. Collapsing economies. Cost of living crises. There is no shortage of real-world contemporary problems.

What does archaeology have to do with the #noDAPL movement and the global issues to which it relates? How can archaeology help address our current environmental crises, the ongoing pernicious violence of settler colonialism, and the ways that late capitalism commodifies and threatens particularly vulnerable groups of humans, like the people of Standing Rock? There are many impactful ways to address these problems. You might financially support activists and charities, write to political leaders, vote, teach young people, make your consumption more thoughtful, or engage in activism and protest. With so many possible ways to act, where does this leave archaeology, or more to the point, a book about archaeology that places special emphasis on, of all things, theory?

DOI: 10.4324/9781003244141-1

Figure 1.1 NODAPL protest.

Image: Pax Ahimsa Gethen, CC BY-SA 4.0 license (https://creativecommons.org/licenses/by-sa/4.0).

Archaeological theory is usually understood as perhaps the most esoteric and "ivory tower" element of the discipline. Wrapped in debates that pitch obscure philosophers against one another or that deploy legions of jargon-infused articles, it can seem obscure. We would be the first to acknowledge that theory can often seem bamboozling to the uninitiated. Yet, as explored later in this chapter, we also argue that theory is always present in archaeology *regardless* of whether we recognize it explicitly or not (Harris and Cipolla 2017; Johnson 2020). Theory here isn't simply the discussions that exist between academics; it is the fundamental approach we take to archaeology. It is the preconceptions, assumptions, and concepts that we bring to bear and use in our engagements with the past. In this book, we suggest that some of the concepts at play in contemporary archaeology have a great deal to offer us in wrestling with the political issues and concerns that shape the world of today and, indeed, of tomorrow. If we, as archaeologists, want to deal with the issues raised by the #noDAPL movement, we need archaeological theory.

Nick Estes' (2019) book, *Our History is the Future*, contextualizes the #noDAPL movement in terms of a history of Indigenous resistance against colonial, genocidal violence. His work bears witness to the violence and injustices of settler colonialism, highlighting many forms of Indigenous activism and resilience. The history that Estes maps is a history of relations between people, water, buffalo, and much more that were violently disrupted by settler colonialism. It is a history of communities rather than individuals. And, in our reading of Estes' work, it is a chronicle of Indigenous histories that offers important new ways to rethink the future of all people. Inspired by the work of Estes and many others, we seek a future-oriented approach to archaeology. This book asks what archaeology brings to the table and how it can be involved in reshaping the worlds of today and tomorrow. It also asks about the role of theory in creating better futures.

Nevertheless, here we must heed the warning of education scholars Eve Tuck and K. Wayne Yang (2012) and remember that the challenges we face are not simply about academic debate; as they put it, decolonization is not a metaphor. Their argument is about the use of the term decolonization, but it applies, more broadly, to any academic discussion of social justice; the notion that you can "free your mind and the rest will follow" (Tuck and Yang 2012, 19) does not chart a clear path to changing colonial structures and could result in simply reifying structural inequalities—a surface change that maintains academic business-as-usual but with new decolonial language. The task of earnestly connecting archaeology and social, political, and environmental justice in the present while devoting oneself to real change seems monumental and—let's be honest here—quite possibly delusional. On the one hand, we have #noDAPL, water protection, the commodification of places and people in the name of capitalism, and genocidal colonial violence. On the other hand, we have the discipline of archaeology, its colonial history and status, and the ivory-tower reputation of archaeological theory. How can we bridge this impasse?

A book like this could never—obviously—be the sole answer to the many troubles of our current world, especially when considering the positionality of the writers. Instead, we offer the book as a small piece in a much wider puzzle. We see it as a stepping stone, amongst many, leading down a winding future path towards new versions of our discipline that are always emerging. The DAPL and the violent attacks on its protesters did not sit well with many peoples across the globe. There was discomfort for all the people who participated directly in this resistance movement, for those who supported it indirectly or simply agreed with it, and even for those who passively followed the news coverage. Of course, there are many people who felt this discomfort in direct, material ways—for instance, those living on the Standing Rock Reservation, those who suffered directly from police violence, those whose ancestors fought hard for treaty rights ignored by the US government, and those who experience the day-to-day and long-term ramifications of a lack of access to clean water. We, the authors, have not experienced any of these things. In consideration of these important differences, we must tread carefully to avoid overstating the mission of this book, but we must also remember that archaeology and archaeological theory are not separate from the "real world" problems introduced here.

Then what are the connections? Like many others, we see archaeology, even academic versions of it, as part of the world, not just a way of describing and commenting on it. This means that it would be irresponsible for its practitioners to falsely sever those connections and pretend that archaeology is not part of our present context, part of our problems, and, at least potentially, part of the solutions to those problems. We conduct our research and write with continued awareness of the privilege involved in practicing archaeology and in working at universities. We are also aware of the differences that our work makes (or fails to make) in the broader world, regardless of our specific intentions. For us, it is important to write not with assumptions that we have complete and god-like understanding of other peoples' positionalities but with empathy, care, and open minds (cf. Supernant et al. 2020). We listen, we write, and then we listen some more. We aim to write archaeologies that make differences that extend beyond the world of archaeologists, field sites, universities, or museums. This book, by itself, is not decolonization, transformation, or restorative justice, but our work does not preclude these things. We hope that at least some readers might view this as a positive step in these complex and drawn-out processes. This is a book about how thinking like an archaeologist can transform our conceptual tools and, with that, contribute to changing the possible futures we can imagine and work towards.

Archaeology: always political, always in the present

What does it mean to take a future-oriented approach to our subject? What does it mean, to take our book's key theme, to make an archaeology for *today and tomorrow*? We suggest that there are critical ways that we can develop this question through an engagement with archaeological theory. As we have already noted, this might seem a world away from the real, on-the-ground concerns of people trying to stop an oil pipeline or to address the many legacies of settler colonialism. Nonetheless, we suggest that an approach to archaeology that situates itself in contemporary theoretical concerns can do much to address recent "real world" concerns and struggles. We see theory as ubiquitous in all forms of archaeology regardless of how much notice practitioners take. To avoid or ignore theory simply allows it to do its work lurking in the shadows. For us, theory is a way, first and foremost, of situating our knowledge and recognizing its limitations. Theory offers a means of thinking differently, helping to identify and challenge aspects of our world that we take for granted. In the twenty-first century, theory offers an important means of continuing to raise our awareness of ethnocentrism, Western[2] defaults, and the continued privileging of only certain forms of humanity. Theory is a key part of the processes that are often labeled "decolonization" in universities (but see Tuck and Yang 2012). Archaeological theory, by itself, is insufficient, but an archaeological engagement with present and past case studies, which is rooted in a cutting-edge, critical, but productive theoretical perspective, can demonstrate its relevance to the challenges facing the world today.

One of the critical reasons that archaeological theory remains so vital to the way our engagements with the past impact on the present is that the theories we work with are thoroughly and inevitably political. This has long been acknowledged by archaeologists. Bruce Trigger (1984) explored how archaeology emerged in relation to differing forms of nationalist, colonialist, and imperialist agendas. Joan Gero and Margaret Conkey (1991) demonstrated that archaeology is always written from a specific standpoint (cf. Haraway 1988; Harding 2004), highlighting the sexist nature of archaeology as a discipline and critiquing the androcentric (male-centered) narratives it produces. Michael Shanks and Christopher Tilley linked theory and politics explicitly in their twin 1987 books. They set out how processual archaeology, which argued for a positivist and scientifically oriented approach to the past, could provide support for capitalism (Shanks and Tilley 1987a, 48–9; see also Chapter 3 of this book), how forms of cultural hegemony shape our encounters with the past, and how, more generally, power relations in the discipline rendered all theoretical approaches fundamentally political (1987b, Chapter 7). They argued that:

> archaeology is an active production of the past, an intellectual and cultural labor. Archaeology is to be situated in the present as discourse in a political field, and as a practice located in relation to structures of power.
>
> (Shanks and Tilley 1987b, 186)

More recently, work by Whitney Battle-Baptiste (2011), Kathleen Sterling (2015), and others (e.g., Flewellen et al. 2021; Franklin et al. 2020) articulates the relationship between archaeology and racism, highlighting the potential of Black Feminist standpoints for crafting radically different pasts (see Chapter 8).

What these archaeologists, and feminist standpoint theory (Harding 2004) more broadly, teach us is that whenever you write a piece of archaeology, you do not do it from a detached, neutral position devoid of politics. You are not cut off from the world that you are writing about or the present in which you find yourself. Our writing is always shaped by who we are, our race, gender, sexuality, class, and more. The feminist philosopher Donna Haraway (1988, 584) makes this clear; we do not write from a position that is separate from the world, somehow above it, able to view the past from a detached location—the view from *nowhere* as she calls it. Nor, to quote her again, are we able to write from any position we choose—the view from *everywhere* (Haraway 1988, 584). Instead, we always write from somewhere, and our locations and perspectives are shaped by those specific orientations and sensibilities (Crellin et al. 2021). In other words, our knowledge is *always* situated (Haraway 1988).

Recent engagements with thinking from science and technology studies, such as the work of Bruno Latour (1999, 2005), and with posthumanist thinking, particularly the work of Karen Barad (2007), have pushed this argument further. Not only are archaeologists entangled in the interpretations they produce, but they are also thoroughly caught up in the production of the data they interpret; data emerges from entanglements between people, microscopes, trowels, buckets, cameras, and isotopes (e.g., Cobb and Croucher 2020; Crellin and Harris 2020; Fowler 2013a; Tsoraki et al. 2020) (see Figure 1.2). Furthermore, archaeology is not just something produced by the interpreting human at the "trowel's edge" (Hodder 1999). It is not an endeavor we begin alone; instead, as Hodder (1999) argued, practical archaeology is always teamwork (see also Cobb and Croucher 2020). We work with and alongside others in the present. Archaeology as a process emerges from the combination of many human hands and many more non-humans. Theory, data, human perspectives, and non-human contributions cannot be disentangled (Pétursdóttir and Olsen 2018). Archaeology is written and produced through collaborations in the present, and the people in those collaborations are thoroughly and inseparably entangled in the present with all its problems and politics.

Figure 1.2 Fieldwork underway in western Scotland.
Image: Oliver J. T. Harris.

Thus, archaeology is always political and always written from somewhere, but it is also always theoretical. There is nowhere from which archaeology escapes theory: from the work we do in the field (Cobb et al. 2012) to our teaching in the classroom (Cobb and Croucher 2020); from the first essay we write as a student to the closing pages of our final book; from public-facing outreach to how media companies repackage and resell our research. The centrality of theory is a standard claim of any introduction to archaeological thought (e.g., Chapman 2023; Harris and Cipolla 2017; Johnson 2020; Lucas 2023), and it remains absolutely and vitally true. This recognition that theory is ubiquitous means we cannot limit theory to the cut-off realms of the ivory tower. Theory is something with which all archaeologists need to wrestle. And this includes those archaeologists who seek to make a real and explicit difference to the world in which we find ourselves today, as much as it does to anyone asking the most esoteric questions imaginable of the distant past. This also means that those of us who remain committed to the essential and unavoidable nature of archaeological theory need to continue to try and convince the rest of the discipline of its centrality and to communicate that in as many different and accessible ways as possible.

Making a difference: mapping different future-oriented archaeologies

Before we get to our own perspectives on what a theoretically centered and future-oriented archaeology might look like, we must first set out the broader disciplinary context for our project. As we have seen, we are certainly not the first archaeologists to declare that archaeology is always political, theoretical, or written in the present. Nor are we the first to ask what our discipline might contribute to the wider problems facing the world today. Here we outline five related but distinctive strands of future-oriented thought in archaeology.

One of the long-standing ways archaeologists have argued for the contemporary relevance of their discipline is by suggesting that information from the past can help us understand the challenges that we face in the present. This is our first strand; we refer to it as *studies of the past for the present*. This general approach relates closely to the adage about studying history to avoid having it "repeat itself." Cautionary tales, if you will. One common example of this is when archaeologists explore how past instances of climate change forced humans to adapt and what this might mean for our current predicament (e.g., Cooper and Peros 2010). In a similar vein, one might use archaeological method to study the emergence of the industrial system that drives the climate crisis (e.g., Rockman and Hritz 2020). Alternatively, archaeologists working in this mode might explore how we can make our food supplies more sustainable by developing long-term agricultural resilience (Guttmann-Bond 2019; Reed and Ryan 2019). Similarly, Jeremy Sabloff (2008) has explored how the ability of the Ancient Maya to adapt and thrive (and eventually collapse) within tropical rainforests has much to teach us about how we can adapt to the challenges that we face today.

Examples like these are sometimes drawn upon in populist rhetoric that calls for people (usually meaning western people) to "learn from the past," specifically from the apparently simpler life of times gone by. Whether this comes in the form of the "paleo diet" or a longing for a more "natural" way of living (cf. Johnson 2015), these latter accounts both idealize or romanticize the past and tend to downplay the way our present understandings are always caught up in the realities of twenty-first-century capitalism. Many of the defining characteristics of the late twentieth and early twenty-first centuries are what afford certain people the privilege of "returning" to the past. For example, arguments for paleo diets and barefoot running only emerge and spread because of scientific means of measuring a food's nutritional content, the powers of social media, or the accumulation of personal wealth made possible through capitalism. On one level, it is unfair to compare these more populist, and often deeply inaccurate, understandings of past societies with the complex scholarly work done by archaeologists themselves. Nonetheless, the central contention is similar—the past is a resource from which we can extract knowledge, which in turn we can apply to improve our conditions in the present.

Our aim in this book is not to establish a primarily extractive relationship with the past in this manner. We reject entirely the notion, inherent in populist conceptions, that one can or should return to a past world where human beings were somehow more in tune with "nature" (see Chapter 9). While there is no doubt, as Sabloff (2008) and others have rightly argued, that there is much to learn from past societies, we suggest there are more critical and productive ways of putting archaeology to work in our battles with contemporary issues. Rather than only learning lessons from the past, this book will think with the past to help us generate new potentials for the future.

Other archaeologists take a future-oriented stance via *pragmatism* (Preucel and Mrozowski 2010; Saitta 2007; see also Rorty 1990), our second strand. Pragmatism focuses its attention on the impacts of knowledge and research practices—that is, *what they do* and the differences that they make in the wider world today. In the United States, for example, a pragmatic approach to Indigenous history might ask how archaeological research could possibly help (or hurt) descendant communities in the present; for instance, archaeological research might help in federal recognition cases for different tribes (cf. Cipolla 2013). In a different place, we might ask what the consequences are of talking about ancient DNA (aDNA) and migration in the European Neolithic, Bronze, and Iron Ages for present-day communities (Hakenbeck 2019; cf. Crellin and Harris 2020). As the post-processual critiques reminded us, archaeology does not occur in a vacuum, so archaeologists need to pay close attention to the relationships their research shares with the rest of the world.

A third but distinct line of future-oriented archaeology frames the discipline as *social activism*, largely via neo-Marxist lines of reasoning (e.g., Atalay et al. 2014; McGuire 2008). As with pragmatism, activist archaeologies pay close attention to their impacts on the world around them (see, for example, Barton 2021; Battle-Baptiste 2011; Kiddey 2017; Little and Zimmerman 2010; Stottman 2010). They prioritize challenging the structural inequalities of late capitalism. For example, archaeologists can excavate fascist histories and add new material textures to our current understanding of fascism (for example, Bernbeck 2018; González-Ruibal 2021). Activist archaeology creates new knowledge about the world, constructs new critiques of the world, and takes action to change it. It strives for a more humane world with less alienation and more emancipation. Like the pragmatists, activist archaeologies focus on the broader social collective, particularly underrepresented groups and groups suffering from the long-term structural violence of capitalism and settler colonialism. The general principles here also often underlie a strand of more participatory activist archaeology working with a range of disenfranchised groups (Darvill et al. 2019 and papers therein; Evans et al. 2019; Ford et al. 2022; Osgood 2023; Winterton 2014).

Our fourth strand, *archaeologies of the contemporary world* (Buchli and Lucas 2001; Graves-Brown et al. 2013; Harrison and Schofield 2010; see also *Journal of Contemporary Archaeology*) is of course, one of the most obvious ways that we can effectively work to build a future-oriented archaeology. Some of this research looks at contemporary life using an archaeological lens and mode of analysis (Cipolla et al. 2021; Hamilakis 2018; Hicks and Mallet 2019; Kiddey 2017, 2018, 2019; McAtackney 2014; McAtackney and McGuire 2020; McGuire 2018; Pétursdóttir and Olsen 2018) and some think particularly about how the general public interacts, engages with, and understands archaeology and heritage (Breithoff and Harrison 2018, 2020; Hicks 2021; Holtorf 2005, 2009; May 2019; Smith 2006; Thomas 2004). The field is far from homogenous, overlapping with disciplines such as sociology, media, museum studies, geography, and even philosophy; interdisciplinarity rules in this field. Contemporary archaeology often, though not always, has a focus on the ephemeral, considering protests, conflicts, and waste. It is also often built around a participatory framework (Kiddey 2020) that works to engage the public in its practice.

Finally, *anarchist* approaches represent a fifth and growing variety of future-oriented archaeologies (Angelbeck and Jones 2018; Borake 2019; Borck 2018; Denham 2018; Flexner and Gonzalez-Tenant 2018). Anarchism has clear connections to grassroots, bottom-up, social critique and transformation; it strives to create different, more egalitarian futures. Many anarchist archaeologies draw directly on the work of the late David Graeber, an anthropologist who played a key role in the *Occupy Wallstreet* movement. The intersection between past, present, and future is a key theme of Graeber's recent co-authored book with David Wengrow, *The Dawn of Everything* (2021). A central concern in anarchist anthropology and archaeology is looking to Indigenous peoples or "non-western" peoples and their respective histories as sources of inspiration for how westerners might change the world; this entails attributing things often only associated with "western" people and history, such as elements of democracy, to Indigenous societies. Clearly, there is a danger here of romanticizing or essentializing Indigenous peoples (for example, by alluding to an idea of noble savagery, see Deloria 1999), but the general spirit of these critiques should be commended for looking beyond a familiar dichotomy of our world—the "West" versus the "rest."

Building our future-oriented archaeology: think like an archaeologist!

So, what does *our* future-oriented archaeology aim to do? Fundamentally we aim to develop an analysis of how archaeological theory, linked to case studies from across archaeology, can make an impact on our capacity to help different futures to emerge. In each of the chapters, we develop specific theoretical tools and deploy them in connection with archaeological case studies. In this part of the chapter, we want to introduce the underlying theoretical approach of the volume. Don't worry if you are unfamiliar with some of our conceptual tools; we will revisit the key tools in greater detail in the chapters that follow. There are also books that engage with the background to these arguments in much greater detail (e.g., Crellin 2020; Crellin et al. 2021; Harris 2021a; Harris and Cipolla 2017; Jervis 2018).

As our first theoretical starting point, we take a relational approach. Relational approaches stress that rather than looking at preformed entities, archaeologists need to understand how the world emerges through webs of relations. This means that rather than things, people, animals, and plants having fixed and eternal identities and properties, these entities emerge in specific sets of connections that are thoroughly historical. When we look at a person, a house, a pot, or a place, we need to think about the actions that have produced them, the places they are connected to, the actions they make possible, and much more.

A consequence of this relational approach is that we adopt a position that can be described as posthumanist, one rooted in feminist critique (e.g., Braidotti 2013,

2022). Posthumanism is a growing and diverse set of critiques in the social sciences, humanities, and beyond (for a discussion of its relationship with archaeology, see Cipolla et al. 2021). An umbrella term, posthumanism aims to disrupt the way the modern West imposes dualist forms of thinking (e.g., that nature and culture or mind and body are opposed to one another). As archaeologists have long pointed out, these dualisms impose very particular ways of thinking onto the world around us that prevent us from appreciating the complexity of how interlinked everything is (Harris and Cipolla 2017; Thomas 2004). Instead of worrying about whether something is "natural" or "cultural," posthumanism explores how the world around us reveals these dualisms to be Western attempts to order and sort the world into bounded categories (Latour 1993). Posthumanism aims to move past the privileging of certain kinds of human beings over others (a topic we return to in Chapters 2 and 8). This ties our posthumanism both to feminism and to anti-racism in its commitment to ensuring that certain kinds of people (White, able-bodied, heterosexual men) are not elevated over others.

Similarly, we draw upon and learn from Indigenous perspectives that encourage us to move beyond Western ways of thinking, to critique and challenge settler colonialism, and to think in ways that require us to critically consider the relationships we share with the world around us (e.g., Atalay 2006a, 2006b, 2019; Deloria 1997, 2001, 2012; Steeves 2015, 2021; Tallbear 2013, 2014, 2017; Watts 2013; Wilson 2020). Our engagement with Indigenous perspectives is a careful one that works to avoid appropriation while still recognizing the importance of Indigenous thinkers and how Indigenous peoples have been working to make the world anew for centuries (Deloria 1997, 2012; Tallbear 2017; also, for examples from the authors, see Cipolla 2019, 2021; Cipolla and Allard 2019; Cipolla et al. 2019; Cobb and Crellin 2022; Crellin 2020; Crellin and Harris 2021; Crellin et al. 2021; Harris 2021a). This engagement with Indigenous thought and posthumanism raises critical questions of ontology—the question of what exists in the world and how we cope with differences in this regard (see Cipolla 2019; Crellin et al. 2021, Chapter 10). Ontological difference is an important part of recent archaeological and anthropological debates; in Chapter 8, we explore how these considerations improve archaeology.

Finally, we aim to be post-anthropocentric. Post-anthropocentrism is a commitment to refusing to see humans as ontologically distinct from the others we share the world with and to no longer making humans the most important protagonists in all that we do. Many of the future-oriented archaeologies reviewed earlier take anthropocentric approaches to make the world anew for the disenfranchised (cf. Joyce 2020; Pétursdóttir 2020). As authors, we believe that a post-anthropocentric approach is the only way we can begin to tackle our climate crisis and the social justice crises that are emerging in its wake, something we explore in detail in Chapter 9. A world without plants, animals, things, and the environment is no world at all. Moreover, it is not a world in which we can all be treated equally. To date, commitments to social justice have often been separated from commitments to environmentalism (there are, of course, exceptions, eco-feminism being a key example explored in Chapter 9); separating these two missions is damaging. They are thoroughly entwined and working to build a better world for all will prove fruitless without action on the climate crisis and vice versa. Our commitment to post-anthropocentrism (and posthumanism) in no way eschews or contradicts our commitment to social justice issues; indeed we argue that it only enhances it (contra van Dyke 2015, 2021; Ribeiro 2016b, 2022).

Post-anthropocentrism means that we need to combine our posthumanism with a clear interrogation and engagement with all the myriad non-humans that exist in the world today and that existed in worlds of the past. To do so, we also draw on related ideas from new materialism. New materialism covers a diverse and wide-ranging set of approaches (see Coole and Frost 2010), but all of them are committed to exploring the complex ways in which non-humans contribute to the production of the world. Matter is "vibrant" here, in Jane Bennett's (2010) terms, and life is not necessarily restricted to the organic sphere but emerges through the complex relations and processes that flow across the boundaries we traditionally try to draw. Within new materialism, we will draw on assemblage theory. In the last ten years, assemblage theory has become a popular archaeological tool (Crellin 2020; Harris 2021a; Hamilakis and Jones 2017 and papers therein; Jervis 2018). Emerging from the work of Gilles Deleuze and Félix Guattari (Deleuze 2004; Deleuze and Guattari 2004; cf. DeLanda 2006), it provides archaeologists with a way of thinking about the relations we identified earlier. Assemblage theory treats everything–people, animals, landscapes, planets–as multi-scalar collections of diverse elements temporarily brought together in specific historical settings. These assemblages include both material and immaterial components and have different properties and capacities. Assemblages are constantly in the process of change and emergence. Thinking in terms of assemblages draws us back constantly to attend to relations, on the one hand, and what things do, on the other. It insists on the historical contingency of everything we study. Assemblages operate at multiple scales, another defining feature that has much to offer the archaeological discipline.

Assemblage thinking, new materialism, posthumanism. These approaches ask us to look at the world again and to attend to its specificity at multiple scales. In this way, our future-oriented archaeologies are firmly rooted in our data. We assemble the best data we can, and we make each step in our research process as secure as possible (cf. Fowler 2013a). As Ian Hodder (1999) has demonstrated, the past is multiple and multi-vocal. Chris Fowler (2013b, 235) builds on this by arguing against the traditional approach to truth where there is a singular "True Past" out there that we are trying to recover (what is sometimes known as the "correspondence theory of truth"). There is no singular truth we reveal about the past, but multiple stories for us to tell. Writing those stories should always involve considering the consequences of how we collect, assemble, analyze, and "become with" our data. We should also consider how we construct narratives from that data, along with the consequences those narratives might have in the world. Instead of finding singular truths, archaeology emerges as a way of exploring and building past worlds, a form of engagement that contributes to our world today and builds toward a future. An ally of other forms of critical contemporary engagement, archaeology is the historical science of posthumanism (Cipolla et al. 2021), with much to teach us about both today and tomorrow.

In the chapters that follow we develop different elements of these theoretical approaches, showing how they can help us, in conjunction with archaeological examples, to develop new ways of thinking and new conceptual tools. Of course, there is much that the modern world can learn directly from the past—how to farm in more sustainable ways, how to manage environments, how to respond to climate change, and more. What has not been fully appreciated is how archaeology as a mode of thinking and a mode of doing can provide us with new tools for conceptualizing the problems themselves. This act of reconceptualization cannot solve the problems we face—the demonization of migrants, the appalling treatment of Indigenous people, climate crisis, patriarchy, or homelessness—by themselves. One of the things that is perhaps most frustrating about the kinds of problems that we face today is that they are not new. Feminists have been fighting against the patriarchy for at least two hundred years, anti-racists and disability activists have been demonstrating structural inequalities for decades, climate scientists have been highlighting the coming crisis for years, and Indigenous peoples have been battling for their own survivance for centuries (Braidotti 2022, 227). Yet the problems remain. In this book, we argue that these problems are material and structural, which is part of the reason why they are so firmly embedded in our world (Cobb and Crellin 2022). But, for us, these are also thinking problems. If we continue to think in the same old ways about these challenges, we cannot hope to meet them. Therefore, we suggest that the first step on the way to dealing with these seemingly intractable problems is to rethink them, and a theoretically informed archaeology is well situated to help with this reassessment.

Conclusion: the view from where we are

These approaches call to us because of who we are, and here we need to confront our standpoints and perspectives explicitly. In a previous book, co-authored with the wonderful Lindsay Montgomery and Sophie Moore, we set out who we were, writing individually. In this text, our authorial voice remains singular, but this singularity disguises the multiplicity that it contains, a multiplicity that exists in each of the three authors. We each work with resources that are both shared and variable, but we share far more than most archaeologists, and this allows us to write together. Collectively our privilege as White, middle-class, able-bodied, cis-gendered academics in permanent positions cannot be ignored in the context of this book. Nor can the fact that two of us are male, and one lives and works on Indigenous land in a settler-colonial society. This privilege allows us the time and space with which to think, to learn from, and to engage with activists, thinkers, colleagues, and friends, and to put that learning and listening to work in this book. We recognize and acknowledge our inescapable privilege, but we try to put that privilege to good use. That, for us, is part of what it means to be future-oriented.

Our shared expertise lies in archaeological theory. It is archaeological theory that allows us to position other accounts in relation to one another and to consider examples from across space and time. We do not claim expertise over the wide range of temporal and geographical case studies we include in this book, from Oceania to North America, and from the Paleolithic to the present. Instead, we draw on the experts in our field who have studied these places and times and situate their accounts within our own theoretical frameworks to allow new concepts to develop. We are clear throughout when we are representing the voices of others or our own perspectives and employ citations to acknowledge our debt to our colleagues.

The theoretical position we take is actively political. We are committed to a perspective that explicitly makes room for different kinds of humanity, for historical actors that are non-humans, and for bodies that can do different kinds of things. Our politics and our theory are feminist and anti-racist. We see the philosophy that we read and write with as thoroughly and inescapably entangled with so-called "real world" problems; there is no divide between philosophy and politics. The philosophies that we engage with fundamentally *drive* our political perspective. They call us to be future-oriented in our thinking.

The structure of the book

The rest of the book explores the challenge we outlined previously, asking how thinking like an archaeologist can help us address future-oriented problems. Each chapter addresses a different theme that we see as crucial to the world of today and tomorrow. It also develops a critical theoretical tool (see Table 1.1). Chapter 2 turns to issues of mobility and migration. Why do we approach examples of historical migration as progressive and positive whilst the politics of today often work to limit migration and the movement of refugees and migrants? We live in a world

Table 1.1 Roadmap of key themes, theoretical tools, and case studies for each chapter.

	Key theme	Theoretical tool	Key case study/ studies
Chapter 2	Mobility and migration	Humanist Man and the non-humans	Sonoran Desert Migrations
Chapter 3	Capitalism	Assemblages and desire	Homeless Archaeology
Chapter 4	Leadership	Potestas/potentia	Tiwanaku and Bronze Age Barrows
Chapter 5	Violence	Virtual/actual	Puhú
Chapter 6	Types	Positive difference	Teotihuacan Figurines
Chapter 7	Truth	Relational and emergent truth	Fingerprints and the Sphinx
Chapter 8	Collaborating across difference	Positive difference, ontological difference	Collaborative Archaeologies
Chapter 9	Anthropocene	Futurity, affect, scale	Waste

that demands the movement of things but often condemns the movement of people. Our climate crisis will cause an increase in forced and unforced migration and movement in coming years as those living in the global south are forced to move to escape our changing climate. Chapter 3 develops these ideas further by considering why having a fixed home and particular kinds of kinship relations has come to be so central to living in the modern capitalist west. We explore these themes through a study of the archaeology of homelessness. In Chapter 4, we consider leaders and leadership in the past and present and suggest archaeologists can construct alternative models of power relationships and leadership. Violence is the key theme of Chapter 5, where we consider how alternative theoretical approaches might open new ways of thinking about the causes and effects of violence. How does violence emerge in specific historical ways? How does it work with and against non-humans?

Chapters 6, 7, and 8 deal with intersecting issues central to archaeological practice but which have significant implications for the contemporary and future world. Chapter 6 explores typology, an archaeological method often presented as relatively neutral yet one with significant relevance today. This chapter considers the philosophical roots of typological thinking and their relationship to the way we categorize different types of people. Chapter 7 explores how we can know the past and construct "truth" in archaeology. It argues that the kinds of relational truth we construct in archaeological arguments have far broader relevance beyond our own subject. Building on the key themes of evidence and truth, Chapter 8 critically considers how we can build collaborative archaeologies and how we can integrate different standpoints and different ontologies within these.

We draw our argument to a close by addressing a topic central to everyone alive today and indeed to future generations: *the Anthropocene and the climate crisis*. Chapter 9 argues that the anthropocentrism that dominates archaeology is reflected in our engagements with the Anthropocene and our ability to challenge climate change; the two are closely tethered (see also Joyce 2020; Pétursdóttir 2020). Our conclusion, Chapter 10, revisits the theoretically engaged and future-oriented archaeologies highlighted throughout the book. It distills key lessons for shaping what archaeology and the broader world can become. It reiterates that this is a book about how archaeological concepts and things work together to reorient our views of the present and future. Chapter 10 emphasizes the role that non-humans need to play in our concepts if we are to face up to the contemporary challenges discussed throughout this book.

Our aim in this book is to convince the reader that an engagement with archaeological theory creates the potential for using archaeology to play its part in making *different* worlds possible. We believe that archaeology encourages us to think differently about the world and that these different modes of thought are what the enduring problems of our present world need and demand. Archaeology provides the stimulus and the materials to allow us to think differently and to develop new concepts with which to approach the worlds of today and tomorrow. This means that this book is not merely an exploration of applying posthumanism or new materialism to archaeology. It is also about what happens when we think about what doing a posthumanist, new materialist, and feminist archaeology means for today. That too is what it means for us to be future-oriented.

Where does this leave us? Archaeology as a process and the present in which we live are co-constitutive. Archaeology is not a discipline of the past, though it is the past that we (the authors) study, it is a discipline of the present. It produces stories about the past firmly rooted in the now. In this book, we argue for the power of archaeology and archaeological theory to change how we approach the present and to help us build better futures. We call, therefore, for an archaeology that studies the past, is rooted in the present, but is oriented towards building better futures. When we accept that we actively intervene in producing and shaping narratives about the past, the next step is to recognize our responsibility to think about the consequences of those stories.

Notes

1 A designation for those protesting the pipeline.
2 Within this book we take the same approach to capitalization taken in a previous volume (Crellin et al. 2021, 13—note 2). For example, when we use the term "Western" with a capital W we are referring to hegemonic positions within the West, those we might associate (in the terms of this book) with humanist Man, discussed further in Chapter 2. When western lacks the capital letter, we are using it for general descriptive purposes. When we discuss Indigenous People (capitalized in both words) we are referring to particular groups, whereas Indigenous people (lower case p) is used as a general term.

Chapter 2

Archaeology and migration
More-than-human movements

Introduction: a world in motion

The world is full of movement. Wind rushes over the trees, blowing leaves. Birds swoop down from the sky. Mushrooms grow and create mycelial networks. Cats shift as they sleep on their beds. Dogs chase after balls. Fingers move over keyboards. Refugees cling to boats as they cross the seas. The molecules that make up the table in front of you move and shift. Movement seems inevitable. Today in many western societies, however, movement is classified and valued in contradictory ways. For some people, movement is celebrated: the arrival of a new signing to your favorite sports team; the politician who completes a foreign tour with a new trade deal; the businessman jetting across the skies to earn *ever more* money; the rockstars preparing for their next tour.

Yet, for others, movement is frowned upon, discouraged, or worse. To give just one example, between 2014 and 2022 the missing migrants project recorded 27,845 people who had disappeared while trying to cross the Mediterranean to get to Europe (Missing Migrant Project 2023). This version of movement is not welcomed or assisted by the countries these migrants seek to reach. Recent political arguments focus on—and demonize—the movement of certain people; these arguments range from Donald Trump describing those crossing the Mexican-US border in unspeakable terms to the racism openly deployed in persuading Britain to vote to leave the European Union in 2016. While the movement of attractive American celebrities to Britain is usually celebrated by the press and the public alike, Meghan Markle's relationship with Prince Harry proved less than popular in the UK for reasons that are all too depressing. So, it is not just wealth or even legality that sometimes determines the way migration is viewed and whether the outcome is successful or even survivable. Indeed, even for those privileged people dwelling in the relative comfort of European modernity, with the right citizenship, name, and skin pigmentation to facilitate mobility, movement is still monitored in a variety of ways; crossing some borders requires passports and visas. Whether lauded or decried, it seems that movement is thoroughly controlled, and denying or resisting that control sometimes has deadly consequences.

DOI: 10.4324/9781003244141-2

Yet, movement in the past appears to be a different matter altogether; the same politicians mentioned earlier tend to frame past population movements, particularly those of the very distant past (see Aldred 2021 for an excellent overview of movement in archaeology), in a different light. For them, movement in the deep past might be brave, dynamic, and daring. Where British politicians debate sending arriving immigrants fleeing persecution to Rwanda, and British conservative commentators bemoan lifeboats saving the lives of drowning people in the English Channel, the colonization of the Pacific is recognized (rightly so) as a "remarkable" human achievement (e.g., Sear et al. 2020, 8813). There is little moral condemnation of people moving around Europe in the middle of the first millennium CE, and newspaper articles report in excited tones the latest archaeological insights into the spread of the Bronze Age via the "Yamnaya Culture." The image of people moving in the past suggests that they were powerful, active individuals, forging their own paths and domesticating the world around them. In these narratives, past migrants have much more in common with businessmen traveling to make money than they do with those squeezing into boats to try and cross the English Channel or the Mediterranean Sea. As we will see, the questions of *who* you are and *when* you move are critical for understanding these different reactions (and the gender that we've associated with the term "business" is anything but accidental).

In this chapter, we explore how thinking like an archaeologist, and especially developing an understanding informed by certain strands of archaeological theory, can help us understand why and how movement is valued in such contradictory ways today. We start by providing some examples of how archaeologists write about migration and movement and how this can help us think about these processes in new ways. We then turn to the theoretical tools that can help us enhance these understandings further, exploring how today's dominant "humanism" enshrines a hierarchy of people that ends up celebrating movement for some and condemning it for others. We also examine how assemblage theory, mentioned in Chapter 1, can add to these discussions by emphasizing how important non-humans are in these processes. Finally, we turn to our key case study, Jason De León's (2012, 2013, 2015) brilliant contemporary archaeological study of migration across the US-Mexico border. Mixing De León's analysis with the theoretical threads introduced in this chapter, we argue that thinking like an archaeologist offers fresh perspectives on movement and migration, today and tomorrow.

Setting the stage: archaeology and migration

Before turning to our theoretical tools, we examine a few different case studies to consider the various ways that archaeologists write and think about migration. Each example from the past provides us with important insights on migration today. They demonstrate how migration and colonization transform all parties involved and how material conditions participate in, enhance, and, of course, hinder mobility in unexpected ways.

To begin, we consider archaeological studies exploring how Europeans migrated around the world over the last one thousand years or so, although this is rarely described as migration. In most cases, these forms of human mobility are seen as the work of explorers or "pioneers." Nonetheless, archaeological studies of various forms of European colonialism provide fascinating examples of the complexities of migration and the usefulness of archaeological toolkits. In today's world, western societies are increasingly forced to reckon with their colonial roots and tendencies. A hallmark of these colonial tendencies is how such societies remember and teach about European colonial history. Strangely, these histories are often framed as beginnings or, for local Indigenous peoples, endings. It is as if, prior to European presence, the lands that Europeans reached had no history (cf. Wolf 2010) and that as soon as they arrived, Indigenous peoples and lifeways came to an end. Contemporary Indigenous perspectives on colonialism provide a much-needed balance to these simplified representations. Indigenous archaeologist Sonya Atalay (2006b) provides an excellent example of one such counternarrative that circulates in popular culture. She writes about a popular meme that critically reframes "western" understandings of North American colonialism by redefining the infamous date of 1492, when Columbus accidentally arrived in the Americas, as the start of foreign invasion and terrorism rather than the beginning of cultural improvements and progress; the meme usually shows Native Americans holding guns alongside the slogan "The original homeland security: Fighting terrorism since 1492."

Settler colonists' sedentary heritage meant that they brought a particular set of ideals with them. They had specific notions about nature, culture, "savagery," "civilization," improvement, land ownership, architecture, and more (Gosden 2004). These arbitrary defaults were immediately challenged when they arrived in places like the Americas or Australia to find the land already occupied by Indigenous nations that practiced different ways of life. Colonists found no evidence of what they thought of as "progressive" and "complex" ways of life (like theirs), so they enacted their "natural rights" to take over and make these places "productive." Of course, we know how mistaken these perspectives were. In Australia, for example, settler colonists encountered a heavily managed landscape (anthropogenic), but one that resembled the parks of England that colonists understood as "natural," for them, the way landscapes "should" look (Rowley-Conwy n.d.). Although these different places were produced in England and Australia via equivalent forms of land management, encroaching colonists could not or did not recognize this complexity in Australian landscapes. Instead, they used the apparent "raw" or unchanged land as evidence of their divine right to rule; from there, as documented by countless archaeologies of settler colonialism (e.g., Panich and Gonzalez 2021), colonists often used violence, coercion, and more to steal Indigenous lands. They claimed ownership, physically planting the flag of their respective nation-states on Indigenous lands. Of course, such acts didn't, in fact, end Indigenous histories at all; the realities here are messier than many would care to admit. The persistence of diverse Indigenous peoples up to the present speaks to the many weaknesses in simplistic narratives of erasure and replacement. Archaeology sheds additional light on the survivance and persistence of Indigenous peoples up to the present *despite* European settler colonialism.

Vanuatu

An excellent example of this comes from the Indigenous-colonial histories of Melanesia, which demonstrate the dynamics of Indigenous persistence in one such setting (see Figure 2.1). Melanesia was a late frontier of European colonialism (Flexner et al. 2015, 5–6); although contact began as early as the sixteenth and seventeenth centuries, prolonged European presence in the area only started in the mid-nineteenth century and consisted mostly of Christian missions and sandalwood traders. Multiple lines of evidence, including archaeology, show how colonialism came to parts of Melanesia *on Indigenous terms*. Often thought of in similar ways as European flags planted on Indigenous land to stake a claim, Christian missions are typically seen as emblems of colonial expansion and the erasure of Indigenous traditions.

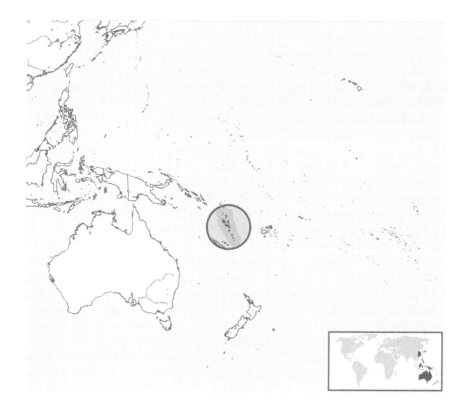

Figure 2.1 Vanuatu map.

Image: TUBS, CC BY-SA 3.0 license (https://creativecommons.org/licenses/by-sa/3.0).

Yet, contemporary ni-Vanuatu peoples (Indigenous People of Vanuatu) value the archaeological remains of Christian missions as important heritage sites, where *their* past as ni-Vanuatu people intersects with *their* present (Flexner and Spriggs 2015).

Not only are missionary sites important to ni-Vanuatu people today, archaeological insights on the history of the missions show that they were indigenized. In other words, missionaries adjusted their practices to fit local ni-Vanuatu belief systems. After building a church, for instance, one missionary found that he had angered the local sacred men because the fence surrounding the church blocked a path that spirits used to access the sea (Flexner and Spriggs 2015, 14); the missionary removed the fence to appease the sacred men. Even apparently strict European styles of architecture are deceiving in Vanuatu. One "western" style church, for instance, is documented as being used in distinct Indigenous ways that relate to local gendered practices. Instead of the typical western approach, where "nuclear" families congregate together, in this church, there were three discrete groupings that followed local gender expectations: adult men, adult women, and children and young mothers (Flexner and Spriggs 2015, 18).

Initial survey and excavation of Indigenous village sites in the same region suggest strong continuity of ni-Vanuatu traditions throughout the twentieth century with very little European influence (Flexner et al. 2015). The archaeology shows continued production of ni-Vanuatu architectural forms, an emphasis on ephemeral forms of artifact and modification to the land, and very few European-produced objects. Taken together, the patterns reviewed in this section show how European settler colonists, even missionaries whose sole purpose was to *change* Indigenous peoples, adapted their practices and developed them *in situ* with local Indigenous peoples.

The Norse

What about earlier forms of European colonialism? To consider this further, we next turn to archaeologies of the Norse. This ability to jump between case studies is a distinct advantage of archaeological perspectives; we can compare and think through very different examples, but we can also consider how processes of migration and movement begin *and end*. Why would a highly mobile and adaptable group of people cease their expansive ways or even retreat? Norse histories offer some answers. Starting in the late eighth century, the Norse spread across much of Europe and into parts of Asia. Between 1200 and 1000 years ago, they also pushed into the North Atlantic, eventually landing in present-day Canada (McGovern 1990; see also Ingstad and Ingstad 2000). According to popular and academic portrayals, mobility is a core defining characteristic of the Norse. In passing, we often call them "Vikings," a term that refers to a trading or raiding trip—meaning that a Norse person might *go Viking*. We revel in archaeological discoveries that speak to just how far they went—the archaeology of L'Anse aux Meadows, a 1000-year-old Norse settlement in Newfoundland (northeastern Canada), is a perfect example. And, of course, we are enchanted by the beauty of their ships and impressed by the dangers we associate with Norse seafaring.

The Norse colonized the North Atlantic from Iceland to Greenland and eventually to the northeast coast of North America (Wallace 2003) (see Figure 2.2). These expansions slowed down after 1000 CE and eventually came to an end. This is the problem we want to start with, the end rather than the beginning. What can archaeological studies of migration tell us about how such processes end? Why did these highly mobile and adaptable peoples stop their expansion? The answers partially lie in the material conditions of sedentism.

Established by the famous Viking Leif Erickson, L'Anse aux Meadows (or Vinland as the Norse referred to it) seems to have functioned as a base camp for further North American exploration (see Ingstad and Ingstad 2000). The presence of plant remains (butternut) indigenous to other parts of northeastern Canada suggests that the Norse did indeed investigate the area to some extent (Wallace 2003). We also know, from Viking Sagas written hundreds of years after the fact, that they failed to establish stable and amicable trade relations with local Indigenous peoples (Wallace 2003). In addition to this, the climate was beginning to change dramatically; for example, the Little Ice Age was not far off, meaning that global temperatures were beginning to drop. After about 20 years, these challenges seem to have pushed residents of L'Anse aux Meadows to abandon their post and retreat to Greenland (but see Ledger et al. 2019 for a new Bayesian model that suggests sporadic occupation for up to 195 years). Scholars still debate exactly why the Norse left Canada,

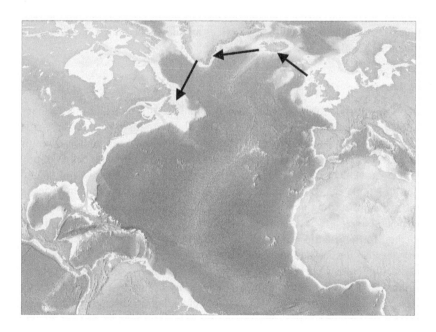

Figure 2.2 Map of North Atlantic. Arrow shows the direction of Norse expansion.

Modified Image: Tom Patterson, Public domain.

but we do know that their settlement was burned down just before or just after they departed; whether this signals hostile relations with local Indigenous groups or a Viking gesture to demonstrate an abrupt end to their North American meddling remains unclear. But scholars are making headway in explaining the slow demise of Viking expansion during this time.

As summarized by McGovern (1990, 333), decade after decade of Norse sedentism in Iceland and Greenland atrophied the flexibility and mobility that we often celebrate. Early Norse colonists in these areas came with a wide variety of skill sets. They were flexible and they had options; depending on the places they chose to occupy and the different resources that were available, they could herd, fish, or hunt, and they could easily shift strategies if resource availability changed. Over the course of about a century of sedentism, however, as Norse Atlantic communities became increasingly stratified and centralized, they also came to rely on comparatively rigid ways of life that were more narrowly focused on specific forms of subsistence and economic activity. In other words, their subsistence strategies became far less resilient as they "slowed down" and stayed in permanent settlements (see also Steinburg et al. 2018). Some of the myriad skills of earlier generations—to herd *or* to fish *or* to hunt—fell out of use in certain places, leaving later generations with fewer options when resource availability changed. Several changes, ranging from a shifting climate (remember, the Little Ice Age was upon them), to unintentional degradation of local resources, to sometimes-violent interactions with Indigenous peoples of northeastern Canada and Greenland, challenged Norse futures in the North Atlantic. These two forces—less flexible ways of life and "external" changes beyond Norse control—seem to have brought Norse expansion in the North Atlantic to an end. As already mentioned, L'Anse aux Meadows lasted until just after 1000 CE. Norse Greenland and Iceland sharply declined during the fifteenth century, with Greenland being largely abandoned and Iceland becoming, at least in the view of some, an "impoverished marginal backwater" (McGovern 1990, 333). These examples show the fallibility of simple notions of improvement, complexity, and cultural evolution. In other words, sedentism and its material trappings sometimes fail to last and blossom in predictable ways, especially when faced with climate change and other challenges.

The Linearbandkeramik

What about an example typically framed as a more clear-cut migration success story? For this, let's consider the first farmers of central Europe, usually referred to as the Linearbandkeramik or LBK. As a way of life, the LBK began somewhere shortly after 5600 cal. BCE in the Carpathian basin, Hungary, and from around 5400, began spreading out across much of central Europe from Ukraine in the east to the Paris basin in the west (Bickle and Whittle 2013; Last 2013; Whittle 1996, 2003) (see Figure 2.3). As already noted, they were the first farmers in these new regions. In the first few hundred years, they lived similar lives based around small villages of longhouses cultivating a range of crops, including emmer, einkorn, pea, lentil, flax, and sometimes oats, naked barley, hulled barley, millet, poppy, rye, free-threshing

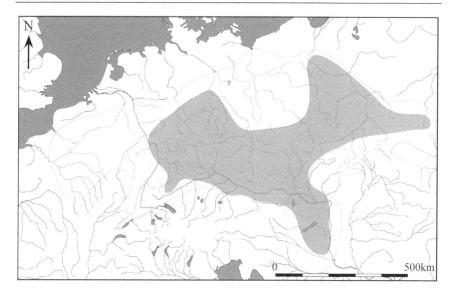

Figure 2.3 The spread of the Linearbandkeramik; dark is the early phase, light is the later phase (after Bickle and Whittle 2013, fig 1.1).

Image: Penny Bickle.

wheat, spelt, bitter vetch, and fava bean; they also raised domestic species of cattle, sheep, goat, pig, and dog, and hunted wild fauna (Bickle and Whittle 2013).

The first farmers are usually thought of as colonizers *from elsewhere*, "an incoming population, bringing sedentism and agriculture" (Bickle and Whittle 2013, 5), which conjures up images of population replacement. Where does this leave the hunter-gatherers who initially occupied these landscapes? Some studies of aDNA have argued that the origins of farming resulted directly from massive migrations of people across Europe, followed by a rapid population replacement in their new "homes" (for example, Brace et al. 2019). But is it plausible that Mesolithic peoples, practices, and places were simply erased and replaced with new farming populations? Other studies have challenged the idea of complete replacement, instead suggesting that farming and hunting and gathering groups lived alongside each other for up to 2000 years. It is also clear that varied processes of interaction took place at the local level (Lipson et al. 2017). Thus, movement here can have outcomes other than population replacement (Bollongino et al. 2013; Immel et al. 2021). The simplified aDNA narrative of population replacement that often characterizes large-scale studies using this technique certainly meshes well with certain political ideas in the present, but that really says more about *our* world than about worlds of the past (Crellin and Harris 2020). In other words, they match modern, Western, ideas of identities, which are easily understood and mapped in specific ways: the incomer/migrant meets the native/local, who is, like DNA, incapable of change. Of course, in reality, both identities and DNA shift all the time, so what might be "population replacement" at a genetic level, can be continuity at another.

In terms of material things, however, perhaps a more interesting conundrum is the tension between an LBK world of sedentary farming—including large long-houses, enclosures, and crops—and how the LBK arrived, namely through mobility and rapid spread. How can we understand this? How was it that these lifeways were both settled and mobile? Here the detailed work by archaeologists looking at isotope evidence shows how specific groups of people were more mobile than others (Bickle 2020; Hofmann 2020), so rather than casting a whole society as either sedentary or mobile, we need to unpick such distinctions (Hofmann 2020). We can also explore how longhouses lived a variety of life cycles (Bickle 2013, 157; Whittle 2003). Some were repaired, others seem to have been allowed to decay at the same time as others were built, and many houses were abandoned before they became structurally unsound (Bickle 2013, 169). This means that, alongside people moving, architectures themselves drifted over time, and the lifecycle of architecture helped spur human mobility. Longhouse orientations in new settlements may have pointed back in the direction from which people had come, linking houses in one place to houses in another, a line of movement and descent captured in architecture as much as people (Bradley 2002). Dani Hofmann (2020) has traced how complex these farmers' practices of movement and migration might have been. All told, the LBK reveals a world in which the opposition between people who move and people who stay home and the kinds of material things that facilitate change and facilitate stasis are not as clear cut as our modern imaginations would have us believe.

This example includes important insights that are applicable to how we think of migration and movement today. First, contact and colonialism are multi-directional, not one-way streets, where powerful colonizers remake or erase passive local or Indigenous peoples. There is rarely a singular origin point or single destination. As postcolonial theorists argue, the complex mixtures that emerge from migration and colonization are much more complicated and nuanced than the language of population replacement or declarations of Indigenous extinction would have us think. Indeed, these complicated encounters have the power to transform all parties involved (Gosden 2004; Lydon and Rizvi 2010; Panich and Gonzalez 2021). Second, material things play critical roles in processes of mobility and movement, including how they end. The shift in Norse lifeways to tools, architecture, and ways of being that were materially enshrined left few options when climate change began or when the Norse exhausted resources. Increasingly inflexible forms of sedentism in the North Atlantic became unsustainable. The lesson here is that material things not only facilitate mobility, in the form of boats in this case, but they can also bring it to a close. With the LBK example, we encounter a different set of circumstances; material patterns there seem to scream of sedentism: longhouses anchored communities in place, surrounded by villages, enclosures, and fields of planted crops. Yet, of course, the LBK communities are best known for their colonization of Europe; here, a set of material patterns that seem to speak of sedentism were also associated with forms of mobility, if in complex ways. These examples suggest that we may need different ways of thinking about the roles that non-humans play in histories of human mobility and movement. Furthermore, we must also ask why, in all three examples, European colonists, Norse settlers, or the first farmers, the people on the move rarely get the kind of bad press and condemnation migrants get today. It seems, despite all that we can learn from these archaeological examples, that we still need some additional theoretical tools to think with. We turn to those now.

Theoretical Toolkit: rethinking non-humans and human hierarchy

Why is it that some examples of human mobility are valued while others are not? The key question seems to be *who* is moving. When people in the present see transnational travelers jetting across the world with all the support of passports, visas, and money, the response is very different from what we see when people with less privilege try to improve their circumstances through relocation. Whilst archaeologists have written about movement in more complex ways, some still presume that the movement of certain people is to be celebrated as pioneering, while other forms of movement are shocking. When archaeologists explored the patterns of mobility through isotopes and aDNA in a Beaker cemetery in Germany, for example, they found that a particular age group of young women were unexpectedly absent, having apparently moved elsewhere (Mittnik et al. 2019). The archaeologists described themselves as "shocked" by this, suggesting the daughters were "given away" (Gibbons 2019). It is interesting to hypothesize how the situation would be interpreted and described if it were young men who were missing; perhaps not as "shocking" or so passively, that is, as being "given away" by some other active party. Spoiler alert: they wouldn't! Again, the movements of one *kind* of people is expected and applauded, while the movements of others are not.

Here we encounter underlying assumptions written into how some archaeologists conceive of people in the past—the same assumptions that also underwrite how many people, thinking in traditional Eurocentric terms, conceptualize people in the present. Although most would insist that all human beings are equal, this "equality" hides a form of hierarchy that privileges particular kinds of people, human beings who are able-bodied, White, cis, heterosexual, male, middle-class, middle-aged, and so on (Braidotti 2013, 2022). These are the humans whose movement is welcome and who, in the past, are seen as pioneers. When others try to move, their efforts are not as celebrated. The assumptions which encode a hierarchy of human beings are what we refer to as *humanist*; at the peak of this hierarchy is the figure of humanist *Man* (Braidotti 2013, 2022, 18–23). Now your first thought might be that surely humanism is the opposite of this—it refers to treating everyone equally, doesn't it? It assumes that all human beings are the same, no?

This is certainly the aim of humanism, and humanism's achievements are many (Braidotti 2022). It is also a complex and broad movement with a long history. Early phases of humanism, sometimes referred to as classical humanism, for example, aimed to unpick the certainties of the Renaissance context in which it emerged (Tully 2008, 104–5). More recently, however, humanism has become increasingly associated with ideas that emphasize a particular and singular version of humanity (Braidotti 2013). In this book, we are going to be critical of this version of humanism. The emphasis that contemporary humanism places on a singular vision of humanity has significant consequences. The version of humanity that humanism uses as an archetype—against which all other people are compared—is *not neutral*, but rather the type of privileged person identified in the previous paragraph, a version of humanity that matches most people who have written about (and from) the humanist tradition. The image of the Vitruvian man (see Figure 2.4) is often evoked here (Braidotti 2013, 14, Fig 1.1); this is what a person is supposed to be, and those who differ will be punished. The legacy of sexism, racism, homophobia, transphobia, and so on that lives alongside the seeming equality of Enlightenment humanism in modern European and American societies is thus not a bug—"Why don't the bigots get it? We're all equal!"—but a feature; if you have a single image of the human to measure everyone against, *people will always differ, and that difference will be seen as a failure and as a lack*. We will return to difference later in this book (Chapters 6 and 8). The key

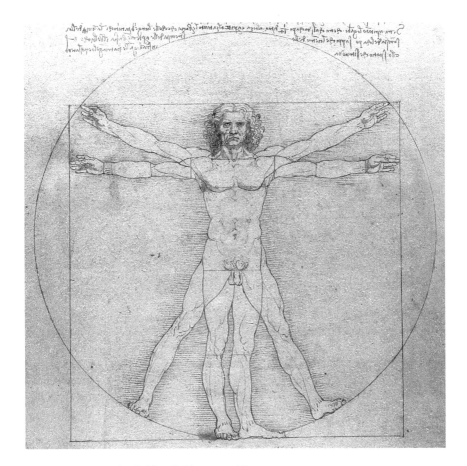

Figure 2.4 Leonardo da Vinci's Vitruvian Man.

Image: Leonardo da Vinci, Public domain.

point here is that this is why we argue that we need a different approach to the question of human identity and diversity; not a humanist one that defaults to privilege *Man*, but, as we saw in the introduction, a posthumanist approach.

Posthumanism is an umbrella term that covers a range of different approaches (Crellin and Harris 2021; Ferrando 2019). One of the critical elements that underlies the kind of feminist posthumanism we draw on in this book, however, is that it seeks to move away from the underlying notion that there is a single category of "human" to which all members of our species aspire (Braidotti 2013, 2022; Cobb and Crellin 2022; Ferrando 2019). Rather than treating the idea of human as something with a set of essential characteristics (free will, mobility, agency, whatever), all of which tend to describe *some* human beings, in *certain* historical contexts, better than others, it explores how human beings are always located relationally (Crellin and Harris 2021). This means not starting with the notion of what a human being is, separated from their historical context, but rather exploring the location of humans within specific historical and material settings. Such an approach would understand the very different sets of options that exist for one group of human beings (say, migrants driven by climate change or war to cross the Mediterranean) than others (western academics sitting in airplane seats typing into their laptops as they jet off to conferences). Recognizing how these differences create different capacities for action for human beings allows us to move away from these essentialist accounts in which certain groups are set up to fail. Such an approach asks us to build on the archaeological accounts we outlined previously to include a more radical rethinking of what the possibilities for being human were amongst the LBK or the Norse. It would mean we might offer differing accounts of Beaker cemeteries in Germany with missing young women—maybe these were pioneers taking opportunities to migrate that were offered to them (and not to young men in their society). A posthumanist approach can help transform how we value the people who move in both the past and the present.

There is, however, a second subset that we need to consider. As our examples of the LBK and the Vikings showed earlier, mobility is not just something that involves humans; it is fundamentally something caught up in the worlds of non-humans as well. Different kinds of technology (boats, longhouses) or animals (fish, cows) can lead to differing forms of mobility or tie people to places in different ways. This allows us to understand movement in ways that are not just posthumanist, then, but also post-anthropocentric, as we defined in Chapter 1. We can explore movement without centering human beings entirely; such an approach is an essential counterpart and collaborator in allowing us to attend to historical specificity and, with that, further disrupt the way humanism privileges certain kinds of people and certain kinds of movement. To explore in more detail the kinds of non-humans involved in movement and the roles that they play, assemblage theory proves a critical addition.

Assemblage theory, a particular element of the theories usually known as "new materialism," offers us both a way of thinking and a methodology for exploring how the world emerges relationally. Rather than starting with ideas of bounded entities—a person, a car, a pot, a boat, a cow—assemblages begin with the understanding that the world emerges through complex gatherings of multiple different elements (DeLanda 2006, 2016). These can include materials and ideas, and they operate at all kinds of scales. A university department is an assemblage of students, staff, buildings, computers, labs, and more. A diamond ring is an assemblage of gold and carbon, but also (in a western society) ideas of wealth and privilege, and potentially violence and theft (depending on the origins of the diamond, for example). Acts of movement always involve non-humans as parts of the assemblage, from the landscapes you move through to the shoes on your feet, the car you drive, or the train you ride.

Here we develop our definition of assemblages a little further before turning to our main case study. As we noted in Chapter 1, the concept of assemblage comes from the work of Gilles Deleuze and Félix Guattari (2004) and has been expanded and developed by Jane Bennett (2010), Manuel DeLanda (2006, 2016), and many others. There are three key things to always keep in mind about assemblages. First, they are always in process, or in flow; that is, they are always changing (Crellin 2020). This process of change happens in two directions, new things become part of assemblages (the technical term for this is "territorialization"), and things are always leaving assemblages (the term for this is "deterritorialization"). Assemblages are also internally organized in specific ways, but these are also in process, so they are both becoming more ordered in some ways and less in others (this is usually referred to as "coding" and "decoding") (for discussion, see Harris 2021a, 62, 237). Second, assemblages include both material and meaningful elements (Deleuze and Guattari call this "machinic" and "enunciative"). This means that assemblages that involve human beings do not only include material relations with non-humans, but also ideas, concepts, and symbols (for discussion, see Harris 2018). Third, as our examples show, assemblages are multi-scalar (for discussion, see Crellin 2017). So, as we walk down the road, we form an assemblage of movement with our bodies, our shoes, the weather as the rain beats down on us, and the social rules of how to cross a road coded in white lines and green lights. But each of these elements is also an assemblage on its own. The road is an assemblage of cars and tarmac; our shoes are assemblages of leather, cord, and so on. Non-human elements in an assemblage of movement are critical to understand how they both facilitate humans moving in some ways (the car that whisks a passenger quickly from one spot to another) and prevent it in others (the same road cuts through a housing estate making crossing difficult for residents). One of the interesting dilemmas raised by recent disputes over movement has been the desire for non-humans to continue to move even as human movement is curtailed. Brexit forms a neat example of this (Carter and Harris 2020). Movement is central to our world today, especially the movement of non-humans, but unless we take an approach like assemblage theory that is post-anthropocentric—that is, one that does not indulge in "human exceptionalism"—this becomes very difficult to recognize.

So far in this chapter, we've argued that archaeology has much to teach us about movement and mobility and that this can help us understand and rethink our contemporary attitudes to these phenomena. In this section, we've made a case for adding posthumanist and post-anthropocentric theories to such considerations. This allows for a better understanding of how different kinds of humanity emerge in specific sets of material circumstances, and it keeps an eye tuned to the critical role of non-humans within these processes. These things are easy to say, of course, but harder to put into practice. To explore what this might look like in more detail, we turn now to our main case study, bringing together these theoretical concerns with the work of the contemporary archaeologist Jason De León (2012, 2013, 2015).

Using our theoretical tools: humans and non-humans at the US-Mexican border

Archaeologist Jason De León's (2012, 2013, 2015; see also Stewart et al. 2016) *Undocumented Migration Project* uses ethnography, archaeology, and forensics to study twenty-first-century migration between Mexico and the United States. His study sits alongside work from other archaeologists exploring the US-Mexican border, such as Randall McGuire (2013, 2018; McGuire and Van Dyke 2019) and those exploring similar migratory contexts elsewhere, such as Yanis Hamilakis (2016), George Tyrikos-Ergas (2016), and Ángela Arbeláez and Edward Mulholland (2016) on the Greek border island of Lesvos, Dan Hicks and Sarah Mallet (2019) at the Calais "Jungle" camp in France, and Rachael Kiddey (2019) studying migrant shelters in Athens. The forms of mobility De León documents are largely motivated by the extreme wealth differentials of global capitalism. Most migrants attempt the move in search of employment opportunities and improved living conditions that are not available to them in their current homes. De León shows how these migration efforts are constrained by border control and the material world in general. The most obvious example of this is the United States of America's "prevention through deterrence" strategy, which is designed to keep undocumented migrants out of the US (US Border Patrol 1994). This strategy employs the Sonoran Desert and all its dangers as a key element in territorializing the border. De León and others argue convincingly that this strategy is ineffective; it does *not* prevent people from attempting the crossing, but it clearly makes the crossing more dangerous, often leading to migrant injuries and deaths (De León 2012, 480). Of note, a parallel approach exists in the UK, where politicians have sought to deter Channel crossings by making them considerably more dangerous.

Understanding migration here requires attention to non-humans. When we think about migration purely as a human process, it is all too easy to write out the deadly effects of the desert, just as, with migration in Europe, we write out the deadly effects of the Mediterranean Sea or the English Channel. If we render the non-human as natural and migration as human and therefore cultural, we might fail to appreciate the capacities the desert brings to this process, or the role it plays in the tragic deaths that often result from attempted crossings. This does *not* somehow distribute blame or make the desert "responsible" for the deaths of migrants, far from it. Rather, assemblage theory demands we think critically about the specific relational context, including the desert in which this migration takes place. Migrants and the desert are territorialized in the process of movement into an assemblage with deadly consequences for some of its components (namely, the migrants).

De León engages critically with some non-human elements of migration through an analysis of the emergent smuggling industry in this area, highlighting human-thing relations and noting the "dialectical and often oppressive" relationship between migrants and the objects they use to cross the desert, including dark-colored clothing and water bottles (De León 2012, 478). "It's better to be hot than caught," is the title of one of De León's (2012) articles, referring to one migrant's response to De León's questioning of his choice to wear black-colored clothing on the crossing. De León considers the standardization of a set of dark colored material tools used by migrants to cross the desert. He notes that the use of dark-colored clothes and equipment is well known by border patrol agents; to them, it is a material sign of the "undocumented migrant assemblage" and is, therefore, often used to profile suspects. Furthermore, he considers how this material assemblage disadvantages the migrants by increasing the physical difficulty of the crossing.

Businesses on the Mexican side of the border market black water bottles, dark-colored clothing, and inexpensive, Chinese- or Mexican-made footwear (sneakers or trainers, but never hiking boots) that mimic styles popular in the US to would-be migrants (De León 2012). These businesses exploit migrant desperation by building upon and reifying local folk understandings of the best equipment for a successful crossing. There are many interesting parallels between the emergence of this industry and "disaster capitalism," where companies and people attempt to make a profit from disasters like floods and earthquakes. In this case, De León shows how this industry, combined with the dangers of the Sonoran Desert, significantly hinders attempted border crossings.

Black water bottles, for example, substantially decrease the likelihood of a successful crossing in several ways. Many migrants prefer black bottles to clear and opaque bottles, which, according to local folk understandings, reflect light and attract unwanted attention from US border patrol. De León notes that black bottles, compared to white and opaque bottles, increase water temperatures significantly when exposed to direct sunlight. Crucially, a higher water temperature increases the drinker's core temperature and forces their body to expend extra energy to cool down (De León 2012, 486). For the same reasons, dark-colored clothing increases the physical difficulty of the crossing. Similarly, cheaply made footwear is not suitable for crossing the desert; these shoes often break down, slowing migrants and causing injuries. As noted, in addition to these physical disadvantages, border patrol agents are also aware of these specialized material assemblages and often profile possible migrants based on spotting these signs, picking potential migrants out of crowds for interrogation. In summary, these specialized material assemblages increase the likelihood of being both "hot" and "caught" while simultaneously helping local business owners turn a profit. The material assemblage directly affects the nature of the migration process and has an effect on the likelihood of success.

The process of migration here includes all the different elements assembled: the dark clothing and water bottles, the temperature and the landscape, the migrant and the authorities. The operation of capitalism here, which we explore in more depth in Chapter 3, shows how these assemblages are multi-scalar. They operate both in the intimate moments of one person's attempted crossing and in the flow of goods and services up to and across the US-Mexico border. The migrant in dark clothes cannot cross the border, but truckloads of avocados can. Differences in economic opportunity attract migrants to the border, and they find ways of creating new economic opportunities once they arrive; none of this is human as opposed to material, it is always the assemblage of both. Migration at the US-Mexico border ties in capitalist processes of production operating at one scale, with the intensive heat and oppressive environment of the desert on the other. These assemblages include material properties, like the way black water bottles gather heat, with social meanings, such as how they mark you as a migrant. Thinking like an archaeologist, as De León does, allows us to understand how humans and non-humans assemble the different modes of migration in the worlds in which they operate. Like the houses of the LBK or the ecologies of Norse worlds, sets of relations both hinder and facilitate different kinds of movement.

Again, to understand the process by which migration happens, we must embrace the important roles that non-humans play. If we don't recognize how materials are caught up in the processes we study, we fail to engage with their complexities and realities on the ground. This move away from anthropocentrism does not *diminish* the suffering of human beings, nor does it deny the active roles of human beings. Assemblage theory demonstrates that causation is not simply about identifying singular individuals for blame nor sharing out responsibility as though there was a fixed share to go around. Embracing the active role of the non-human, as De León shows, does not diminish the role of US border policy; *it actively identifies why and how it operates in the way that it does*. It recognizes how the deaths of these migrants, indeed the very process of migration, can only be understood by including non-humans, such as landscapes, in our understanding.

Conclusion: learning from archaeology and looking forward to migration

Movement is everywhere, and migration is inevitable. From the origins of our species, via the histories revealed in isotopic and genetic studies of our past to the histories of colonialism, there has never been a period or a people without movement and migration. What is relatively recent, however, is the suggestion that mobility is somehow abnormal or wrong. Although migration and movement are common in human history, they happen within very specific historical contexts, and they involve different non-human partners. One of the notable elements of our current world is the ranking of migrants. At the top stands proudly the White, middle-class, European, heterosexual male. Due to his capacity to fulfill these societal expectations, his ability to move is supported in many ways by society—he can move from country to country seeking economic or social gain, or merely entertainment. At the bottom, people with different skin pigmentation or ethnic identities are denied any right to movement at all and will be left to drown or die of thirst if they attempt it. In the middle of these two sit a host of others who are evaluated on their economic usefulness; someone with a medical degree might be welcome across a border where someone who simply wants to survive will not. Our current economic system is perhaps the most dependent on mobility of all time.

This contrast between those who are set in place and those who move does not survive an encounter with archaeology. When we look at the movement of European colonists into Vanuatu, we see that the missions they brought with them were transformed by the encounters there and that differing iterations of Christianity emerged. We can see how the different worlds of the farmers of central Europe emerged from both differences within LBK societies and between the LBK and others. We see here, too, how forms of architecture that seem to suggest stability can also drive movement; for example, the moment of long-house decay marking the time to start a new act of building somewhere else. Just as relations with non-humans can drive movement, so they can tie people into place, as we saw with the Norse. In each of these cases, movement and stasis, change and continuity, inside and outside, are part of complex and historically emergent relations. These relations challenge us to rethink mobility in our own time. It is here where De León's work on the US-Mexican border is so crucial. Set within an understanding that embraces the complex role of non-humans, from deserts to water bottles, we can use archaeology to reconceptualize the complexity of modern migration and to challenge the way we conceptualize and write about it.

In this chapter, we argued that thinking like an archaeologist has much to teach us about mobility. It reminds us how central it is to human lives, how it has specific rhythms, how it can involve non-humans that allow us to move more freely, like boats, and others that spur movement on even as they tie us to place, like the longhouses of the LBK. It is when we combine archaeology with an attention to the role of these non-humans, and a recognition of the emergence of particular kinds of people and mobility in certain contexts, that it has the most to teach us. We looked at how assemblage theory can help us appreciate how humans have never moved alone. Human lives and human movements always intersect with a host of non-humans that form assemblages of historically specific modes of migration. The importance of engaging the role of the non-human here enhances the second theoretical emphasis of this chapter, the importance of posthumanism. It is posthumanism that insists we reject a singular standard against which everyone is measured. Posthumanism does not measure the bodies of migrants and find them wanting, and it does not require them to be settled or to possess passports, visas, and the other trappings of those whose movement is deemed acceptable today. Posthumanism embraces the emergence of multiple kinds of humanity in different material contexts. Of course, many humanists would argue that they, too, value all humans equally, but in their insistence that humans can be separated from the context of their emergence, and that they transcend their historical contexts, they create a barrier that always results, in the end, in a refusal to engage fully with the non-human. This, in turn, sows the seeds that allow some to make certain people, those that most resemble humanist Man, more human than others.

Chapter 3

Archaeology and capitalism

Flows and desires

Introduction: you are what you own?

The message shown in Figure 3.1 is perhaps off-putting for some, especially for those living in capitalist worlds—and, let's face it, that would be most, if not all, of our readers. Capitalism tells us just the opposite of this message. *Capitalism* is an economic system that makes anything exchangeable through commodification, that places no limit on the accumulation of wealth through the "free" market, that frames nature only as a place to extract human value, and that played (and continues to play) a massive role in countless atrocities over the last 500 years or so. That we *are* what we own[1]—or that our worth as people is directly reflected in the things that we've accumulated (especially land)—is an old capitalist incantation that most of us continue to experience, navigate, and unfortunately reproduce daily. This capitalist incantation surrounds us, even follows us; this is perhaps most obvious in the advertisements that pop up as you search the internet. You pull up your social media account and find an advertisement for beanie hats—it's cold outside this winter, and you've been thinking about buying a new one. Well, this advert shows you who you could become if you only clicked a few buttons and ordered one. You go to another site (this one is much more serious and devoted to sharing your academic writing with the world), but there, too, you are shown a variety of commodities blinking in the background, ranging from academic books to skateboards, that you could purchase to become a better version of yourself. Given the ubiquity of capitalism in our lives—it's even prying into my computer as I write this paragraph (well, maybe I do need a new beanie)—it is a vitally important subject of archaeological study.

Each of our relationships with capitalism is multi-faceted and complex. We tend to think of it as something produced by the mega-rich: captains of industry, factory owners, and big bosses. We guess that very few of our readers are part of the so-called 1% of the richest people in the world, who we might most readily refer to as capitalists. As we pay our bills, manage our money, and purchase things like the beanie hat mentioned in the previous paragraph, or more appropriately, desire things that we cannot afford, we might well feel that capitalists are "someone else." Yet many of us are privileged enough that we are not among the 828 million people

DOI: 10.4324/9781003244141-3

Figure 3.1 Anti-capitalist message.
Image: Craig N. Cipolla.

the World Food Program categorizes as not having enough food or the 43.3 million people at risk of famine (World Food Programme n.d.). The capitalist system that surrounds us makes most of us capitalists; it is just that we are different kinds of capitalists (cf. Braidotti 2022, where she argues that *we* are all in this together, but *we* are not all the same). In short, our place in the system and our classification as capitalists become starkly obvious when we compare our situation to that of some-one who doesn't have enough food or who lives in constant fear of famine, but our importance in upholding the system pales in comparison to that of the mega-rich.

Without a doubt, archaeology with its attention to the material world has shed new and valuable light on capitalism and its varied histories. It offers us opportu-nities to reassess the worlds in which we live and to rethink what we would like them to become in the future. A key component and contribution of this work is documenting how capitalism emerged (Johnson 1996) and took shape in differ-ent places and times. The archaeological gaze on things, that is, telling histories via the material traces left behind, provides a powerful corrective to the histories of capitalism that are only told through texts or representations. As detailed later, archaeologists have made great strides in telling these histories via the study of materials and material relations, in documenting resistance to capitalism, and in calling for future-oriented, anti-capitalist praxis. After dealing with each of these, we consider alternative approaches from our theoretical toolkit and introduce a few conceptual tools that offer fresh and helpful perspectives on capitalism. After establishing these, we move on to explore how they inform our understanding of a pervasive issue in today's world—homelessness.

Setting the stage: archaeological perspectives on capitalism, commodification, and ideology

The archaeological gaze offers important insights into capitalist relations. As an example, Stephen Mrozowski's environmental approach to the study of urban colonial contexts in New England (USA) documented important differences in the general health status of different social classes. His use of parasitology to study soils collected from privies revealed how all people living in nineteenth-century urban environments played host to a varied list of parasites (Mrozowski 2006a, 32, 2006b, 37–62) and, because of this, almost certainly lived with multiple health issues, including various digestive discomforts. Yet, the severity of infection and access to medical care cleaved themselves along the lines of social class. Those of "lesser means" suffered more and had fewer opportunities to improve their health. This structural difference between class groups certainly shaped how well members of different social classes felt day-to-day. Here we are reminded of the arbitrariness of the "pull yourself up by your bootstraps" narrative of American capitalism. Contrary to the narrative of the American dream—that you are what you make of yourself—archaeology shows that not everyone approached their bootstraps on equal ground, in this case, suffering from the same health problems. In contrast, as in today's world, one's economic status determined how many parasites and health ailments one had to live with while making a paycheck. Even though many capitalists see themselves as apart from and above nature, the workers that they employed clearly suffered from more "nature" than they did, thus making company owners' paths to wealth accumulation all the easier. Here again, the capitalist ethic of "you are what you own" (in this case, affording access to proper healthcare) reigns supreme and justifies the mistreatment of those with *less than*, glossing them as the unfortunate losers in capitalist competition. This is part of the cycle: you don't have access to healthcare because you don't work as hard as us (who have proper access), and you must therefore endure a harder life (which, of course, limits your ability to succeed). A single capitalist "success story" is thus contingent upon the suffering of large numbers of people.

In other words, capitalism involves relationships between different groups of people and typically results in different forms of dependency between those people. The parasitic relationship between company owners and workers is well documented; the owners depend on the workers and the workers' sale of their labor for much less than the owners earn from exploiting and harnessing it. Christopher Matthews (2010) provides a compelling example of how a once self-sufficient group of "workers" rapidly became entrapped in—and dependent upon—relationships with company owners. In this example, the "workers" were various Indigenous peoples of northeastern North America (especially the Great Lakes region) who became involved in the fur trade of the seventeenth and eighteenth centuries. Initially, the fur trade was just that; Indigenous trappers exchanged excess furs that they had accumulated as part of their typical subsistence practices and ecological relations. Of note, these typical practices seem to have a very long-term history in North America that certainly preceded European settler-colonial presence. This, of course, is *not* to say that everything in North America was static or unchanging before Euro-colonialism, but to recognize that Indigenous peoples like the Haudenosaunee of what we now call upstate New York and Ontario maintained sustainable ecological relations—taking furs in numbers that sustained populations of fur-bearing animals. Furs were traded for imported glass beads, marine shell beads acquired from coastal Indigenous groups, and other commodities like brass kettles. Early examples of fur trading represented what we might today call a "side hustle" in an otherwise traditional subsistence pattern.

Things changed, however, as furs became popular in European markets and trading companies increased in scale (Matthews 2010, Chapter 2; see also Cronon 1983). The water-resistant qualities of beaver furs made them a popular material for making hats. As their popularity increased, so did the profits made by company owners, increasing the desire to rapidly step up "production." On the North American side of this trade, Indigenous peoples were given more incentive to focus narrowly on only obtaining furs rather than other subsistence practices. Instead of fishing, hunting, gathering, and cultivating, Indigenous trappers came to specialize in acquiring fur for the trade and often exchanged fur for subsistence-related items from European traders. The growing power of the fur trade effectively led to a shift from self-sufficient Indigenous communities who obtained their own food to Indigenous communities who "worked" as trappers to obtain food from Euro-colonial sources. This led to the loss of certain forms of ecological engagement; it interrupted the flow of knowledge about how to live on the land from one generation to the next, and, within a matter of decades, the dependency on Euro-colonial traders had increased exponentially.

Matthews (2010) goes on to explore how and why Euro-colonial peoples felt little obligation to help Indigenous communities and nations that began to struggle with subsistence in the eighteenth century, oftentimes primarily *because of* the growing global fur trade and shifting relations that emerged alongside it. Even though there was a clear relationship between Indigenous and Euro-colonial traders, those relationships of obligation were glossed over. This is yet another key component of capitalism. It is contingent upon relations, but these are often downplayed or completely ignored by those in power. This point is articulated nicely in the work of Matthew Johnson (1996), who discussed a host of related issues in terms of enclosure in late medieval to early modern England and Wales. The physical enclosure of field systems and private property emerged with nascent forms of capitalism in these areas, but this is not the only form of bounding that Johnson attended to in his archaeology of capitalism. He took an interest in forms of material *and mental* enclosure, the latter partially resonating with Bruno Latour's (1993) concept of purification. For Johnson (1996, 2), nascent forms of capitalism emerged alongside worldviews that erroneously cleaved up the relationality of the world, leaving us with neat and tidy boxes for religious, agrarian, public, and domestic spheres (cf. Latour 1993).

Similarly, Matthews (2010) documented how the worldview of traders falsely divided economic exchange and moral obligation as well as Euro-colonial and Indigenous worlds, all of which were deeply entangled in the eighteenth-century fur trade. The world is relational, but capitalism seems to domesticate us to see it as increasingly fractured and disconnected—made up of autonomous bits that relate to one another only in terms of exchange value (see Cipolla 2017); this is what Karl Marx referred to as commodity fetishism. A key characteristic of capitalism is that *everything* is exchangeable, and exchange relations are short-term and tidy transactions, meaning that once you complete the exchange, your obligations to the other party end (as opposed to gift exchange systems that have enduring social obligations and debts; see Mauss 1990). This pattern meshes well with the emergence of notions of individuality and individual freedom. You are what you own, and you certainly aren't responsible for others who have failed to accumulate.

This level of exchangeability or commodification is one of the unique and defining characteristics of capitalism. Nowhere is this more apparent than in the commodification and dehumanization of people caught up in acts of slavery and human trafficking. Archaeology and anthropology have revealed much about abhorrent histories like the Atlantic slave trade and the notions of race that emerged within it (Agbe-Davies 2015; Hayes 2013). We discuss these histories in greater detail in Chapter 6, but for now, it is important to emphasize how the institution of slavery created, perpetuated, and enhanced structural inequalities. Anna Agbe-Davies notes, for example, how land ownership in the colony of Virginia was directly correlated to owning other human beings. The more people a person owned, the more land they were entitled to claim in the colony. The more land they had, the more power they had to influence legislation—much of which concerned the codification of race and the institutionalization of race-based slavery. Here we see the codification of a hierarchy of humanity based on power, which connects directly to the ownership of land, of people, and more. As discussed in Chapter 9, capitalism also divides the world into commodities and makes no obligations to care for it once value has been extracted.

Yet, how is it that people stood by while workers were mistreated, environments were desecrated, and other human beings were enslaved? Archaeologists have addressed questions like this head-on, usually in discussions concerning ideology, a critical concept in Marxism and Marxist archaeology (Leone 1988, 1995, 2010; McGuire 1992). Ideologies mask social contradictions and naturalize inequality. Consider, for instance, the "pull yourself up by your bootstraps" mentality discussed earlier and how it naturalized different levels of access to healthcare for different social classes. You must deal with a harder life, but that's because you didn't pull yourself up as hard as those of us with adequate healthcare. Fault lies with the individual (who failed) rather than the system that produced—and benefited from—this inequality. The archaeological gaze has much to offer in studies of ideology as it considers much more than the things that people say and write down. Mark Leone's (e.g., 1988, 2010) pathbreaking work in Annapolis, Maryland, serves as an excellent example. He showed how seemingly miscellaneous things—garden designs, table settings, clocks, or scientific instruments displayed in the home—all actively performed capitalist ideology. To take two of these, table settings became individualized, meaning every person at the table came to have their own plate, flatware, etc., around the same time that clocks became popular. The individual table settings helped to reinforce just how much of an individual you were, responsible for your own fate in the emergent capitalist world of Annapolis, while the clocks helped establish routines that forced workers to discipline themselves to show up on time (Leone 1988). If you were late, it was no one's fault but your own, and company owners or bosses felt justified in penalizing you. Although these approaches have proven incredibly useful for archaeology's engagement with capitalism, in what follows we ask if there is a need for new ways of thinking that move beyond ideology.

Resistance and praxis

Another key strength of archaeologies of capitalism is their ability to identify and study instances of resistance. Many (perhaps most) examples of resistance to capitalist power structures have gone undocumented, but the archaeological lens helps us learn about these struggles. Some forms of resistance involve covertly breaking rules and laws (e.g., Shackel 2000). On eighteenth-century Chesapeake plantations, for example, slave dwellings often contained sub-floor pits or small square holes dug under floors after houses were built (Singleton 2006; see also chapters in Singleton 1999). Archaeologists find myriad items in these pits—animal bones, broken white pottery, and even grape pollen interpreted as traces of wine offerings (Singleton 2006, 322–3). Many archaeologists see sub-floor pits as forms of resistance; perhaps they were secret places, not directly visible to those in power, where enslaved people could store away important resources like food or even make religious and spiritual offerings.

Other notable examples of resistance include studies of moonshine production and prostitution. Even though there were laws in place prohibiting the production of moonshine in twentieth-century North Carolina, Kirk French (2022) finds numerous traces of illicit moonshine production. He notes how North American moonshine production has a deep history that stretches back at least 1,000 years (from England and Scotland) and how US prohibition legislation in 1818 attempted to outlaw such practices. The illicit moonshine economy that continued at this time was an example of an "intimate economy" that operated outside the boundaries of capitalism and in direct defiance of US law. Similarly, Jade Luiz (2022) and other historical archaeologists find ample evidence for brothels and prostitution in places and times where prostitution was illegal. Luiz (2022) studies a nineteenth-century brothel in Boston, documenting another illicit economy that operated under the radar and distanced from capitalism.

In other cases, resistance was much more explicit (e.g., Shackel 1994). The Colorado Coal Field War (1913–1914) is an obvious example, where workers stood up for their rights and attempted to improve their conditions, challenging the grip that capitalism had on their lives (Ludlow Collective 2001; McGuire 2006; McGuire and Reckner 2002). The Ludlow Massacre, one of the bloodiest incidents of the Coal Field War, has received a great deal of archaeological attention. In 1914, the Colorado National Guard engaged in a battle with armed strikers near Ludlow, Colorado; this occurred at a tent settlement of strikers and their families. Hundreds of guards fired on the camp with machine guns for an entire day before looting the settlement and setting it on fire. Twenty people in the strikers' camp died that day, including women and children, some of whom suffocated under burning tents. This violent altercation was a watershed moment in the history of US workers' rights.

In the case of the Ludlow Massacre, archaeology is not just about the past. It is about using the past to help shape a better future through *praxis*. Praxis is strategically informed action, usually of a group, and typically designed to challenge social hierarchies. Randall McGuire (2006, 141) elegantly describes the mission of studying the Ludlow Massacre archaeologically:

> The project's message is simple. Labour's rights to a safe workplace, benefits, reasonable wages, a forty-hour week and dignity were won with blood. They were not freely given by capitalists but bought with the lives of working people like those who died at Ludlow.

Archaeologies of capitalism are thus firmly situated in the here and now (and in the future). Whether studying structural inequality, relational dependency, the lack of obligation felt for other people with *less than*, the commodification of people, places, or things, ideologies, resistance, or the violation of workers' rights, archaeologies of capitalism give us much to contemplate about our current dilemma. They offer firm ground from which to question the "you are what you own" ethic of capitalism. Indeed, today archaeology is thoroughly entangled with capitalism as it is often the commercial development of a site (to create some form of profit) that provides the impetus for archaeology to happen, creating jobs for archaeologists (see Wurst 2019). Next, we experiment with other ideas that complement and expand upon some of the approaches outlined here.

Theoretical toolkit: capitalism as flow and desire

One of the key things that these critical archaeologies demonstrate is that capitalism is not a single overarching edifice; it isn't a malevolent entity lurking somewhere in a dark alley, ready to pounce. Nor will removing specific capitalists defeat capitalism altogether; the mega-rich, the bosses, the factory owners, and the business leaders are not the only sources. Things are more complicated than that. Capitalism is widespread and sticky, and it involves much more than people.

In common parlance, especially if you are on the left of the political spectrum, it is easy to refer to capitalism in generic terms: "the trouble with university education is capitalism," "we must bring down capitalism," or "we have to keep capitalism out of the National Health Service." These statements treat capitalism as a single thing, what the philosopher Manuel DeLanda (2006, 28) calls a "reified generality," a thing that is somehow external to the very processes it is trying to explain. Something that is, to evoke another philosophical term, "transcendent." Rendering capitalism transcendent severs it from its historical connections, from the social and material relations that constitute it daily. This framing makes capitalism seem unbeatable and eternal, an encircling force that is inescapable. No wonder Frederic Jameson (1994, xii) said that it is easier to imagine the end of the world than the end of capitalism.

Archaeologists, especially historical archaeologists, have long abandoned viewing capitalism simply as an external force (e.g., Leone 1995; McGuire 1992). Influenced by Marxism, they view capitalism as a particular set of economic relations, grouped around the private ownership of means of production, guarded by an ideology that precisely renders it ahistorical and, therefore, unavailable to critique. There are other ways of understanding capitalism, too, though, which in some ways complement these approaches and in other ways take us in a different direction. Here we want to draw on the analysis of capitalism offered by Gilles Deleuze and Félix Guattari (2013), whose concept of assemblage we discussed in Chapters 1 and 2. Deleuze and Guattari's work is famously complex but has increasingly influenced archaeologists (e.g., Crellin 2020; Harris 2021a; Jervis 2018). Writing their first book together in the late 1960s, they connected Marxist understandings of the economy and capitalism with psychoanalytic ideas derived from the writings of Sigmund Freud and others. They sought to understand how the economy and the mind could be understood together. Rather than seeing two separate sets of processes, one affecting the mind, our desires, and our family lives (traditionally the focus of psychology and psychiatry), and another shaping our economies, working lives, and society (the domain of economic analyses), they saw these two areas as thoroughly interlinked. Rather than placing certain concepts outside of time and space (as psychoanalysis tried to do in particular), they aimed to set out a thoroughly historicized—or immanent—understanding of capitalist society and its past, present, and future. Far from being against either Marxism or psychoanalysis, although critical of both, Deleuze and Guattari thought that by bringing them together, one could understand the dominance of capitalism in helpful new ways.

Rather than concentrating on issues like the means of production, Deleuze and Guattari (2013) approached capitalism in terms of how it emerges through setting up new kinds of *flows* through society and across the world—flows of things, flows of people, and, most of all, flows of capital. For them, capitalism works when money and capital get separated from the contexts in which they are produced; the meanings attached to objects and practices therefore become "decoded" and "deterritorialized" in their terms, allowing the flows to crisscross societies and the world (Deleuze and Guattari 2013, 259). These flows push at their limits constantly, allowing them to flow more quickly. At the same time, Deleuze and Guattari (2013, 289) argued other forces act to control these flows to ensure they can be managed and put to use. Consider the flows of furs discussed earlier and the slowing and ceasing of Indigenous subsistence practices to allow those flows to increase. Here we can also see the contrast we encountered in Chapter 2. On the one hand, the celebration of the movement of non-humans, shredded of meaning, consumed far from where they were produced (and, with this, the movement of those "good migrant" humans who bring capital with them). On the other hand, social forces push back against this, cutting and stopping other flows of migrants or refugees.

One of the ways that capitalism controls these flows, bringing them back down to earth, is through the family, or rather, the way that many of us are taught to understand families. For Deleuze and Guattari (2013), the classic "nuclear" family is not simply a natural entity or a harmless byproduct of our current social setting; on the contrary, this model of the family sits at the heart of capitalism. To understand this, they critique the way psychoanalysis has traditionally thought about the family. In classic Freudian analysis, at the heart of the family is the Oedipus complex, the idea that there lies a fundamental tension between the mother, father, and child where the child must learn to suppress its sexual desire for its mother and its wish to replace its father (note the way gender and heteronormativity are implied here). For Freud, and others, these tensions are an eternal element of human existence; accordingly, for them, it explains how the potential for incest is controlled, how sexual desire works, how family lives are reproduced, and more. For Deleuze and Guattari, however, this model of the family is not ahistorical nor universal. Instead, it emerges specifically through capitalism. These forms of family protect property, power, and the interests of capital. As they rather evocatively describe, "it is not via a flow of shit or a wave of incest that Oedipus arrives, but via the decoded flows of capital-money" (Deleuze and Guattari 2013, 306). These families shape both how money is passed on and also help to produce the kinds of subjectivities that sustain capitalism. This framework makes us internalize our own fathers, who we try to live up to by being successful capitalist citizens, capturing and focusing flows of desire in ways that help sustain capitalism (Deleuze and Guattari 2013, 304). Their point here is that capitalism doesn't just shape our economies, it shapes how our families function. It shapes our relationships with our partners, our parents, our siblings, and our children. Homeownership, success, children—everything you think or want for your own life—are all caught up with the flows of capital that Deleuze and Guattari mapped.

Does this render the nuclear family another example of ideology, like the American Dream we encountered earlier? That is, is it an example of *false consciousness*? Think about your own family or friends. Are people tricked into wanting children? Even if you don't have or want children, do you think all parents have been tricked into it? Or that they don't love their children? More broadly, if ideas like the American Dream or wanting to be rich, successful, and famous are just tricks of capitalism, how come we *actually* seem to want them? And how come, even after understanding that they don't work, are unfair, or are part of a way of doing things that involves destroying the planet (Chapter 9), many people *really* do still want them? We saw at the start of the chapter how the different processes that make up capitalism rig things to ensure that the bodies of most people will be poorer, more ill, and less well-cared-for than the bodies of a wealthy minority. Why do we put up with this? As Deleuze and Guattari (2013, 42) say:

> the astonishing thing is not that some people steal or that others occasionally go out on strike, but rather that all those who are starving do not steal as a regular practice, and all those who are exploited are not continually out on strike.

To understand this, they argue, we need to get away from the concept of ideology. As they rather baldly put it, "the concept of ideology is an execrable concept that hides the real problems" (Deleuze and Guattari 2013, 392). By thinking of ideology as a set of beliefs or a form of false consciousness (you don't really want a family or a good job, you just *think* you do), they argue that this element of Marxism fails to understand *desire*.

Desire, or what we want, is usually taken to be something connected to two things. First, it is linked to something inside us, something that makes us who we really are. Second, it is understood in relation to lack—when you desire or want something that you don't currently have. This relation of desire and lack is at the heart of how psychiatrists have understood family relations through the Oedipus complex. In contrast to this, Deleuze and Guattari (2013) argue that desire drives the kinds of flows that underlie both societies (capitalist or otherwise) and the emergence of people as particular kinds of subjects. The flows of capital that help form specific kinds of families pre-exist your emergence as a person with a particular form of subjectivity, and the same is true of desire. The desires, these positive forces, create subjects through the process Deleuze and Guattari (2013, 43) call "desiring-production." In capitalism, the Oedipal relations psychiatrists have identified are the means of capturing these flows of desire and creating a particular kind of subject. This means that rather than being fooled into wanting things by capitalism, or by the ruling classes, as mainstream Marxist analysis might contend, we are created through specific forms of desire. As they put it, "the fundamental problem of political philosophy is still precisely the one that Spinoza saw so clearly, and that Wilhelm Reich rediscovered: 'Why do men fight *for* their servitude as stubbornly as though it were their salvation?'" (Deleuze and Guattari 2013, 42, original emphasis). In other words, the question isn't why do we put up with a system that punishes so many of us; it is why do we actively desire that system? As people, we emerge from the flows of desire that are always already encoded and entwined via relations with our family members with flows of capital; these desires actively produce us, pushing us in particular directions.

What does this mean for us as archaeologists wrestling with contemporary issues? First and foremost, thinking in these terms can add to our repertoire of ways of understanding capitalist societies. Furthermore, they can help us reconceptualize people who live in such societies but outside of these capitalist norms. One such group is homeless people. In the next section, we examine how archaeological engagements with homelessness combine with the theoretical concepts discussed thus far in the chapter to provide useful, future-oriented ways of thinking.

Using our toolkit: the archaeology of homelessness

How have archaeologists discussed homelessness, and what might the previously presented reading of desire, flow, and capitalism add? In 2010, Larry Zimmerman and colleagues published an agenda-setting paper about the material culture of homelessness. The authors proposed that archaeologists work with homeless people, using the discipline to make positive contributions to the world at large, or to "real world" problems. Zimmerman and colleagues (2010) described how, accidentally, they came to study homelessness. They had been excavating the overgrown garden of an historic mansion in St. Paul, Minnesota. As the team arrived on site each day, they noticed homeless people sheltering in different parts of the garden, and their survey work revealed a distinct material culture of homelessness: "cast-off clothing, sleeping bags, alcohol bottles and evidence of cooking" (Zimmerman et al. 2010, 446). That archaeologists effectively "stumbled upon" homelessness as a research topic is indicative of social attitudes to homelessness—all too often, it is something we choose to ignore. Archaeologists who study homelessness point this out repeatedly; many western societies conventionally ignore and Other homeless people (see, for example, Kiddey 2018, 701; Kiddey and Schofield 2011, 20; Zimmerman et al. 2010, 445).

We can think about this Othering process in relation to the concept of humanist Man, introduced in Chapter 2. Homeless people are regularly ignored and sometimes viewed as threatening. We often hold stereotypes about them. For example, Zimmerman and colleagues (2010, 449–50) remarked on their surprise that homeless people had books and were educated or that they used blogs to record their lives and offer advice to others experiencing homelessness. In our thinking, these communities differ from the humanist ideal because they are un-homed and are then painted as less human, as outside of—and threatening to—the norms of their respective societies. There are strong parallels here to the undocumented migrants discussed in Chapter 2. For homeless people in particular, the kinds of family life discussed before as central to capitalism are often absent and disrupted; this is far from coincidental.

A clear material culture of homelessness emerges from the literature (Kiddey 2017; Zimmerman et al. 2010, 446). This material culture is used by those experiencing homelessness to construct "homes" for themselves and to produce the places they live in, making them more than mere shelters (see Figure 3.2). As an example, Zimmerman and colleagues (2010, 449; plate 1) describe a camp with a mattress and pillow covered by a bedspread with a rug laid out at the foot of the bed and a sheet of cardboard placed to stop car lights (effectively acting like curtains). Drawing on work by Valado (2006), the authors argue that homeless people use

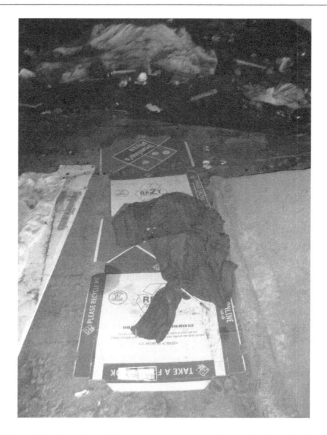

Figure 3.2 Materials abandoned by mainstream capitalism (a pizza box) re-purposed to form a bed for a person experiencing homelessness.

Image: Rachael Kiddey.

material culture to make safe, comfortable, and supportive homes despite the wider city and society that works to exclude them. Courtney Singleton (2021, 9) refers to this practice as "alternative forms of home." Homeless peoples' desires flow and produce subjectivities in ways that are different from, but not unrelated to, those within mainstream capitalist society. Alternative kinds of home, family, and relatedness emerge from these desires, showing how particular (and arbitrary) ideas of nuclear families are, even in modern western societies.

Zimmerman and colleagues (2010) identified three kinds of homeless sites in Indianapolis: 1) route sites where there is evidence that those experiencing homelessness have been passing through; 2) short-term sites that have been used for a night or two; and 3) long-term campsites where people have been making their own homes. They note that these sites often emerge in "places poorly maintained by landowners and less frequently scrutinized by law enforcement" (Zimmerman et al. 2010, 447).

This is a theme that emerges in other archaeologies of homelessness; people—though not the people who live there—refer to the places occupied by those experiencing homelessness as "non-places" and "liminal" locations. This is the case for Stelios Lekakis (2019), who studied the area under the Anapafseos Street Bridge in Athens, Greece. Lekakis (2019) talks about the area as an in-between place, arguing that neo-liberalism and policing have effectively pushed flows of subaltern people there; a range of different people, including undocumented migrants, refugees, prostitutes, and drug dealers, use the space. Lekakis (2019, 152) also writes about Pedion Areos Park in Athens. It has a long history of use by a variety of different groups. Yet, after its budget was cut, visitor numbers declined, and the park eventually became a "liminal" place. As a result, in 2015, it became home to 50 refugee families from Afghanistan and, more recently, became a site for prostitution and drug dealing. These kinds of places, abandoned by mainstream capitalism, become liminal places or non-places that are reproduced as such every day by most citizens. But when we look at the archaeology of homelessness, these are clearly not non-places for the people who live in them.

The history of Turbo Island—a homeless site in Bristol (UK) studied and excavated as part of a collaborative project with those experiencing homelessness— allows us to take our thinking further (Kiddey 2017; Kiddey and Schofield 2009, 2010, 2011). The site sits in the middle of Bristol, a prosperous city in southern England. First, how would such a place become a non-place and thereby a place for those experiencing homelessness? Turbo Island was once comprised of three Georgian townhouses; today, if the houses were still intact, they would doubtless be of high rental and commercial value (Crea et al. 2014, 134–6). During World War II, the houses were bombed and left in a ruined state, and, in 1961, they were demolished as part of a road-widening project. As a result, the space came to have no commercial value and was bought by an advertising company that simply used it to put up billboards. Turbo Island effectively became a place of no significant value to capitalism, a place through which flows of capital and profit could not be moved, and, as a result, it was abandoned and became a place into which homeless people moved. In these ruins of capitalism, people who exist outside of its mainstream flows find spaces to call home (cf. Tsing 2015).

When we consider the evidence from Indianapolis, Athens, and Bristol together, some key themes emerge. To the homed population, the places that those experiencing homelessness live appear to be non-places, or liminal places abandoned by "normal" flows of people and capital. Yet, in each case flows of people and desire are still circulating through these places. In all three cases, the authors discuss flows of people through spaces and financial exchanges—flows of capital still happen there, and homes are still built, just not of the kind most people expect. Lekakis' (2019) work came about after they participated in a project to "clean" up parts of Athens. This collective grassroots project aimed to tidy marginal areas to increase general wellbeing. Lekakis (2019, 153; 157) discusses how this kind of work, to clean away the debris of life that lies outside of traditional bounds, is often seen as apolitical and categorically a "good thing." The traces of these non-people, in their non-places, need to be tidied away so that the spaces can become useful for "proper" citizens once again. Gabriel Moshenska and Shaun Shelly (2020) present a parallel example from Oxford (UK), where they used archaeological recording techniques to capture abandoned drug paraphernalia. They note that the next step when discovering such a collection of objects is usually to call the council, many of whom employ "cleaning teams" to remove the material culture of drugs. On the one hand, it is easy to see why this kind of tidying can be seen as generally good and helpful behavior and might be seen as apolitical. In some cases, however, this would serve to erase the lives of homeless people, removing them from cityscapes and possibly even disposing of their possessions, including, for example, vital medicines and treasured objects that they both need and want to retain (Zimmerman et al. 2010).

Here we see the intersection of capitalism and flows of desire. The reality is that people, governments, and societies do not desire the presence of homeless people; quite the opposite, they desire their erasure. The dirt, the smells, the evidence (cf. Zimmerman et al. 2010, who discuss the smell of urine and accumulation of rubbish that characterizes the places that homeless people often pass through); each is swept away by flows of desire that constitute concepts of "clean," "tidy" and "prosperous"—the economies of cities are not somehow operating in a different sphere from the desires of its "successful" capitalist citizens. Courtney Singleton (2017) provides another example of this from Zuccotti Park in New York. The park has a regular homeless population but was also the site of an Occupy Wallstreet protest. The left-leaning protestors were forced to engage with the homeless population but saw them as quite separate from themselves and excluded them from the Occupy protest (Singleton 2017). One might have expected both groups to form an alliance given their interactions with capitalism, yet the protestors excluded the homeless population.

Here again, a traditional notion of ideology isn't very helpful. In a nice, leafy middle-class suburb, it isn't the case that the people who are homed there are "fooled" or "duped" into demanding the absence of homeless people; being this kind of "middle-class" person means not wanting homeless people living on your doorstep, and erasing their heritage, their materials, and their connection. Similarly, the protestors in New York who camped in the park, just as the homeless community did, saw themselves as separate from the homeless community. The affective senses of cleanliness and order that come from not having the presence of homeless people and their material culture are real, and they comprise middle-class subjectivities. In contrast, oral testimony from homeless participants in the Turbo Island project detail how they felt about the notion that they have no part in the history or heritage of the place (Crea et al. 2014, 145–7). This notion implies that they were unimportant—that their lives did not matter. Their desires are denied as the mainstream economies and subjectivities of our cities over-code the spaces. Those experiencing homelessness take up a position outside of the flows of Oedipal family life; they connect to capitalism and place differently, their desires are not middle-class desires, and so others want this alternative subjectivity, one that lies outside the humanist definition of Man, to be swept away.

Conclusion

In this chapter, we sought new perspectives on capitalism and homelessness—interrelated themes that continue to shape our world. We explored the usefulness of the archaeological lens, discussing how historical and contemporary archaeologists weave multiple lines of evidence together to offer fresh perspectives on how things were (or are) rather than only what people wrote or said about them. By connecting archaeologies of capitalism and homelessness with the understanding of humanist Man developed in Chapter 2 and a reading of capitalism, desire, and the family that takes influence from Deleuze and Guattari, we are now in a position to rethink several key issues.

First, we can see how the excellent work of historical archaeologists who study capitalism might be augmented with new conceptual tools that further challenge traditional Marxist notions of "ideology." Rather than imagining that people have been duped into supporting capitalism, or wanting homeless people to be cleared away, we can see this is what people *really* want—we know this because this is how they vote, this is how they act, and this is what they say. The work of thinkers like Deleuze and Guattari thus has important implications for how we think and write about archaeologies of capitalism.

Second, we can see how, in contrast to the kinds of familial and economic life that the flows of capitalism try to instantiate, homelessness operates *differently* (cf. Chapter 8). Other kinds of heritage, homes, family lives, and more come into being in places where homeless people live. The intention here is not to romanticize homelessness. This perspective does not mean celebrating the differences these lives involve or essentializing the desires that constitute them as unchanging. Put bluntly, this isn't an argument that says homelessness is okay or an argument that we should not invest in creating safe and pleasant places for people to live in; it is an argument that we should listen and take seriously what homeless people say, and that we should not simply clear away their belongings, or present the act of moving them on as anything other than the imposition of one set of powerful desires over another.

Third, we can consider how all the pasts and presents that we investigate operate through multiple flows of desire, which are unlikely to be uniform in any past world that archaeologists investigate.

By thinking about desire, capitalism, and the family as specific historical institutions, archaeologists can engage in new ways with contemporary issues like homelessness. To return to a key theme of this book, the archaeology of homelessness shows us that just like having a home, being human always involves non-humans, which range from places to personal paraphernalia. Thinking about human-non-human relationships and how they relate to subjectivity and desire—the flows that constitute both capitalism and what it leaves behind—can help us understand the places that homelessness creates and the way in which non-homeless people react to them. Archaeology's material emphasis really helps here, but it needs to focus on understandings that not only historicize economies (we all know capitalism isn't universal) but ones that historicize the desires that make up the people who operate within and around the boundaries of these economies. Our families and our feelings are not somehow separate from the flows of capital and money that surround and permeate our world.

These points have wider implications beyond just the study of homelessness. Archaeology reveals the ways that capitalism is an unfair process. As seen in the privies of New England (Mrozowski 2006a, 2006b) or in the ruins of historic mansions in St. Paul, Minnesota (Zimmerman et al. 2010), capitalism is not the American Dream. In stark contrast to this notion, archaeologies of capitalism and homelessness identify and document the way that particular historical circumstances make certain kinds of subjectivities more likely to emerge than others. Capitalism does not just demand that you are "good" with your money; the interconnectedness of family, mental health, and circumstances that Deleuze and Guattari's work highlights shows that not being left behind in the ruins of capitalism takes *far more* than a savvy use of your bank account. That does not mean, however, that those who do not measure up to capitalism's norms and demands have failed or are less-than the homeowner with his wife, 1.13 kids (based on 2021 US census data), and cute dog. Rather, they are often those who have been most exploited by the imposition of humanist Man as the measure of all things. Next, in Chapter 4, we explore how this ever-more historicized vision of humanity changes the ways we conceptualize another element of society: leadership.

Note

1 Incidentally, this concept should not be confused with "things are us" from symmetrical archaeology (Webmoor and Witmore 2008); the key aspect of the capitalist mantra is the relationship of ownership.

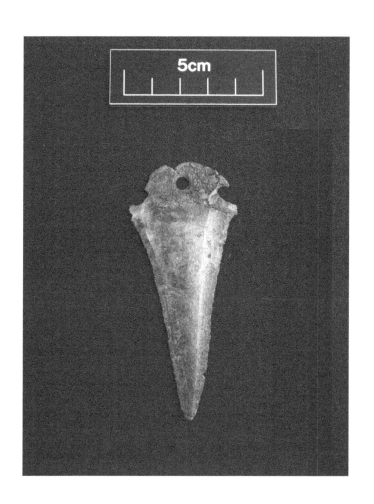

Chapter 4

Leaders of the past, leaders in the future

Rethinking power

Introduction: we need a leader!

What makes a good leader? Who do we think of as leaders? In an average week, we see many different forms of leadership: the fitness instructor who leads through enthusiasm, encouragement, and support, knowing just what to say to get the best out of everyone in her class; the chair in a meeting who works to let everyone speak and find a way forward that blends different opinions; the person who blocks the corridor of a train to make sure that a wheelchair user has the time and space they need to exit; the boy on the playground that goes to talk to the quiet child and includes them in their play. We often think of leadership in terms of elected officials like prime ministers and presidents or as appointed positions in a variety of different organizations such as directors, chairs, and managers. Perhaps more than some archaeologists would like to admit, this vision of leadership often colors how we think about and characterize leadership in the past. In the Neolithic and Bronze Age of Europe, for example, we frequently see arguments about the emergence of leaders in relation to the creation of monuments (Parker Pearson 2012; Renfrew 1973a; but see Pauketat 2007). These arguments typically hinge on the fact that monuments require large amounts of labor and planning. To achieve such projects, *someone* had to be in charge—a leader! From the concept of an activity leader (the person who coordinated the making of a monument, for example), we slide into a concept of political leadership and hierarchy (the monument leader becomes the political leader who must have been more important than the people that they led). We then might take a further step and suggest perhaps this leadership was transferable to the leader's children, meaning that those children were inherently privileged. In contrast to this well-worn and rather narrow narrative of political ascendance, the examples at the start of this paragraph show the breadth of different forms of leadership that we encounter in our daily lives. This means, of course, that leaders are not just elites and those who occupy the top rungs in hierarchies.

All too often, when we think of leaders, we envisage the humanist character of Man outlined in Chapter 2. We think of a White man, someone with authority and agency, someone who is bold, someone who has a loud (literally and metaphorically) voice and is listened to, someone who is charismatic, well-educated,

DOI: 10.4324/9781003244141-4

and powerful. Feminists have spent decades critiquing this problematic image of leadership and highlighting alternatives. Perhaps you can think of examples of how people use discussion and consensus-building to become a leader? Or you can think of how people might use humor or kindness to bring you along in their projects? When we discuss leaders in this chapter, we are thinking of those who take you with them—those that make you part of their projects. There are many ways they might do this. This basic definition leaves space for more traditional ideas about leadership performed through power and coercion or the deployment of ritual authority. Additionally, it allows us to think about alternative ways of organizing and leading based on charisma, humor, kindness, and encouragement or through the creation of shared projects so inspiring that we feel compelled to follow. We can also consider how non-humans might lead. This definition both allows for a traditional image of leadership shaped after humanist Man and permits us to develop alternative approaches that leave room for a far more diverse cast of characters to occupy leadership roles.

In this chapter, we explore leadership through an archaeological lens. We also necessarily touch on the topics of power and politics. We take a critical approach to power that sees it not just as "power over" but also as "power to" (Thomas 2002). We move beyond seeing power as something that is fixed, possessed by humans, and used to control others, but instead, following Rosi Braidotti (2011, 4, 2019, 33), we approach power as both what she terms *potestas* and *potentia*. *Potestas* captures the negative, repressive, and entrapping aspects of power, while *potentia* refers to the positive, affirmative, empowering aspects of power. We can think of a day at work when, at some moments, we have the *potentia* to bring about an affirmative and positive result in a meeting and other moments, when the *potestas* of the university crushes our aspirations and forces us to conform. These two concepts do not exist in a binary; rather, power always has these two elements to it, and the freedom to act for one person can limit and control the capacity of others. Building on this, we approach power as something relational, multiple, and dynamic (see discussion in Crellin et al. 2021, Chapter 8). Power is always entangled with politics, and our approach sees politics not as a separate sphere of action but as something embedded and entangled in the flow of life more broadly. Politics is about the negotiation of different relationships and the power this inevitably involves. Thus, instead of seeing politics as a separate sphere of human activity, we approach it as part of the organization of all human relationships. This wider reading also makes space for non-humans in politics (Carter and Harris 2020), as discussed later in the chapter.

Our goal is to show how archaeological approaches to leadership, power, and politics in the past can create new ways of thinking about these things in the present and future. By touching on different examples of leadership and social organization from other times and places, we aim to consider how archaeology challenges us to think through these themes and what the value of that process of thinking and theorizing archaeologically can bring to the worlds of today and tomorrow. The chapter begins by exploring the concept of heterarchy and the writings of anarchist thinkers. We discuss how archaeologists apply these theories in the study of the

Andean city of Tiwanaku (500 to 1100 CE). The site raises important questions about standard narratives of leadership, opening new spaces for us to consider how non-humans—from stones to flows of water—also participate in political projects. We conclude by bringing our observations from Tiwanaku into dialogue with a case study from Bronze Age Britain, where instead of humans, non-humans seem to have served as the key "power brokers."

Setting the stage: heterarchy and anarchy

Archaeologists have long attempted to think beyond the characterization of the leader as the elite who rules *his* subjects. One of the key concepts used to address these challenges is *heterarchy*. Heterarchy is often thought of in opposition to hierarchy, where societies are stratified into different groups of people with more or less power, prestige, and wealth. The development of hierarchy is entangled with progressive narratives about the development of so-called "complex socie-ties." One of the main reasons that progressive narratives are deeply problematic is because they assume that the world is becoming more complex and undergoing a process of improvement (see Crellin 2020, 7–9). At their core, they present the cur-rent western world as the apex of human achievement and suggest that alternative forms of social organization and politics in other places represent simpler stages of development (cf. our discussion of settler colonialism in Chapter 2). This kind of thinking is locked into Sahlins and Service's (1960) four-stage model that sug-gests that societies progress from bands to tribes to chiefdoms to states. Hierarchy and leadership, in this kind of thinking, are indelibly linked to ideas of progress; more "complex" societies require stratification, social differentiation, and firmer or institutionalized leadership roles.

Heterarchy has been used to critique this model by looking at alternative ways of organizing social groups (Brumfiel 1995; Crumley 1979, 2007; see also Janusek 2004a, 20–5 for an example from the Andes). Carole Crumley's (1979, 144) foun-dational work defined heterarchy as an organizational structure where "each ele-ment possessed the potential of being unranked (relative to the other elements) or ranked in a number of ways." As Elizabeth Brumfiel (1995, 125) outlines, heter-archy counters the idea that ranking need always be present in a society, that it is permanent or institutionalized, and thus transcendent; this is what Graeber and Wengrow (2021) recently referred to as "arbitrary power." Crumley's definition could be used to describe societies where multiple different forms of "ranking" exist, where ranking shifts and changes, and where it might be situational or con-textual (for example, different hierarchies for religious versus construction pro-jects). It could also be applied to egalitarian relations between and within groups. Heterarchy has been used to describe less fixed forms of social organization, and this often leads to alternative approaches to leadership where we might focus on the role of cooperation, coalition, and consensus building rather than coercion (DeMarrais 2016 and papers therein). Whereas in a hierarchical society, where one individual oversees all areas of life, a heterarchical society might have different and non-commensurate forms of leadership in trade, warfare, ritual, and more. Discussions of heterarchy have undoubtedly created productive spaces for rethinking different forms of leadership and their dynamics.

Taking inspiration from—or at least developing in parallel with—these discussions of heterarchy is the recent rise of anarchist archaeologies briefly introduced in Chapter 1 (Angelbeck and Jones 2018; Angelbeck et al. 2018; Borake 2019; Borck 2018; Denham 2018; Eddisford and Morgan 2018; Flexner 2018; Flexner and Gonzalez-Tenant 2018; Gonzalez-Tenant 2018; Graeber and Wengrow 2021; Jamieson 2018; Rathbone 2017). Themes of power, leadership, and social organization sit at the core of anarchist concerns. For some readers, the concept of anarchy likely conjures up some very specific images. Perhaps you think only of violence, graffiti-covered and trash-strewn streets, or young people simply fed up with—and rebelling against—the system. It is true that anarchism has clear connections to grassroots, bottom-up, social critique and transformation; it strives to create different, more egalitarian futures. Anarchism is not, however, a gloss for "chaos" or "anything goes." Instead, it is a way to rethink social hierarchy and inequality, especially those forms associated with late capitalism. Anarchist thought urges us to conceive of a different way of organizing our world today, which, of course, relates to how archaeologists study leadership in the past.

Archaeology provides powerful material for anarchists to think with because our field has access to the entirety of global human history—different times, different societies, and perhaps different worlds (cf. Alberti et al. 2011). Anarchists ask whether we can learn from those pasts (particularly egalitarian and non-hierarchical societies) in the hope of rethinking our present and future. They also highlight how anarchist thinking can help us escape traditional top-down models of power and leadership that have their roots in capitalism (Chapter 3). Of course, this means that the general concerns of anarchists overlap with the various forms of Marxist thought employed in archaeology. Before getting into any more theory, however, we first introduce some archaeological patterns at the site of Tiwanaku to help us think further about archaeological conceptions of leadership.

Power and leadership at Tiwanaku

In the mid-sixteenth century, a Spanish conquistador named Pedro de Cieza León ventured into the current-day Bolivian highlands (Kolata 1993, 1–4; see also Vranich 2004); there, on the southern shore of Lake Titicaca bounded by mountain ranges, he observed the remains of an impressive and ancient human settlement—Tiwanaku. Today, this is the name of both an archaeological site and the unique political formation with which it emerged. Cieza León initially considered the likelihood that this place was part of the Inka empire, but its ruined state suggested otherwise; furthermore, when Cieza León inquired with local peoples, they reportedly laughed at the idea that the remains could have been built by the Inka (Kolata 1993, 1–4). Instead, it seemed, this place had a much deeper history. One of the earliest researchers of Tiwanaku was Arthur Posnansky (1945), who, in the early twentieth century, saw strong evidence in the archaeological remains of an ancient and influential political entity; indeed, he wrote about Tiwanaku as the "cradle of American man," arguing that it was the source of all complex societies across the Americas; for him, everything began in Tiwanaku and diffused outward. Today, scholars reject Posnansky's ambitious (and largely unsupported) theories. There is, however, much still to learn from—and debate about—Tiwanaku. Depending on what source you read, scholars studying Tiwanaku describe it as a state, a polity, or an expansive empire.[1] Although the broader region of the Titicaca basin saw earlier signs of proto-urbanism and political experimentation,[2] scholars recognize Tiwanaku as one of the earliest so-called "complex societies" to develop in the high Andes. Its monumental period dates between 600–1000 CE, and its impressive architecture includes a variety of different structures that unequivocally required massive amounts of organized labor.

The Akapana (see Figure 4.1), the largest single structure at Tiwanaku, is a stepped pyramid made from transported earth and stone; it is approximately 200 meters wide on each side and about 17 meters tall (Kolata 1993, 104). To the southwest of the Akapana is the Puma Punku, a T-shaped stepped platform that includes monumental stone block-facings; sharing many characteristics with the Akapana, it contains courts, terraces, and numerous stone gateways (Kolata 1993, 129–30). Of note, according to some specialists, the Akapana and the Puma Punku mirror surrounding mountains (Kolata 2003). Also found in Tiwanaku's center is the Kalasasaya, a large,

Figure 4.1 The northwest corner of the Akapana at Tiwanaku.

Image: Noa Corcoran-Tadd.

low rectangular platform mound approximately 130 meters by 140 meters in size; it includes a central sunken court and walls built from sandstone pillars (Kolata 1993, 143–5). These structures and more[3] form what specialists interpret as the ceremonial core of Tiwanaku, places where large-scale public rituals took place.

The archaeology also offers information on the daily lives of Tiwanaku's residents, offering glimpses into more private and smaller-scale ritual practices. One such place where this is possible is the Putuni, a later period (800–1150 CE) residential and ceremonial complex occupied by what some experts (e.g., Couture and Sampeck 2003; Kolata 1993, 149) see as Tiwanaku's emergent elites. The Putuni sat within Tiwanaku's central monumental area (Couture and Sampeck 2003), suggesting that the people who lived there had a close connection to the city's impressive built landscape. These patterns alone raise important questions about social relations at Tiwanaku. Who lived at the site, and why did some residents get to live so close to the monumental core? Why did so many people contribute their labor to building structures like the Akapana? More to the point of this chapter, how did leadership and power work at Tiwanaku?

Tiwanaku challenges standardized social evolutionary narratives about the rise of social complexity while offering opportunities to think beyond the models of hierarchical power and leadership introduced at the start of this chapter. Evidence of state-like hierarchical power is lacking in Tiwanaku's early history; in fact, these forms of power did not manifest themselves for about 300 years after the city was founded (e.g., Jennings and Earle 2016; cf. Clastres 1977); this is evident in debates surrounding potential elite burials associated with Tiwanaku (Janusek 2004a, 2008; Couture and Sampeck 2003; Isbell and Korpisaari 2015). Furthermore, although expansion and colonization were a part of the story around Tiwanaku's core, evidence of militaristic conquest outside this area is absent, and evidence of violence is generally rare (Becker 2020, 935). There is also no evidence of warehouses or expansive transport networks (Bandy 2013, 135).

Since scholars generally interpret the population of Tiwanaku as diverse or multiethnic (Becker 2017, 2020; Blom 2005; Isbell and Korpisaari 2015; Janusek 2005), perhaps it was a shared understanding of the world and the cosmos that brought them together. This is born out in Tiwanaku's many sprawling compounds, potentially occupied by different communities drawn to the urban center for its ritual significance. Janusek (2006) has explored the significance of religion and ritual in driving the development of Tiwanaku (see also Kolata 1993, 2003), suggesting that a religion tied into the landscape and celestial cycles played a key role at the site. As highlighted further later, Janusek's innovative thinking considers much more than hierarchical power and much more than humans as the key drivers behind this unique political formation. His work reframes power in ways that parallel some of our key concerns in archaeological theory, discussed in the following section.

To sample some of the innovative archaeological thinking about leadership prompted by Tiwanaku's complicated archaeological record, we consider two recent examples, respectively exploring hospitality and heterarchy. Matthew Bandy (2013) roots his explanation of Tiwanaku's political organization in the concept of hospitality rather than strong hierarchical leadership. Bandy (2013) suggests that multiple social groups might have offered hospitality and feasting at the site and that this is evidenced in the monolith sculptural figures found there. The monoliths depict a being standing upright with both hands at their chest (see Figure 4.2); in the left hand, the being holds a *kero* cup containing *chica*. Drawing on Inka traditions, Bandy argues that the placement of the *kero* in the left hand indicates that the viewer of the statue was seen as an inferior person to whom the statue was offering hospitality. In its right hand, the statue holds a snuff tablet; Bandy notes, however, that the right hands of these statues are in an anatomically impossible position, with palms outwards and thumbs upwards. For him, this unexpected anomaly means that people were supposed to view the statue from the front and perceive the left hand as indicating the hospitality of the statue towards us as inferiors, but read the right hand as being at the back of the statue and being in receipt of a gift from a superior source—someone from the divine realm (Bandy 2013, 137–8). Read this way, the statue is the central conduit in the relationship between the divine and the inferior. For Bandy (2013, 139–40), hospitality sat at the core of Tiwanaku society.

Figure 4.2 Monolith from Tiwanaku.

Image: SodaCan, CC by 4.0 license (https://creativecommons.org/licenses/by-sa/4.0).

A second alternative comes from Sara Becker (2020), who uses anarchist theory to rethink Tiwanaku as a heterarchical society. She draws on bioarchaeological data to explore the impact of social organization on Tiwanaku's residents. More specifically, she looks at the development of osteoarthritis and entheseal changes (the part of the bone to which tendons attach) as a means of assessing the physical impact of labor and activity on human bodies. Her work reveals that there was a reduction in the amount of labor that people carried out once Tiwanaku was established; she sees this pattern as evidence that people at Tiwanaku experienced a higher quality of life. Becker (2020) argues that the multiethnic groups at Tiwanaku might have been organized according to the principles of *allyu*. This is an Andean kinship-based system of social organization characterized by fluctuating hierarchies with impermanent control exercised by leaders; they operate as reciprocal networks of support, closely connected to the land. From Becker's (2020, 936) perspective, the reciprocity and cooperation associated with the *allyu* is part of the explanation for how Tiwanaku came to flourish without clear evidence for violent control of hierarchy. Anarchist theory draws Becker away from hierarchical explanations and towards further consideration of how living within different power structures might impact people's lives.

Theoretical toolkit: post-anthropocentrism, potentia, potestas

In each of these accounts, humans play crucial roles. In other words, humans' power moves, relationships, and decisions about cooperating (or not) shaped— even defined—the political field. How does the story change if we bring the contributions of non-humans more squarely into focus? Our aim is not to simply dismiss the important insights from existing approaches of experts in these areas, but to investigate other dimensions and angles of approach, further developing our thinking about power and politics. We are particularly interested in exploring how concepts from new materialism and posthumanism help to shift our understanding of places like Tiwanaku.

Just as anarchism has a great deal in common with Marxism (cf. Chapter 3), it also overlaps with new materialism (introduced in Chapter 1 and discussed in the form of assemblage theory in Chapter 2). This should come as no surprise; the very name, "new materialism," indicates the debt this form of thinking owes to Marx, and, thus, a potential overlap with anarchism as well. Anarchism emphasizes the poverty of assuming that power only flows in one direction and stresses the need to explore the multiple ways in which resistance might operate. In parallel with this, new materialists explore how power operates in ways that both create possibilities for action and constrain and limit what it is we can do—*potentia* and *potestas* (Braidotti 2011, 4, 2019, 33). Furthermore, new materialism calls for similar forms of experimental and creative responses to political situations, what anarchists refer to as "prefigurative" politics (Borck 2018). Two key inspirations for new materialism, Gilles Deleuze and Félix Guattari (2004, 178–9), argue that we need to experiment with ways of creating new forms of social and material relationships which allow desire and power to flow in new ways. In his work as a psychoanalyst at La Borde Clinic outside of Paris, Guattari experimented with alternative groupings of patients and physicians that undermined the classic hierarchies of Freudian analysis—an experiment with what we might call heterarchy. He developed this as part of what he called a "transversal approach," where power and connections crosscut and undermine top-down structures (Guattari 1984).

The analysis of power and potentiality, and the need to construct new connections and ways of doing things here in the present, link across new materialism, heterarchy, and anarchist theory (cf. Rathbone 2017; Van Heerden and Eloff 2019). There are, however, important differences. Most striking are their different orientations to non-humans, whether materials, places, animals, plants, or anything else. Heterarchical analyses focus on the relationships between humans. Anarchism is often anthropocentric, that is, it places humans at its center; although Flexner and Gonzalez-Tenant (2018, 213) note that anarchist approaches seek to redefine social and ecological relationships, "including with non-humans," most anarchist archaeologies appear to elevate humans over other beings and things. There are powerful traditions of green and eco-anarchism that work to help fight the climate crisis, but such projects remain focused (ontologically) on humans as primary and exceptional. This contrasts with the "flat" ontology of new materialism, which argues that we need to start with a position where no single element of the universe—an earthworm, a mushroom, a carbon atom, an elephant, or a blackhole—is necessarily *more real*, or more ontologically significant, than any other (Cipolla 2021). Rather than a position that assumes that human beings, always and forever, are central, new materialism demands a more radical approach that argues that we should explore how things relate, what matters, and how different parts of the world operate in specific historical and material settings. No form of humanity—competitive, egalitarian, heterarchical, or anything else—can operate outside of history here. Thus, while anarchism offers us excellent counter-narratives to stories of universal progress, or the inevitability of hierarchy, it remains firmly located within the same fundamental set of perspectives as the approaches it seeks to critique.

Power and politics provide excellent examples of how important it is to consider non-humans. It is quite normal in Western society to presume that politics is a matter for human beings: voters queuing up in an election, senators debating laws in Congress, prime ministers making screeching u-turns on recent policy announcements. Similarly, when things are difficult, we often blame the power that media moguls or bosses have over the conditions of our lives. New materialism does not deny the critical role of people within power relations and politics. It does suggest, however, that we cannot truly understand these things if we leave them to people alone (Carter and Harris 2020). If we think critically about any politician, the ways that their power depends upon non-humans becomes obvious. This ranges from the buildings where they reside (the White House or 10 Downing Street, for example) to the vehicles that transport them in their day-to-day work. Similarly, their ability to engage with us relies on non-humans, like the forms of media that we consume, the constant availability of social media, and much more. As algorithms on social media increasingly define our engagement with politics, the role of non-humans in our own world is impossible to deny. Might we even need to think of them as performing forms of leadership?

The insistence that human beings are central to everything ontologically, however, is not just an issue of accuracy. It also has political connotations. As we saw in Chapters 2 and 3, the humans that get positioned as central are rarely neutral figures. With their desire for freedom, or justice, or democracy, the people identified by anarchism remain like those of the modern west. The anarchist literature also draws distinctions between "natural" as opposed to "artificial" authority (e.g., Angelbeck and Grier 2012, 552). This distinction relies both on inherited Enlightenment dualisms (natural versus artificial in this case) and an ahistorical approach to critical questions. The evocation of a warrior's leadership as natural, for example, because it comes from an authority based on skill, overlooks the question of *who* becomes a warrior in the first place. How does this relate to class, gender, background, and more? What makes becoming a warrior natural in one case but not in another? Again, these categories rest on a particular way of understanding and conceptualizing human beings. The point here is not to argue that we should elevate artificial authority over the natural but rather to do away with this dualism altogether.

From a posthumanist or new materialist standpoint, no form of authority, social organization, leadership, or humanity is any more or less natural or artificial. All are historically emergent. Instead, these approaches embrace a much more open version of humanity. Recognizing all humans as historically situated and emergent means that we cannot be certain, in advance, what characteristics they will have or what they can and cannot accomplish. Thus, ironically, an insistence on the historical importance of non-humans in power relations does not diminish what we think of human beings but rather allows them to become fully historically situated (Harris 2021a, 24).

Using our theoretical tools: from Tiwanaku to Bronze Age Britain

Tiwanaku

With these ideas in mind, let us return to Tiwanaku. John Janusek (2020, 120; see also Roddick and Janusek 2018) recently noted that "most archaeological interpretations of Tiwanaku restrict themselves to the domain of human relations and activities." He experimented with an alternative approach, focusing on the flows of water and stone at Tiwanaku. In other words, for Janusek and others, water and stone were key players in the assemblage of Tiwanaku. Tiwanaku's emergence began with the local ecosystem and its subterranean aquifers and continued through the construction of monumental hydraulic networks linking the city to far-off locations. Passages of water divided the city and "directed human flows" (Janusek 2020, 99; see also Janusek 2015; Roddick and Janusek 2018); in other words, these flows exhibited what Braidotti would term *potestas* over humans. Similarly, stone quarried from the broader landscape was essential to the emergence of ritual at Tiwanaku. This is exemplified in the monoliths discussed in the first part of this chapter, which Janusek (2020, 117) referred to as "key nonhuman operators." For the people of Tiwanaku, water and stone were not "dead utilitarian resources" but "vital matters that manifested the telluric power of the mountains, springs, and other animate earthly features they derived from and indexed" (Janusek 2020, 121).

Janusek's reinterpretation of the city demonstrates just how complicated it is to define urban boundaries; when one considers the non-human flows which they depend upon, cities extend far beyond classically defined urban centers. As humans come into relation with new landscapes and materials, new configurations and capacities emerge to form wondrous collectives such as the city of Tiwanaku. And, of course, leadership and power at these places rely upon non-living matter like water and stone. Janusek's work goes a long way in recognizing the more-than-human assemblages at the heart of cities, but much of his focus remains on how these non-human forces shaped and factored into Tiwanaku worldviews (cf. Cipolla 2019; see also Crellin et al. 2021, Chapter 10), i.e., what these things came to *mean* or *represent* for the people of Tiwanaku (but see Janusek 2015 for a discussion of material qualities). There is still room to explore what water, stone, and myriad other non-human entities *did* at Tiwanaku. How, for instance, did the qualities, affordances, and geological histories of the sandstone used to make monoliths factor into the solidification of political power and hierarchy at Tiwanaku? Did these "raw materials" simply represent the world that would-be elites wanted? Or did they act back and afford new possibilities that were unforeseen by their human makers?

For us, questions like these are key for future-oriented archaeologies that seek to imagine future worlds potentially very different from our own. There remains space for a further new materialist inquiry into how non-humans participated in flows of power, as well as water, at a site like Tiwanaku. We saw how monoliths at Tiwanaku interceded between different worlds (Bandy 2013). What would happen if we no longer addressed this as a representation of a religious belief but the active construction of politics? Bandy (2013) argued that the monoliths at Tiwanaku took a position between one world and the next that offered hospitality to humans while receiving it from the gods. What would our narratives of Tiwanaku look like if, rather than seeing these monoliths as representing these kinds of interactions, they were performing them (cf. Chapter 8's discussion of the ontological turn)? Alongside the humanoid figures offering kero and receiving snuff discussed earlier, other monoliths at Tiwanaku depict human/feline hybrids, often holding an axe and a severed human head (Janusek 2020, 119). These "chachapumas" stand outside temples in Tiwanaku; Janusek (2020, 119) argues that they helped to shape the experience and subjectivity of those who encountered them. These human/feline/stone sculptures intervened in the political worlds of Tiwanaku not merely as objects to be viewed but as political players shaping and reorienting the humans who encountered them. Next, we consider an example from the British Bronze Age to think further about the leadership capabilities of non-humans.

Bronze Age Britain

There is a long-standing argument in European Neolithic and Bronze Age archaeology that the transition in burial practices from the former to the latter is associated with a change in social structure. Neolithic burial practices are mixed and complicated, and they changed over time (for a discussion of their variety, see Harris 2021a, Chapter 5), but they are often characterized as focusing on communal forms of burial (Shanks and Tilley 1982). At sites like long barrows and chambered tombs, for example, archaeologists often find the remains of multiple individuals inserted into single monuments with little sense of one person being treated any differently from another; in fact, in many cases, it seems that skeletal remains were intentionally disarticulated and mixed up (see for example, Wayland's Smithy, Wiltshire, UK (Whittle et al. 2007)). The traditional interpretation is that these patterns were made by egalitarian communities lacking clear institutionalized leadership.

At the start of the Bronze Age, however, a tradition emerged involving singular burials containing Beaker vessels (though note that this is also mixed and complicated). Archaeologists often interpret the frequent placement of individuals within singular graves containing grave goods as indicative of a change in social organization and leadership roles. Here, singular burials point to a shift to more individualistic and less egalitarian social collectives (e.g., Earle 1991; Renfrew 1973a). Important people, like leaders, required their own special burials. This argument relates to the broad evolutionary frameworks discussed earlier that assume that human societies universally progress from simple to complex (e.g., Sahlins and Service 1960).

There are countless arguments that aim to disrupt this grand narrative. Some point out that, in fact, multiple burials remained a common practice during the Bronze Age (Appleby 2013; Bloxam and Parker Pearson 2022; Gibson 2007), while others critique the idea that any Neolithic burials were egalitarian (Shanks and Tilley 1982). Others focus on anthropological concepts of individuality, critiquing its application to pre-Enlightenment contexts (Brück 2019; Fowler 2013a). Our point here is not that the contrast between an egalitarian Neolithic and a more hierarchical Bronze Age is true, but rather to emphasize that this is how archaeologists typically think of these complicated transitions.

What happens when, instead of assuming that single burials *represent* new forms of leadership, we ask what these new kinds of burials *did* in the past? What happens when we explore them, like the monoliths at Tiwanaku, as political actors? To address this question, we turn to a Bronze Age burial landscape in southern Britain, Andover Airfield, Penton Mewsey, in Hampshire (Howell et al. 2019). There, archaeologists recorded seven barrows or burial mounds as well as a pit burial, cremations, and other features. Only one of the barrows survived as a physical mound. The others had no upstanding layers and were identified from their surrounding circular ditches; the site was damaged by plowing, meaning that we cannot know if the others were also once covered by earthen mounds. At least 43 people were buried across the site. Due to dating complications, there are instances when the precise sequence of events is unclear. In the following discussion, we do not tell the whole story of the site (if such a thing were possible) but rather focus on select burial patterns to rethink how leadership and power work.

The main barrow group at the site consists of a cluster of five barrows (see Figure 4.3) that vary in size from 32 meters to 16.5 meters in diameter. The barrows are tightly packed, each surrounded by a ditch. The biggest of the barrows, Structure 1 (also referred to as the Mark Lane barrow), included a small central scoop containing cremated remains and a re-hafted bronze knife-dagger. Fragments of two other pottery vessels and some cremated remains were also discovered. One reading of this barrow might paint the individual buried with the knife-dagger as an important leader, and the object as a sign of his power (though the sex of the remains is unknown). His importance in life brought people together to labor, digging chalk and earth, and piling it high to create a monument to mark his grave.

This example speaks to possibilities for both *potestas* and *potentia*. The knife-dagger could be read as a sign of the leader's power over a social collective, his *potestas,* demanding the community to build his monument. We, of course, might also wonder whether someone else was forcing people to build the mound after the leader's death. Beyond this, however, we could also think about *potentia* (power to),

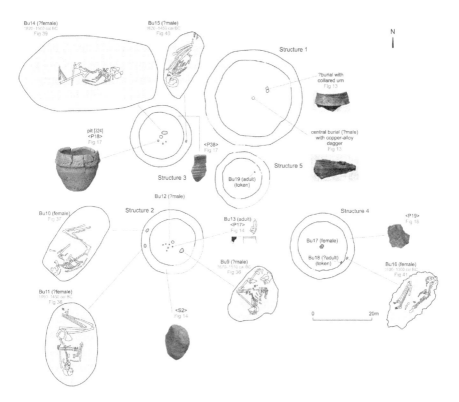

Figure 4.3 Plan of Andover Airfield. ©MOLA.

asking how those that came together to build the mound might have done so for certain benefits, such as associating themselves with a powerful leader and their achievements. The knife-dagger is interesting here; some interpretations frame it as an instrument of violence (a weapon) used in combat (Needham et al. 2017) and thus associated with a leader's violent or controlling methods of accruing power. Alternative interpretations pose questions about the knife-dagger's potential ritual uses (Skak-Nielsen 2009), perhaps in bloodletting. Similarly, others ask if the knife-dagger could have been used metaphorically to cut ties between the living and the dead (Fowler 2013a). These possibilities shift how we think about leadership, moving away from top-down, violent control over a social collective towards more complicated and communal activities and practices where the knife-dagger's user performed leadership through their parts in rituals or funerary processes. Here, the narratives shift from asking just about what the knife-dagger represented to what it did and how it performed, raising different possibilities about how leadership works.

It appears that Structure 1 might have been the first barrow constructed in the cluster. The knife-dagger burial thus seems to have attracted other burials toward it. Perhaps it was the leader's power that attracted later burials. Yet, the construction of the barrow group and the burial of multiple individuals in association with the five barrows covers a long stretch of time, spanning approximately 100–220 years (Howell et al. 2019, 40). When considering pottery finds associated with cremations in the broader landscape, this duration appears to be even greater. Since people returned to the site many times over the course of many generations, we must ask whether it was the power and leadership of the first person interred in Structure 1 that continued to attract people to the area. Even if we want to tell the story of a powerful leader *starting* the burial cluster, that need not be the case as time, including multiple human generations, passed. Instead, perhaps the barrows *themselves* provided a form of leadership. Although, as established in this chapter, archaeologists tend to associate power with humans, compared to some non-humans, human beings live relatively short lives. Some barrows and knife-daggers, for example, often have far longer durations. Perhaps paralleling the emergence of Tiwanaku, non-human entities like barrows take on projects and afford new possibilities unforeseen by the people who built them. Later burials and barrows might have gravitated to the mounds themselves, continually drawing communities to the site and nudging them to re-engage.

Read in the longer-term, architecture offers a very different form of leadership than the ones introduced at the start of this chapter. It shapes and channels human action, it attracts maintenance, it draws in practice, and it shapes the decisions of communities (Harris 2021a, 183–92). Barrows make you part of their projects; they are leaders and political actors. They have *potestas* and *potentia* by demanding and encouraging action—digging more burials, re-digging ditches, or constructing new monuments. This is far more than the familiar archaeological claim that objects can have a form of "secondary" agency (Gell 1998), with the primary ability to act remaining with human beings. Instead, it is to claim that flows of power circulate across humans and non-humans with no clear division possible. At times, the leadership of the barrows might have been experienced positively, a familiar place people were happy to labor in; at other times, however, barrows might have been negative spaces, where people sweated and toiled to maintain ditches or construct mounds.

Away from the main barrow group, there exist other intriguing patterns. Structure 6 was a lone barrow at the head of a valley, 28.5 meters in diameter, with a slot-like ditch surrounding it. Seen from the valley bottom, it dominated the skyline (Howell et al. 2019, 22). About 7 meters southwest of the surrounding ditch, archaeologists identified an adult male cremation under an inverted food vessel. They found a second pit containing a second inverted food vessel 1 meter away from the cremation, but with no human remains. The second vessel is described as an accessory deposit. We might, for example, imagine a return to the place of the grave and the vessel being added in an act of remembrance. But what if the burial of the lone food vessel came first? Could it have provided the impetus for the cremation deposit? Although we can't know for sure, if we adjust how we think about leaders to consider leadership as a more-than-human process, this alternative possibility is equally as likely as the first scenario.

Structure 6 itself contains no clear primary burial. Instead, the southeast quadrant of the barrow contained an arc of small, shallow, circular, or oval pits containing 24 cremation burials. Most of the burials were packed together within an area about 8 meters in diameter. With a few exceptions that intercut, the burials largely avoided each other. The weight of cremated remains varied between small token deposits of 22 grams to substantial deposits weighing nearly 2 kilograms (Howell et al. 2019, 26–8; 76–7). Although there were few grave goods associated with these burials, some people were buried *with* sherds of pottery and others *in* pottery vessels, all dating to the Middle Bronze Age (c.1500–1150 BCE) (Howell et al. 2019, 28; 53–5). A capping layer of flint and chalk sat over most burials, with another cremation burial on top of the capping layer. These cremations certainly cluster together, but not around a clear leader. They tell potential stories of other kinds of leadership. Was this a more egalitarian deposit, where a sense of shared community rather than a shared leader bound these people together? Perhaps a location or a shared landscape or sense of place is what drew them together. Or was it a series of relationships between the different individuals that drew others to be buried there? Leadership and power work differently in this context, disrupting the narratives about a shift toward a more individualized society.

Conclusion: power and the future

Our models of past leadership, hierarchy, power, and politics are not arbitrary. They reflect and reinforce the ideas of the present, just as our present shapes the pasts that we write. It is little wonder, therefore, that the leaders and forms of hierarchy that populate our past seem so familiar. Male, middle-aged, power-hungry, and individualistic, most archaeological leaders—whether commanding bands of

Bronze Age warriors around Europe, ordering the building of a monument in the Mississippi basin, or constructing a city-state in the Andes—resemble the leaders we know from our world. These images reinforce our inability to shift our models of leadership today. Of course, as the standard argument goes, we need leaders who are charismatic, decisive, powerful, and egotistical; after all, that is what has existed throughout all of history the world over, at least according to most popular accounts. Leaders today sometimes even draw explicitly on the power of archaeology, pitching political broadcasts from ancient monuments, encasing their promises on a standing stone, and more.[4]

If we, as archaeologists, want to change the world of the future, that means changing how we write about the past. We need to explore new models of leadership and power relations and disrupt the comfortable notion that things have always been this way. In this chapter, we explored how concepts like heterarchy and anarchism can begin this process of disruption. In place of universal ideas of leadership and singular forms of hierarchy, heterarchy offers a way of thinking through the multiple and complex trajectories of power and leadership in a society. Authority in a heterarchical world isn't singular but rather multiple, contextual, and contingent. Anarchism goes further still, offering both an emphasis on how we can change the world as archaeologists, here and now, through prefiguring the world we want to build, but can also explore past contexts to see how hierarchy, organizations like the state, and centralized politics, were actively contested and resisted.

As sympathetic as we are to such approaches, from the perspectives advanced in this book, they could go further. If we really want to disrupt ideas of leadership, hierarchy, and authority, it is not enough to appeal to universal ideas of the human, to ideas that if it weren't for "the State," we would all be free, or that some forms of authority are somehow "natural" rather than "artificial." Leaning on this concept of universal anarchism, as seductive as it sounds, does little to disrupt the underlying notions that, in the end, human beings are all the same and all resemble the Western figure of "Man." Instead, we advocate a move to analyze politics and power that embraces the non-human. What worlds could we imagine if, as at Tiwanaku, monoliths were the key political players? What happens if we imagine that monuments, instead of people, generated power in Bronze Age Europe? At the start of the chapter, we defined leaders as those who take you with them—those that make you part of their projects. When considered from this point of view, there is no reason for leaders to be human and certainly not *only human*. Now the chachapumas of Tiwanaku, the Bronze Age barrows that call you to add to them, and the car that requires maintenance, roads to be built, and oil to be extracted can be leaders too. From this perspective, it is not that humans don't lead, that they can't be leaders, or that somehow their power is diminished. In the complex interweaving worlds of *potentia* and *potestas*, power is multiple and relational. People can be leaders, places can be leaders, and so much more. Imagining the complex amalgamations of power and leadership in the past could suggest to us how much more complicated, interesting, and open our ideas of leadership in the future might be too.

Notes

1 In some cases, the name is spelled "Tiahuanaco," whereas other authors use "Tiwanaku" to refer to the state and "Tiahuanaco" to refer to the urban center (e.g., Jennings and Earle 2016).
2 These often involve carved stone monoliths such as at those at the site of Khonkho Wankane (Janusek 2015; see also Janusek 2004b).
3 See Young-Sánchez's (2004) edited collection for excellent images and descriptions of Tiwanaku's architecture.
4 These are all actual examples from the UK.

Chapter 5

Violence across the human/
non-human divide

The virtual and the actual

Introduction: approaching violence

In the last three chapters, we considered mobility and migration (Chapter 2), capitalism (Chapter 3), and political leadership (Chapter 4), noting how each of these phenomena involves complicated, more-than-human assemblages and histories. We discussed, for example, how a stone statue can lead and amass political power and how non-humans, like water bottles, afford or restrict human mobility. As already discussed, popular and academic perspectives on these topics tacitly recognize—but almost always diminish—the role that non-humans play in these phenomena, and they often do so while naturalizing western capitalist modes of social life as eternal. In comparison to migration, homelessness, or political leadership, there is considerably more widespread acceptance of the critical role that non-humans play in the focus of this chapter—violence.

On the surface, this is an uncontroversial position. We've all read the headlines—firearms, nuclear weapons, shoe bombs! Rightfully so, the non-humans just listed are sources of anxiety and handwringing. But how does all of this relate to archaeology? We find and study stuff, right? This means that we should be in a good position to at least document archaeological histories of violence (more on this in what follows). Several recent developments in archaeological theory, like posthumanism, relational archaeologies, and new materialism, also shine new light on humanity's deep connections to—and reliance upon—non-human things like weapons. From these perspectives, we cannot understand or historicize violence without incorporating a more complete understanding of the role played by non-humans. Yet, this argument has proved controversial. Some archaeologists read theories like the ones just listed as convoluted ways of using non-humans as scapegoats in place of the people who might be responsible for doing harmful things, like hurting other people or destroying the environment. Does recognizing that a murderous human can do much more damage with a sharp knife or a machine gun take the blame away from that which deserves it most—the murderous human? Or is the concept of "murderous human" also comprised of a complicated set of relations consisting of both a human and many non-humans? What made them murderous in the first place? Is that solely a human issue? Or could non-humans play a

DOI: 10.4324/9781003244141-5

part? By recognizing these interconnections, are archaeologists and philosophers truly displacing human blame? We'll address complicated questions like these at the end of the chapter.

Before that, we need to spend some time scrutinizing how archaeologists generally approach the study of violence and conflict. In the next section of the chapter, we examine the relationship between archaeologists and violence (as a subject of study). Here, of course, we will rely on our preferred theoretical toolkit to shed some new light on the topic. We'll revisit some posthumanist concepts—particularly critiques of humanist Man (see Chapters 2 and 3) and the Othering and xenophobic values it often conceals. From there, we integrate the relational and post-anthropocentric approaches set out in earlier chapters to rethink the myriad roles that non-humans play in acts of violence. It is not simply a matter of recognizing the weapons that people use to hurt one another. We need to think of acts of violence as historically particular or singular; in so doing, we must understand the relationality of the world, where humans and non-humans join up to accomplish new things that they couldn't do on their own. Yet, we'll also have to think about how non-human things sometimes call violence to them—think of the Black Lives Matter (hereafter BLM) movement and its impacts on racist and colonial statues. Here it helps to remember that violence is dependent on perspective, so we'll also consider Indigenous views that sometimes see archaeology and museum collecting themselves as forms of violence. Finally, we'll turn to our main case study, recent archaeological research on Puhú, a nineteenth-century multi-ethnic Indigenous village in current-day California that was eventually destroyed via colonial violence (Acebo 2020). To understand this history in a new way, we introduce some new tools—the philosophical concepts of *the virtual* and *the actual*. Nathan Acebo's (2020) work at Puhú shows how these concepts shed valuable new light on colonial violence. Finally, we conclude the chapter with a return to the problem introduced earlier—how do we place blame as we come to grips with acts of violence? Does a posthumanist and new materialist standpoint truly divert blame from people by considering the roles that non-humans play in acts of violence? We'll address these questions and many more as we work through the chapter.

Setting the stage: archaeology and violence

Archaeology has a mixed relationship with violence. In some of the narratives we write about the past, violence is downplayed or even absent. In other versions, it is emphasized and presented as an explanatory device. Archaeological evidence for violence is also usually complicated and difficult to identify. Imagine, for example, a small skirmish between two groups of people using wooden weapons and hand-to-hand combat. Both parties land blows, but everyone survives. The event itself leaves little trace, and the wooden weapons might not survive archaeologically. Of course, repeated bouts of violence reshape human bodies, but that does not necessarily mean a future archaeologist will be able to "see" this. They might find healed signs of trauma on the body, but one can also land a fatal blow that leaves no mark on the victim's skeleton. There are, however, also cases of clear evidence of violence in the archaeological record. Over the last few decades, "conflict archaeology" has grown significantly; working across different periods and places, archaeologies of conflict identify and study material traces of violence, ranging from studying defensive sites and forts to weapons, depictions of violence, and battlefields themselves (for an overview see papers in the *Journal of Conflict Archaeology*).

While the archaeological evidence for violence is not necessarily simple, the archaeological imagination itself has an even bigger effect on how we approach this topic. In what follows, we explore how common assumptions about violence, including how many archaeologists conceptualize the category "human," structure the kinds of narratives that we write about violence, conflict, and warfare in the human past. Debates about violence in archaeology and anthropology often gravitate around one core question: are humans inherently violent or not? The answer to this question is often binary; violence is either posited as a fundamental part of what it means to be human or it is presented as something that emerges in tandem with the development of larger, more "complex" societies (see Chapter 4). For those that might be referred to as "hawks" (see Otterbein 1997, 2004), violence is part of what makes us human; the ability to kill other humans evolved alongside our DNA and our technology. In contrast, so-called "doves" argue that early humans, who lived in smaller groups, were not violent at all. These debates often link to the political arguments of Thomas Hobbes (1996 [1651]) and Jean-Jacques Rousseau (1984 [1755]) (Dolfini et al. 2018, 1–2; Keeley 1996; Graeber and Wengrow 2021, Chapter 1). Hobbes argued that humans are inherently selfish and prone to violence, whereas Rousseau argued that humans were naturally peaceful but were corrupted by the emergence of the state.

In the wake of the themes identified by Hobbes and Rousseau, archaeologists have tried to identify ever earlier examples of violence in the history of human evolution. The Kenyan site of Nataruk is a case in point. There, archaeologists uncovered evidence for what is presented as a late Pleistocene/early Holocene massacre site; it included 12 skeletons, ten of which showed clear signs of violent death (Mirazón Lahr et al. 2016). Academics and popular writers alike link the site to questions surrounding the origins of warfare and compare it with the scale of violence seen in chimpanzee populations. This is a long-standing topic of archaeological debate. Culture historical models, such as those of V. Gordon Childe, foregrounded diffusion and the spread of culture, which at least suggested possibilities for violent encounters in the past. Did cultures "diffuse" because of violent invasion or peaceful interaction and expansion? More recently, evidence from aDNA research reinvigorated these debates and themes. Researchers identified large-scale shifts in the genetic makeup of populations over time (see, for example, Brace et al. 2019; Haak et al. 2015; Olalde et al. 2018); these findings feed into narratives where either a genetic, technological, or violent advantage explains the replacement of one population with another. As an example, consider a recent popular press article that presented aDNA data relating to the spread of the Yamnaya culture across Europe; it appeared in *New Scientist* under the title, "Story of most murderous people of all time revealed in ancient DNA" (Barras 2019). Graeber and Wengrow (2021, 3) argue that this binary approach—violence as inherent or not—is far from satisfactory on three grounds: first, it isn't true; second, it has dire political consequences; and third, it makes the past unnecessarily dull.

In Europe, there is another factor that shapes archaeological thinking about violence—the specter of the World Wars. John Carman (1997, 2) argues that although violence often surrounds us, it is unpleasant, abnormal, and unacceptable to talk about it. The bloodshed and destruction of the World Wars and the pacifist movements that emerged in their wake gave the deep past of Europe a particularly uneasy relationship with violence. Lawrence Keeley (1996) argued that the intellectual legacy of this phenomenon is an implicit bias toward finding a peaceful European past. Archaeologists often work to show that Europe had not always been, and need not be again, an inherently violent place (see also Vandkilde 2013). Archaeological materials, such as weapons, are interpreted *not* as evidence for actual violence but instead as symbols of power. Those people associated with swords, spears, and shields were not warriors but rather elites who symbolically marked their status with weapons. When evidence of conflict does emerge in these settings, it is often explained away as resulting from highly choreographed and controlled battles (Dolfini et al. 2018, 3). The argument that archaeologists have pacified the European past has spawned a plethora of new research, pulling in new scientific techniques, and asking if the evidence for violence is real or not. Were the people who were buried with weapons violent warriors, or was that just an identity that they adopted without participating in violent acts?

Violence as historically specific and more-than-human

What happens if we move away from these essentialized approaches to "human nature" and rethink violence as historically and culturally specific rather than universal? A serious consideration of historic specificity suggests that violence and conflict can be both chaotic *and* highly structured and rule-driven (Jones 1980). Today, we have international laws about what is and is not acceptable in the field of human conflict. Look, for example, at the bans on chemical and biological weapons following World War I; those who use them are now defined as war criminals who can be tried at the International Criminal Court (hereafter ICC) in the Hague. The existence of the ICC itself is, of course, predicated on a set of culturally constructed rules about what counts as acceptable and unacceptable violence. This is not, however, something that we should only associate with recent times. Rules, often unwritten but practiced, governed which weapons could be used in which ways—these conventions have varied significantly through time, and archaeologists can develop research to partially uncover them. A study of swords from Bronze Age Britain and Italy, for example, reveals that the marks left on their surface cluster and pattern in highly specific ways; the marks are *not* randomly distributed, indicating that there was a clear style of fighting that changed over time (Hermann et al. 2020); here "style" is a set of rules that defines acceptable forms of conflict.

Since conflict is historically specific, it is crucial that we reflect on how our ideas about conflict today shape our understanding of the past. Attitudes towards the wars in Syria, Iraq, or Yemen form a contrast to reactions to the Russian invasion of Ukraine in 2022, illuminating the shape of Western biases. Journalists in Europe and America initially talked about how "like us" the people of Ukraine are—how this was "war in Europe" (as Moustafa Bayoumi (2022) pointed out in *The Guardian*). These representations contrast starkly with attitudes to the wars in Syria, Iraq, or Yemen, where the implication is that these people are not "like us." Those who fight back in Ukraine are protecting their homeland; those who fought back in Iraq were insurgents. These different representations stem from the problems of humanist Man (introduced in Chapter 2). In other words, conflict that affects White, western, educated men is treated differently than that which affects Indigenous, Black, or people of color. Think also of media representation of gun violence in America. Black and brown bodies are coded as criminals or terrorists, while white bodies are labeled as mentally unwell school shooters, even when their violence might involve the same types of weapons or tactics, invoke the same kinds of terror, and have the same devastating outcomes.

In these examples, violence is predicated on the construction of an Other—someone to whom we oppose ourselves. Not only are Others opposed to those in power, but they are also essentialized; for example, all members of the collective are represented as the same, that is, sharing the same views and tendencies. Further than this, Others are often thought of, and treated as, subhuman, lacking the civilized and positive characteristics of the dominant group (cf. Chapters 2 and 3). Jasbir Puar (2017), a queer theorist and professor of women and gender studies, offers a powerful and important reading of attitudes towards difference and violence in the present. Drawing on assemblage theory (discussed in Chapter 2) and queer theory, she considers how western conflicts in Iraq and Afghanistan have often been justified as being about bringing freedom and education to local women. Puar (2017, 5) notes how Americans and Europeans were presented as participating in conflict for virtuous reasons, ignoring both the ongoing work by feminists within these countries and the disadvantages faced by women in America and Europe. Humanist ideals about who is stronger and more capable shape how we define a "legitimate" warrior and a "legitimate" subject of protection, just as the same forms of humanism define who is "more civilized" and, thus, more human. These values intersect with ideas about whiteness to shape how societies imagine and construct "enemy" Others.

Having now established a clear link to the problem of humanist Man, let's think more about how non-humans participate in acts of violence. We'll do this by mixing a few examples that help us to establish a better understanding of the breadth of different forms of violence; the diverse roles played by non-humans in acts of violence; and, following from our points here, how our views of violence are typically colored by false universals and unfair, hierarchical valuations. As already established, popular concerns and debates are open to the idea that non-humans sometimes play big parts in acts of violence and conflict. Yet, this premise is not applied consistently. Think back to the previous discussion of humanist Man and the arbitrary hierarchies associated with this worldview. When it comes to acts of violence, societies generally place blame asymmetrically, especially when influenced by xenophobic values such as the ones discussed earlier regarding representations of warfare in Syria, Iraq, or Yemen. Although it is not a hard and fast rule, when xenophobia and fear of difference come into play, humans are often blamed; for instance, think of acts of international terrorism and world conflict. In those cases, blame is typically attached firmly to an Other (cf. Puar 2017). When acts of violence take place within one's own community and society, however, non-human things sometimes receive the lion's share of blame—think of how school shootings in the US are typically associated with guns or how gang violence in Britain is often associated with knives and drugs. As already noted, humanist Man and dualist thinking clearly play important roles in how social collectives identify, understand, and attempt to protect against violence.

In our view, this coin-flip approach to placing blame is reductionist and potentially dangerous. Philosopher of science Bruno Latour (1999) drove these points home with his discussion of gun control debates. Should we blame gun violence on the guns or on the people? In other words, do *guns* kill people, or do *people* kill people? Latour showed that such questions are fundamentally flawed in how they characterize the world. While one side of this debate recognizes the crucial role played by non-humans in these problems, both sides tend to represent humans and guns as if they were hermetically sealed off from one another, denying the complicated relationality of the world. According to Latour, we shouldn't fixate on one thing or the other but instead explore how the two sometimes act together as one (i.e., a gun-human network) and do things (often violent things) that neither humans nor guns could achieve apart from one another (cf. Fowles 2010; Harris and Cipolla 2017). This means that we should think of violence *relationally*. That is, instead of thinking of it in ways that neatly divide the world into human agents versus tools that human agents use (weapons in this case).

Further complicating matters, humans aren't always the victims; non-human things attract violence too. Consider the Protestant Reformation. During the sixteenth and seventeenth centuries, Europeans came to question and challenge the Catholic Church and its role as the sole mediator between people and God. Part of this upheaval involved iconoclasm, the destruction or vandalization of public icons—statues and images representing political or religious figures. This period saw widespread violence toward (non-human) representations of Catholic saints. Pamela Graves (2008) studied Reformation-era iconoclasm in England and observed some interesting patterns. She noted, for example, that most iconoclastic violence at the time targeted the heads and hands of statues and paintings, leaving the rest of the bodies untouched (see Figure 5.1). Graves emphasized how this treatment of icons mirrored how society punished criminals at the time. She explained the focus on heads and hands in terms of conceptions of personhood and the body. For example, according to Graves (2008, 38), people of sixteenth- and seventeenth-century England regarded representations of heads and hands as centers of "symbolic life-force." Many people at this time made sense of the church and of society in general through a body metaphor; leaders were the heads (where

Figure 5.1 Iconoclasm to the faces and some of the hands of saints on the rood
          screen of Great Snoring parish church, Norfolk, England.

Image: Pamela Graves.

ideas were formulated), while those who carried out the leaders' ideas or orders
(church or state officials) were the hands, and members of the church or citizens
were the feet (cf. Graves 2008, 42). Fascinatingly, Nugent (2019, 118–19) developed this idea further by demonstrating how it varied, meaning that different body
parts represented in statues/effigies were targeted differently depending on the time
and place; here again, violence has its own historical valency.

    For a more familiar example of violence toward nonhumans, consider the BLM
movement and its recent targeting of racist and colonial monuments. As Flewellen
and colleagues (2021, 230) note, BLM and its focus on the destruction or removal
of such monuments from public view "challenges us to consider the political implications of one of the most essential principles of archaeology and heritage work—
preservation." Beginning in mid-2020 as a part of widespread public backlash to
the brutal murder of George Floyd in Minneapolis, Minnesota (USA), these forms
of iconoclasm focus on publicly monumentalized slaveholders and colonists—their

statues are being removed, burned, beheaded, and much more (see Figure 5.2). The monuments commemorate white supremacy; they were created to maintain the status quo (structural inequalities) and to intentionally intimidate structurally disadvantaged and disenfranchised communities. The blatant iconoclasm of 2020 and beyond, however, were not the first examples of violence toward such monuments. There is a deep and complex history of covert defacement and damage to colonial and racist monuments (cf. Thompson 2022). This is part of the long history of Black resistance in places like the US. The difference in 2020 and beyond is that communities and preservationists stopped trying to erase material evidence of these forms of iconoclasm, the idea being that leaving damaged monuments in public view will help to commemorate this turning point in the resistance movement and the vast structural inequalities and racism that it rejected (see Figure 5.3).

As already noted, how one identifies or sees violence depends upon one's perspective. Many Indigenous peoples, for example, see the conventional methods of archaeology and museology as forms of violence that hurt Indigenous lands and belongings (cf. Colwell 2017; see also Cipolla et al. 2019). The collection and theft of Ahayu:da (War gods) from Zuni lands in the southwestern US stand out as powerful reminders of this point. Ahayu:da are wooden carvings placed strategically on

Figure 5.2 Edward Colston statue on display in the M Shed Museum in Bristol. Colston was a celebrated philanthropist, but his money came from the slave trade. The statue was pulled down, vandalized, and then thrown into the harbor. It was then removed from the harbor and displayed lying down covered in paint.

Image: Adrian Bolston, CC license 2.0 license (https://creativecommons.org/licenses/by/2.0).

Figure 5.3 Empty pedestal. The empty plinth after the Colston statue was removed. The plinth was covered in banners and posters from the protest, later gathered by Bristol Museums to record this event.

Image: Caitlin Hobbs, CC 3.0 license (https://creativecommons.org/licenses/by/3.0).

Zuni lands and left exposed to the elements. For Zuni people, Ahayu:da are meant to turn to dust; this process of naturally wearing away ensures a healthy world with a hopeful future. Unfortunately, during the nineteenth century, collectors began removing Ahayu:da from the land. To make things worse, they sometimes treated Ahayu:da with toxic preservatives that prevented or significantly slowed their decay. After this, they often placed these sacred items in sealed glass museum cases—cutting them off from their relations to the land and to the Zuni people—for the "education" of the general (White, western) public. Early collectors saw these efforts as for the "greater good" of humanity, but this idea of "humanity" excluded Zuni peoples (cf. Chapter 2). Although most collectors were clearly aware that they were going against the collective wishes of Zuni peoples, they almost certainly did not see their collection practices as forms of violence.

The brief examples considered here help us to think through the relationality of violence and how violence always operates as a confluence of humans and

non-humans—as a *becoming*. In most cases described here, acts of violence conflated humans and non-humans, in some instances with non-humans standing in for
or representing humans. They "stood for" members of the Catholic Church or for
racist and colonial figures, but they were distinctly different from the people that
they represented (cf. Chapter 7). They invited violence to them via their material
statuses; iconoclasm is a means of doing violence without directly hurting actual
people, and in the cases of both the Reformation and the BLM movement, iconoclasm has an enduring material presence whether in the form of scratched-out faces
and hands or empty plinths that once held statues. These material modifications and
absences have the potential to serve as long-term reminders of resistance movements and of the forms of discord with which they emerged.

In contrast to the examples of iconoclasm we considered, the violence perpetuated by archaeologists and museum collectors certainly did not conflate humans
and non-humans. Collecting practices maintained a strict divide between humans
and non-humans, and collectors seemingly felt free to explore the world and sample
what they found regardless of Zuni perspectives. For those who removed Ahayu:da
from the land, there was a universalized preservation ethic that is quite common for
museum professionals, even today (Cipolla et al. 2021; see also Crellin 2020). It
involves stopping the flow of time for collected objects to preserve them for future
generations. This contrasts sharply with Zuni perspectives; for them, the key to
maintaining equilibrium and to ensuring a positive future is to let Ahayu:da time
flow at its own pace—letting them go back to the earth and turn to dust.

This discussion opens us up to new and different ways of thinking about what
violence is, how and why it erupts, and how non-humans play crucial roles in both
doing violence but also in calling violence to them. In the next section, we expand
our discussion to move beyond specific instances and outcomes of violence and to
rethink the broader settings and histories through which violence emerges.

Theoretical toolkit: the virtual and the actual

Thus far in the chapter, we expanded our ideas about violence. To do this, we both
challenged how our standard concepts rest on arbitrary models of humanity and
explored how non-humans can be both the victims and the perpetrators of violence.
Finally, we looked at how archaeology itself can be a form of violence. Yet, something is still missing in all of this. We need conceptual tools to help explain why it
is that iconoclasm becomes necessary, why it is that violence can make our streets
seem unsafe, and why violence sometimes erupts spectacularly. When we think
about violence, we tend to concentrate on the act itself—the moment when the statue
is destroyed, the person stabbed, the punch thrown. But violence doesn't just lie in
the moments when it is carried out; it rests in the awareness of its potential, in its
threat, and in its capacity to take place. A crowd surges down a street; it isn't a riot
yet, but it might become one. The atmosphere switches, swells, and flows. A person
pulls out a knife or a gun. No violence has yet taken place, but its threat, or its potential, is as real as the act itself. The threat of violence can call violence into reality, as
exemplified in media coverage of police violence (e.g., the murder of George Floyd).

These threats of violence—its potential—are not generic. Instead, as with our discussion of the rules of conflict, threats of violence are specific and historically emergent. As with our discussion of Puar's work earlier in the chapter, they differ depending on which people are involved and how they understand each other. A Black man is at a much greater threat of violence from a police officer than a White woman (Lett et al. 2021). That same woman, walking through a dark street in a UK city, is threatened by far greater violence than a man in the same place at the same time (UN Women 2021). This makes it apparent how central and real the potential of violence is; trying to understand the experience of a woman walking through a dark street is impossible without an appreciation of the reality of the violence latent in the time of day, the location, the history of misogyny, and more. Furthermore, the threat and potential of violence are far more omnipresent than violent acts themselves. Only one woman needs to be attacked for all women to feel in danger. Writing this chapter in 2023, the threatening presence of nuclear weapons is unquestionably real, the potential for their use shaping war in Ukraine and the EU and American responses to it. If we don't think about the role of the *potential* dimensions in violence, we don't just miss half of the picture, we miss most of it!

In what follows we look at how embracing the potential for violence and its historical emergence can help us think through an archaeological case study. Before that, however, we need to explore the theoretical tools that can help us understand this interplay between the act of violence itself and the potential for it to take place. Specifically, we suggest that, within the perspectives advocated for in this book, we can draw on a pair of concepts from the work of the philosopher Gilles Deleuze (2004): the virtual and the actual.

We can start with the latter; the actual refers to what is happening right here, right now. Take the example of a knife; it has a range of properties, including size and mass, which are present in the world at a particular moment (DeLanda 2002). These are what Deleuze would call *actual*. Someone might use the knife to chop up food or peel a potato. In the moment that these things happen, they, too, are actual. At the same time, however, a knife also has a set of capacities for which it is *not* currently being used; these are what Deleuze would call *virtual*. To be clear from the outset, the term virtual here does not relate to the internet, to social media, or to any popular understandings of the term. Instead, Deleuze (1991) developed the concept from his reading of the nineteenth- to twentieth-century philosopher Henri Bergson. The virtual, for Deleuze, captures the range of potentials that exist in the world that are entirely real but not yet actual. Returning to our example, a knife has a range of what we can call virtual capacities; it could slice through an apple, it could spread butter, it could stab someone, and much more, even when it is *not* doing these things. The capacities of different kinds of knives might be suited to do these different things, and the context in which you encounter them makes a virtual capacity more or less likely to be actualized. A butter knife, for example, in the hands of your partner at the breakfast table, could be used—just about—to stab you, but unless things have gotten out of hand, this is probably not something you worry about. In contrast, a person holding a large sharp knife in a dark alleyway reveals a very different set of virtual potentials. Deleuze's (2004, 260) key point is that the virtual is just as real as the actual. That means we cannot understand a context, an object, or a set of relationships unless we think about these unactualized capacities.

When it comes to violence, we need to include the virtual for three reasons. First, as we saw in the experience of women moving through dark spaces in the UK, it allows us to appreciate how violence permeates contexts without needing to be actualized. Second, it allows us to appreciate how people's perceptions of the virtual—even if not voiced in those terms—affects how violence comes into being. Because of the history of racism, Black men are seen by White people in many parts of Europe and America as more violent than their White counterparts (Wilson et al. 2017). This (mis)understanding of the virtual capacity for violence possessed by Black men is one reason for the far more violent treatment they receive from police forces (Lett et al. 2021). Thus, actual violence erupts because of mistaken readings of the virtual (cf. Puar 2017). Finally, this shows us how the virtual and the actual are both always historically specific. The emergence of violence between police forces and ethnic minorities is the product of historical systems of racism, xenophobia, colonialism, capitalism, and more. It is not a transcendent truth.

What can archaeology add to this understanding of violence and the virtual? We suggest that it opens new ways of thinking about why moments of past violence erupted and thus helps shape how we understand violence in the present and in the future. We will turn to that latter argument in the final part of the chapter, but first, we want to explore a case study where an archaeologist has used the concept of the virtual to rethink violence.

Using our theoretical tools: resistance, violence, and the virtual at Puhú

The work of Nathan Acebo (2020) provides a critical example of how using the concept of the virtual can help us reconceptualize past moments of violence. Acebo explores the multi-ethnic Indigenous village of Puhú in California (see Figure 5.4), occupied through both precolonial and colonial periods. Today Puhú is memorialized as the scene of a massacre of its inhabitants by frontiersmen in 1832, allegedly avenging the theft of horses. This event is conventionally represented as an example of straightforward European colonialism and domination, where a struggling village, barely on the edge of survival, was forced into thievery and then swept away by the violent backlash; it is typically told as a tale of European domination of the American West. In contrast, Acebo draws on Indigenous perspectives, oral histories, and archaeological evidence to provide a different account. Alongside these elements, the concepts of the virtual and the actual provide critical ways of opening a very different understanding of these historical events, one in which the people of Puhú are no longer simply the victims of inevitable demise as their lifeways fail but one in which their success created the context in which the massacre took place.

Figure 5.4 The archaeological site of Puhú.

Image: Nathan Acebo.

By the nineteenth century, the traditional image of Indigenous lifeways in California is one of increasing marginalization, poverty, and submission to European domination. Both historians and archaeologists saw Puhú as a small and impoverished village (Acebo 2020, 369). In contrast, Acebo (2020) traces a process at Puhú not just of survival in the face of European colonists, but active, as he terms it, "thriveance." The term thriveance goes beyond the more-familiar concept of survivance, developed by Gerald Vizenor (1994). Archaeologists tend to use the concept of survivance to emphasize how Indigenous peoples did not simply die out in the face of European colonization but actively worked to survive and to resist colonialism. Thriveance pushes this concept even further by arguing that Indigenous peoples at sites like Puhú were not only surviving but were actively thriving in colonial contexts. As Acebo (2020, 15) puts it, thriveance is "a condition of Indigenous existence that exceeds the boundaries of bare survival and resistance focused on politically radical dimensions of communal prosperity." By working closely with contemporary Indigenous descendant groups and by drawing on the results of excavations at the site, Acebo examines how Indigenous peoples gathered all kinds of resources, including food stuffs, projectiles, and more. This included evidence for widespread and successful trading networks with both colonists and other Indigenous peoples over a wide area and a density of materials that far exceeded other contemporaneous villages (e.g., Acebo 2020, 376). These materials also comprised items that would appear in expressions of wealth, shaman's medicine bundles, and other material forms of power and authority. Combined with large-scale evidence for pendant production, these patterns suggest that Puhú was a wealthy and powerful place (Acebo 2020, 378). The traded items also speak to the existence of robust social networks linking the settlement to the wider world. The people of Puhú were connected and entwined across the landscape, and these networks did not fade during the colonial period. Instead, they intensified (Acebo 2020, 388).

At Puhú, Acebo (2020, 186) identifies the ability to resist colonialism as a critical virtual capacity. This capacity to resist was virtual and made actual in materials. This capacity increased as items like firearms became part of villagers' lives (Acebo 2020, 385). Secured for hunting and used in that (actual) capacity, firearms also created the capacity for greater levels of resistance and violence to be undertaken by the inhabitants. These new materials enhanced the virtual capacity for resistance, and thus violence, without it being actualized (Acebo 2020, 364). In turn, the gathering of rich, decorated, and complex materials created the virtual capacity for new kinds of leadership, potentially at the regional level, to emerge at Puhú. It was not that the residents at Puhú were actively working to resist colonial rule via tactical planning and grand design. Instead, it is more likely that they simply avoided engagement with Spanish missions and other expressions of European occupation. There is no evidence that they threatened colonists, carried out attacks, or acted violently. Nothing in the virtual capacity to resist had to be actualized, but, as noted in our theoretical toolkit discussion, it was nonetheless real.

Wealth and autonomy emerged at Puhú through a combination of strong regional political networks and non-humans like arrows and guns. These relations created the capacity for resistance but also something even more powerful—the capacity for war itself (Acebo 2020, 391). The fact that Puhú was *thriving* created this *virtual* capacity, one which posed a serious threat to local settler colonists. This does not mean that the residents of Puhú would have actualized this capacity, any more than having a knife in your house means you are going to stab your partner, but this capacity created a threat or a target for colonial violence (Acebo 2020, 187). The virtual capacity for resistance, for violence, for war, that was present at Puhú— real but not actual—made the village a logical target for colonial authorities. It is unclear whether the putative horse stealing that allegedly sparked the massacre took place or not; there is no evidence of horses in the archaeological record of the site. What is clear, however, is that one set of virtual capacities (the ability to resist or the ability to wage war) changed the way in which settler colonists acted and helped to actualize one of *their* virtual capacities for violence—to kill and to massacre. Far from the narrative of impoverished horse thieves clinging on to the last vestiges of Indigenous lifeways, finally perishing as inevitable victims of a colonizing power, we can now understand how violence at Puhú played out in a complex interplay of actual properties—a thriving village—and virtual capacities for resistance (by the residents of Puhú) and massacre (by the colonial authorities). Without this complex interplay of actual and virtual (alongside the role of non-humans as active players and Indigenous knowledge in understanding the past) the archaeology would have told a very different story.

Conclusion: violence and the future

As with our earlier chapters, we conclude here with a consideration of what archaeology has to say about the future of violence. It would be foolhardy to suggest that archaeology has the potential to reduce violence, but it can help us think about it, and conceptualize it, differently. In this chapter, we explored archaeological approaches to the study of violence in the past and how these are shaped by the ways that we think about violence and about the category Human in the present. Taking a theoretical position that doesn't essentialize human beings in the manner that concepts of Man do, we can sidestep debates about whether humans are "naturally" violent or not. Instead, violence is always historically specific. As a key part of this reorientation, we considered the key role of non-humans in violence—not only do they participate in acts of violence, they are often the focus of violent relationships themselves; think back, for example, to the defacement of Medieval icons or the destruction of colonial statues. Non-humans make different kinds of violence possible; for example, cutting off water, gas, electricity, food, or medicines in a besieged city is a brutal form of violence, just as carrying a knife or a gun changes the capacity for violence. The role of threat, and the potential for violence, brought us to a critical consideration of the virtual and the actual. Instead of considering violence only as actual acts that occur, we must consider the virtual capacities for violence. When we focus only on what actual violence is happening—dreadful, terrifying, and catastrophic as it might be—we are distracted from the role that the virtual plays. What virtual capacities for violence exist? How do people respond to those virtual possibilities? These factors shape the potential for violence to escalate further or to be wound down.

At the start of the chapter, we raised a key critique brought up in relation to approaches like the ones we have set out here. Some argue that an appreciation of the role of non-humans in acts of violence—that is, as helping to carry out violence or as the victims of violence—could be read as letting human beings "off the hook." Authors like Andreas Malm (2019) and Alf Hornberg (2021) suggest that relational approaches prevent us from ever blaming anyone for the acts that people perpetrate. Similarly, Artur Ribeiro (2016a) argued that including non-humans in our explanations risks blaming them for atrocities, including finding railway tracks culpable for transporting Jews to their murder in concentration camps during the Holocaust (cf. Thomas 2015, 1294). This parallels a related critique by those who argue that attention to non-humans inevitably prevents us from truly attending to the suffering of human beings (e.g., Van Dyke 2015, 2021). In other words, if we argue for a relational approach or if we suggest that attention to non-humans receiving violence might be worthy of our time, we risk diverting our attention away from those who really need it, the human beings. These thinkers argue that the logical endpoint of an argument that distributes agency between humans and non-humans is that it is not just people we should lock up in prison but non-humans as well.

Here we need to separate two very different issues: explanation and blame. The former is a question of historical importance; how can we explain how, when, where, and why violence took place? Demanding that we explain violence solely by reference to human beings is not, for the reasons we have been through in this chapter, sufficient. First, it prevents us from understanding the historical nature of violence because it demands that we exclude some of the context. Thus, for example, to exclude non-humans would mean we have to explain high levels of violence against women in modern western society without linking it to how women's bodies are depicted in imagery. To go beyond the people immediately responsible in this context inevitably involves non-humans, including forms of media, and more. Second, this anthropocentric approach prevents us from understanding the virtual as well as the actual components of violence and how these are never located in human beings alone but in the spaces, materials, and capacities that are brought into existence alongside humans. If people alone were solely responsible for violence, it would be much easier to stop—lock up all the bad guys, and you'll only have good guys left. Yet, as we know, increasing prison sentences and locking up more people rarely reduces broader levels of crime (Mears et al. 2016).

None of this is the same as the issue of blame. Blame, we suggest, is not an attempt to understand why something happened but an effort to identify human perpetrators. It operates within a different set of logics from historical explanation, within a different "mode of existence," to quote Latour (2013). In western societies, blame operates as a critical means of assigning human culpability to ensure that a perceived form of social justice is met. If someone suffering from drug addiction mugs a stranger on the street, we can certainly blame them for that act. If we want to understand it or explain it historically, refusing to include the chemical properties of drugs, the histories of criminalization, and the role of humans and non-humans in transporting and selling the substance, will mean we won't get very far. To give another contemporary example, Vladimir Putin may be to *blame* for Russia invading Ukraine, but simply reducing analysis of the war to his role alone is obviously insufficient where historical explanation is concerned.

Outside of the specific notion of blame, though, we would resist most strongly the argument that attention to non-humans prevents us from attending to human suffering. First, the notion that we can easily separate humans and non-humans flies in the face of what Indigenous peoples, let alone new materialist philosophers, teach us. The removal of Zuni Ahayu:da is a violent act against both humans *and* non-humans. The only way to neatly, and in advance of exploring a specific context, restore the easy separation of humans and non-humans is to return to the kinds of humanism and its logical consequences we critiqued earlier in Chapters 2 and 3. Extending care beyond the human does not automatically mean reducing care for human beings. In fact, when we blur the boundaries of what we count as human, it can extend and enhance that care.

As argued in this chapter, thinking archaeologically about violence has much to offer. More specifically, by approaching violence as something that is historically emergent (rather than transcendent, essential, or universal), by exploring the critical role of non-humans in acts of violence, and by emphasizing the virtual and the actual dimensions of violence, we can develop much more nuanced explanations for how and why violence happens. In turn, by undermining the links between our understandings of violence and the xenophobia that traditional humanist versions of Man create, we can forge a better understanding of how and why violence takes the forms it does. Fundamentally, both ancient and modern violence can be reappraised from this archaeological perspective, providing tools for us to understand how and why it erupts in the way that it does. And that, perhaps, may help us understand how to prevent it.

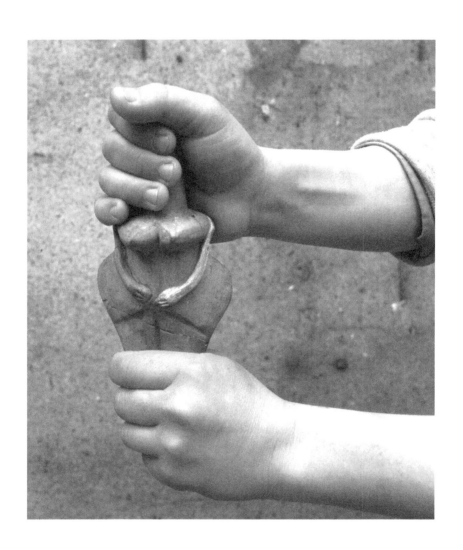

Chapter 6

All the world's a type

Rethinking difference and taxonomy

Introduction: cabinets of curiosities

The roots of archaeology lie in collecting—gathering unique objects from different times and places. In Europe, people we would today call "antiquarians" amassed large personal collections of rare material culture. Cabinets of curiosities capture this early spirit of collecting. In these spaces, a crocodile might sit between a Neolithic axe and a Medieval floor tile (see Figure 6.1).

The discipline of archaeology emerged as people began to sort through and organize these large personal collections. In European archaeology, we often reference the work of Christian Jürgensen Thomsen to think through this process (Rowley-Conwy 2007; Trigger 2006). Thomsen famously developed the Three Age System as he set about trying to organize the large assemblage of objects that would eventually form the collection of the National Museum of Denmark. He organized objects by material, also considering which types of objects were frequently found together. This kind of work always involves comparison—looking for similarities and differences between artifacts.

The Pitt Rivers Museum at Oxford (see Figure 6.2) embodies a similar process. There, diverse objects are lumped together by functional types rather than by date or geography; this means that a cabinet of spearheads might contain examples from Zambia and Denmark next to one another, united by their shared function. Pitt Rivers' aim was to use these groupings to show how human cultures evolved from simple to complex. Today, we might critique the Three Age System for the way it has become not just a *description* of change but an *explanation* of change (Crellin 2020). Similarly, we might criticize the problematic evolutionary ideas that sit behind the Pitt Rivers Museum's organizational scheme (Thomas 2004). In both cases, it is clear how particular worldviews (in this case, of Pitt Rivers and Thomsen) came to shape how collections were (universally) organized and thought about.

Organizing and sorting artifacts are cornerstones of archaeology. We sort finds from a dig, or we classify objects in the museum. Typology is a key part of this process—defining and organizing different kinds of objects, often into chronological sequences. We can, for example, trace changes in the shapes of axes, noting that

DOI: 10.4324/9781003244141-6

Figure 6.1 A cabinet of curiosity, Natural History Museum of Ole Worm, Museum Wormiani Historia Engraving Museum Wormianum Published: 1655.

Image: Wellcome Library, London, CC BY 4.0 license http://wellcomeimages.org).

Figure 6.2 The interior of the Pitt Rivers Museum, Oxford. Objects are organized by type and boxed into separate cabinets.

Image: Einsamer Schütze, CC BY-SA 3.0 license (https://creativecommons.org/licenses/by-sa/3.0).

their forms relate closely to changes in how they were hafted. For specific places and time periods, typology is an important, perhaps even dominant, way of understanding the past. One might argue that typology is simply a way of describing and ordering what archaeologists find—a neutral and scientific technique. In this chapter, we explore this argument further, asking if it really holds up and investigating how it relates to broader patterns of thought in western intellectual traditions. We begin with a brief history of typology (and debates about it!) and then consider how typologizing objects compares with some of the damaging ways that people have been classified. We consider the theoretical underpinnings of typologies, tracing connections to the concept of "ideal types" (cf. Chapter 2) before developing an alternative approach to thinking about difference. We argue for a more positive approach to difference, first, by thinking about the relationship between the autism spectrum and evolution and, second, through a study of figurines from the region we know today as Mexico.

Setting the stage: a history of types

Archaeologists generally love their types. Is that Beaker pot "all over cord" decorated or a "maritime" type? Does that projectile point have side notches or a flute? Archaeologists have debated the nature of questions like these for a long time now. And indeed, typologies continue to occupy a central place in many archaeologists' toolkits. In this section of the chapter, we provide a brief capsule history of typological debates in archaeology, distilling some theoretical concerns and following the story up to the present, including discussions of object "biographies" and how these reorientations intersect with recent archaeological concerns about non-human things and vibrant matter.

In the middle of the twentieth century, American archaeologists James Ford and Albert Spaulding engaged in a blistering and now infamous debate concerning the nature of typological thought in their discipline (Ford and Steward 1954; Ford et al. 1954; see also Bordes and Sonneville-Bordes 1970; Binford and Binford 1969; Rolland and Dibble 1990 for another excellent debate over typology, the Mousterian debate). Spaulding, prefiguring what would become a mainstay of processual archaeologies, argued that typologies are what we might call "ontological." In other words, he saw typologies as singular, "True," and often beyond the understanding of the people who originally made and used the artifacts in question. According to Spaulding, people of the past were likely unaware (or wrong) about the artifact categories that he derived. This was because, for him, real typologies are only accessible through complicated quantitative analyses.

Ford, on the other hand, problematized the concept of types altogether; for our purposes, he raised four key challenges for Spaulding and for typological thinking, more broadly (Ford and Steward 1954; Ford et al. 1954). First, he argued that archaeologists should indeed care about what people thought about in the past; we should consider how they might have categorized artifacts even if we might not succeed in accessing their precise viewpoint. Second, he disregarded many traditional archaeological assumptions about the "normativity" of typologies, asking archaeologists to think about how classification really works for communities or societies (Ford et al. 1954). Does every member of a society share an understanding of how to divide the world into categories? He argued that types do not exist uniformly for all members of a group; in other words, they are *not* normative. Third, according to Ford, types are not timeless—they change as time passes and as different people and things interact with them. Finally, Ford (Ford et al. 1954, 109) questioned the nature of Spaulding's "objectivity" and his self-proclaimed ability to access the real "reality" of types. Truths, like archaeological types, are thus subject to change and partially shaped by the typologist and the assumptions that they bring to the sorting table (see Chapter 7 for more about truth). For Spaulding, the researcher does not shape the categories because, for him, the two exist independently of one another. In contrast, Ford recognized that the researcher and the material world being classified actively influence one another (cf. Barad 2007). Because of this, there is no single correct type for Ford; instead, types or categories are inherently multiple and depend upon the purpose and motivation of their creator.

Many of the challenges that Ford laid out for typology are still important today. As the discipline came to lean less on typologies for relative chronological context thanks to breakthroughs in radiometric dating, new questions emerged, some of which took shape from—or at least resembled—Ford's points from the 1950s. For instance, in the wake of the postprocessual critiques' embrace of the multiple meanings of artifacts and archaeological patterns, archaeologists came to question typologies all over again. Harkening back to Ford's third point about the passage of time, Gosden and Marshall (1999; see also Gosden 2005) looked at how material things outlast human lives (individuals and even generations, cf. Chapter 4). From this perspective, instead of arguing about singular, essential types, archaeologists could follow the artifacts as they aged, encountered new people and places, and transformed. For these thinkers, archaeologists need to continually scrutinize an artifact's shifting contexts, considering the relationships it has with the world in all periods of its existence, including the relationships it has in the present.

These questions and concerns gathered momentum in the last 20 years of archaeological theory. This is especially so with recent concerns over *hylomorphism* (e.g., Alberti and Marshall 2009; Ingold 2007; see also Cipolla and Gallo 2021; Harris and Cipolla 2017; see also Gallo and Cipolla n.d.). Hylomorphism involves the relationship between form and substance or, for our purposes, mind versus matter. A hylomorphic approach assumes that these two realms are opposites of one another (a dualism) and that the mind shapes matter when it comes to the final form of an artifact. In other words, a hylomorphic approach to classification assumes that a group of people share an ideal mental template for what an object should look like, and they simply realize that ideal in passive matter. A social group shares a singular, uniform idea about what a projectile point should look like, they go out and find some stone, and they shape the stone to conform to the ideal they have in their heads.

Here lies a major liability of most typological thought—the yearning for the existence of an ideal! The idea of types, whether archaeological or otherwise, tends to imply the notion that, just off-screen, just out of reach, lies that ideal version of the thing you are looking at: the perfect pint glass, of which yours is a disappointing copy; the perfect Neolithic figurine, by comparison to which yours seems a little cruddy. Indeed, this is a very ancient idea; the Greek philosopher Plato developed this argument explicitly. He suggested that there were eternal, unchanging, and perfect "Ideas" of which the material stuff of the world we encounter were merely disappointing copies, and here we see a direct link to our hylomorphic problem.

The relationship between the perfect idea and the imperfect material copy might seem like a distant fragment of Greek philosophy (after all, do any archaeologists *really* believe that there is a perfect ideal version of whatever object they happen to be looking at?). Nonetheless, like many forms of unexamined theory that seem bizarre when you burrow down to their core, this is what underpins some of the basics of how archaeologists think about the world and supports all the issues with typology we have outlined earlier. It doesn't matter whether an archaeologist explicitly declares their faith in the Platonic ideal version of whichever type of flints they happen to be sorting. The act of creating typologies rests upon these ideas *whether the archaeologist chooses to believe in them or not,* and this just cements the crucial role that theory and theorization play in our discipline.

Note a critical issue hidden in this account of types—it is not just that there are ideal originals and material copies; it is that the material copies are somehow *worse* than the ideal original. They *lack* something that the original has. As noted by thinkers like Ben Alberti, Yvonne Marshall, Tim Ingold, and more (e.g., Conneller 2011; Jones 2012), this approach doesn't give enough credit to inorganic matter and its different properties. For instance, it would be incredibly difficult, if not impossible, for most of us to create a "Clovis" spearpoint using any form of matter that we get our hands on. We can't make it from wood or water. Instead, we need access to specific varieties of stone. Moreover, once we begin chipping that stone, the stone itself acts back upon us and shapes how we think about the spearpoint we want; the stone helps determine what the point looks like in the end. If we choose the "wrong" stone, say one with a structural weakness or unexpected inclusion, it won't behave as we want it to. One of the biggest challenges of archaeological typologies is that archaeologists tend to discuss types as if they worked in a straightforward hylomorphic way. This means that archaeological typologies tend to treat the world as strictly divided into ideas versus materials. They tend to place most emphasis on ideas or ideal types assumed to exist "normatively" in the heads of a group of people. And in so doing, they often overlook the vibrancy and potential of matter to give shape to the world.

Types in the wider world

Perhaps these typological debates in archaeology seem harmless, but they relate directly to assumptions that can be quite dangerous and dehumanizing. This is because archaeologists aren't the only people who like to create typologies; there is a long-running Western tradition of sorting and essentializing—the most egregious examples of which involve the categorization of people into "different" groups that are assumed to have distinctive and timeless traits, limitations, and possibilities (cf. Fowles 2010; Voss 2008; see also Chapter 3). This problem connects directly to our previous discussion of another universalized and idealized concept against which *people*, in this case, are measured, humanist Man (Chapter 2). As we argued, the concept of Man rests on the notion that there is an ideal human who happens to be male, rational, White, heterosexual, able-bodied, and so on. In comparison, other humans *lack* these critical characteristics. They lack a penis, white skin, or the "ability to think rationally." So, while it might seem harmless to bemoan the fact that your "rusticated Beaker" lacks all the class and finish of the perfect pot you have imagined in your mind, this is precisely the same logic that suggests women are "too emotional" or any other number of stereotypes that negatively contrast the idealized Man with the real people that live in the world.

Remember in Chapter 4 where we took on assumptions inherent in cultural evolution, where Western peoples looked around the world and concluded that they sat at the apex of cultural progression while they judged many colonized peoples as "stuck" on lower rungs of the evolutionary ladder? As with many of the typological problems already discussed, this worldview assumes the existence of "ideal" types, and it operationalizes these fictions by way of *negative difference*. In other words, cultural evolution tends to categorize and rank the world based on strict hierarchies, the assumption being that all forms must be compared to the ideals and judged according to what the ideal *has* and what other ("less-than-ideal") examples *lack*. Western societies were assumed to have certain essential traits (e.g., centralized governments, specific notions of landownership and environmental improvement, standing armies, metal smelting, etc.), whereas non-western, colonized societies were seen as lacking these things (Fowles 2010); in other words, what was missing was not judged according to local reasoning, it was judged against a Western universal based on the assumption that all societies would (if they could) become like Western, colonizing nation-states. These patterns mirror traditional Linnaean taxonomy—how biologists sort living things (Agbe-Davies 2015).

As discussed in the previous section, it is important to remember that typologies should be considered in relation to their respective histories and purposes. To put this another way, we must consider the positionality and the motivations of the person or group who created and used the classification system (see also Chapter 8). As an example, archaeologist Anna Agbe-Davies (2015) provides a compelling analysis of seventeenth-century texts that speak to the emergence of racial classifications in the Middle Atlantic region of the US. As mentioned in Chapter 3, the racialized "types" used and discussed today to sort humans into different groups, such as Black or White people, are *not* eternal categories. Instead, as already noted, these forms of classification emerged alongside capitalism and colonialism. This means that early on in colonial Virginia, designations of "black" or "white" people did *not* exist. Agbe-Davies shows how this quickly changed as tobacco plantations grew via the global market. To use the language of Chapter 3, the increased flow of tobacco stopped or curtailed other types of flow—in this case, the freedom of a diverse group of people that would come to be called "Black." Being English and Christian were the default standards for those keeping records at the time (Agbe-Davies 2015, 181–2); anyone lacking these qualities was treated as less than the ideal and thus subject to different (and worse) treatment. As the need for a large, cheap labor force increased with the flows of tobacco and capital, colonists in power moved toward institutionalizing slavery or bondage as a permanent status for their laborers. At first, the criteria for making someone a slave depended on factors that were *not* linked to racial classifications. Instead, it was permissible at the time to enslave a person if: 1) they were *not* Christian; and 2) they had been forcibly shipped to the colony (Agbe-Davies 2015, 186) rather than coming by choice or via self-funded means. These criteria left out many of the early plantation labor force—namely English indentured servants. Plantation owners and colonial officials initially referred to these various types of laborers by status (servants, etc.), but these categories were eventually replaced with what we today would consider "racial" terms. Whiteness became associated with servitude (a non-permanent status), whereas blackness came to be associated with slavery (a permanent and heritable status) (cf. Hayes 2013). Thus, as Hayes puts it, *slavery came before race*, the latter emerging with capitalist desires and needs to transform the status of slaves into something timeless and essential.

Here we see how a complicated range of characteristics (let's take skin pigmentation as an example) became essentialized and forced into two boxes—people were classified as either Black or White. These designations were (racistly) assumed to come packaged with a suite of other characteristics. The Platonic ideal was the White plantation owner or colonial official (cf. discussions of humanist Man). People that were classified as Black were clearly treated as less than human and this was because they were represented as lacking the intellect and complexity of "White" people. This example shares much in common with archaeological and anthropological discussions of cultural evolution. This is because both models default to something resembling a Linnaean mode of classification (Agbe-Davies 2015, 67–8; Brew 1971). Linnaean categories are arranged hierarchically, with higher-order categories including lower-order categories. This means, for example, that the genus category "Homo" includes several sub-categories (e.g., *Homo sapiens, Homo neanderthalensis, Homo erectus,* and more). Examples in any one of these categories (for example, comparing two Neanderthals) are assumed to be more alike one another and less like any example from another category (for example, comparing a Neanderthal with an "anatomically modern human," cf. Sterling 2015 and Chapter 8).

Generations of biological anthropologists have noted how the racial designations that were codified long ago on tobacco plantations and *still* impacting today's world do not work as a Linnaean category! Genetic evidence (e.g., Lewonton 1972) shows that there is *more* diversity or difference between people classified into any one racial category (like Caucasian) than there is between people in *different* categories. Just because race has no biological basis, of course, does not mean that

it isn't "real" (Franklin et al. 2020); as demonstrated earlier, it is a system of classification initially constructed to enslave certain people. This problematic way of
sorting and thinking about variability and difference is, of course, the same model
that many archaeologists use to categorize artifacts. As Agbe-Davies (2015, 68)
notes, "we model our treatment of artifacts on the species concept." So, if we want
archaeology to have ways of thinking about objects that do not rest on these rather
problematic assumptions, and if we want to challenge how we think about people
in both the past and the present, then we will need an alternative starting point, an
alternative way to conceptualize *difference*.

Theoretical toolkit: from identity to difference

As our analysis shows, whether it's the history of how archaeologists think about
objects, how we categorize our data, or much wider issues of how societies conceptualize and act upon ideas of race, typology presents us with some thorny issues. To
unpick this, we need to further explore how and why types exert such power on our
imagination and how they depend upon assumptions and specific ways of thinking.
The approach to types we have seen so far in the chapter operates within a particular understanding of both identity and difference. Identity rests on a presumed
singular point of comparison, the ideal pot, the ideal person, and then difference
emerges as a way of capturing how the object or person in question differs *from*
that ideal. Imagine a pretty much perfect barbed and tanged arrowhead, and then
the disappointment when the one you find *lacks* a barb (see Figure 6.3). As with the
examples of racial classifications presented earlier, difference here is negative;
therefore, it compares how one thing has something that another lacks. One person
is shorter than another, lacking height; one person is fatter than another, lacking the
discipline to stop eating or to make themselves exercise.

Here, we argue that there is an alternative way of thinking about difference
(Bickle 2020; Crellin and Harris 2021; Harris 2021a) that offers helpful new perspectives on typology. In the second half of the twentieth century, feminist and

Figure 6.3 Two barbed and tanged arrowheads—the one on the left is close to
perfect, and the one on the right is lacking a barb.

Image: Peter Reavill, Birmingham Museums Trust, Creative Commons 2.0 license (https://
creativecommons.org/licenses/by/2.0).

other philosophers became interested in how difference could be repurposed, not as a negative question of lack, but rather as a productive force that helped to create the world (Deleuze 2004; Irigaray 1985). These ideas continue to permeate debates today and play a critical role in the kinds of feminist posthumanism we looked at in Chapter 2 (Braidotti 2011; Grosz 1994). For thinkers like Gilles Deleuze (2004), difference wasn't something secondary, working as a tool of comparison. Instead, it was a creative force that was primary. Rather than starting with the identity of two things, whether pots or people, and comparing them, Deleuze suggested that we start with difference and map how it helps to produce the things we would later go on to compare.

How does a river create its course? It does so as the energy of its flow wears away at the banks that surround it, carving out and shaping the world of which it is part. What was originally a blank canvas becoming defined, *differentiated,* we might say, by the flow of water. Through time, the power of the water, the draw of gravity that lures it to the sea, can have a major impact on shaping the landscape through this process of difference-making. What about a more archaeological example? How does a potter make a pot? An undifferentiated lump of clay has force applied to it; this might be by hand alone or with the clay spinning on a wheel. The different forces applied shape the pot through a process of difference-making. The addition of pressure, abrasion, and the use of hands or tools shape how the pot emerges in conjunction with the clay itself. Here, potter and clay work together. The difference is emergent between them; in other words, it is *relational* (Chapter 1). The same is true of rivers, which emerge through the relationships between clouds, gravity, the varied geology of the area that helps shape the direction the water takes, how easily eroded that earth is, and more (cf. Allard and Cipolla 2021; Cipolla and Allard 2019).

These relations mean that difference is never simply a wild and unstructured force flowing through the universe. Rivers don't wear away at their banks at random because they are always operating within the relations we discussed. This critical point brings us back to the issue of types. Rivers resemble one another, not because they were designed as an attempt to match a mythical perfect river, but because the same process, one based on the act of difference-making, produced and reproduced them through time. As we saw, as the potter's hands shape the clay they impart pressure and force in particular ways, shaping the clay and the eventual pot. This means that when we encounter pots that look like one another, and date to similar periods, we are not looking at copies of an ideal type—as the logic that underpins most archaeological typologies would suggest. Instead, we are looking at the outcome of repeated acts of difference-making. None of this is to deny intentionality on the part of a potter, that they wanted the pot to look a particular way and took certain actions to make that happen. Instead, it is to understand that beneath the production of similarity lies the primary and primordial force of difference. Here process, how things come into existence, becomes much more important than the notion of a finished project, an ideal type, or a longed-for design (Gosden and Malafouris 2015). When archaeologists think of the types *we* identify as defining the forms of materials people worked with in the past, we are placing the cart before the horse. We are taking the *outcome* of a set of processes and implying that the result somehow came first. We are ignoring and bracketing the detailed processes, all the relations that helped guide that process, and the flow and force of difference itself.[1]

Using our toolkit: positive difference from autistic traits to gendered figurines

Autistic traits and human evolution

How do the concepts and approaches described in this chapter help us to rethink the categories we often force on human variability? To think about this further, we turn to an excellent study of human evolution where differences, ones normally perceived in terms of *lack*, are instead framed as a positive force of creativity. When it comes to human evolution, the long-standing proposition has been that human beings evolved to attend in increasingly sophisticated ways to what other people are thinking and feeling (Dunbar 1998)—a sense of empathy for fellow humans. This is what cognitive archaeologists and anthropologists mean when they discuss the emergence of a "theory of mind" in human beings, the ability to recognize that other people have thoughts. This general quality is present in many animals but reaches an unparalleled level of complexity in our own species. The idea is that to form the complex social groups in which our species live, and to attend to the complex rituals that make those groups work, people must imagine what others are thinking in a far more detailed manner than our evolutionary relations, like chimpanzees. The correlate of this is that hominins would be more likely to be reproductively successful—having babies that survive to have their own babies—if they were capable of this kind of empathy.

Of course, you might already note how this appears to position the *idealized* modern human, one which again seems to bear a somewhat significant similarity to humanist Man, at the end of this line of progress. Traits that are seen as being critical to the successful politician or business*man* today, not to mention the charming gentleman sitting at the end of the bar, somehow turn out to be the ones evolution has been selecting for all along. One question we might immediately pose, therefore, is where this leaves people who don't match up to this ideal, people who seem to differ from the norm or *lack* the social skills evolution seemingly deemed so central.

One group this might apply to are people within the autism spectrum, including what is known as autism without intellectual impairment or Asperger's Syndrome (hereafter AS). People with AS tend to have difficulties in social interactions and sometimes struggle with non-verbal communication (Spikins et al. 2016; Baron-Cohen 2009). In short, they seem to lack the kinds of skills that the typical story of human evolution has sought to select. People with AS are different, and that difference is typically understood negatively as a *lack* of social skills.

In a striking account, however, Penny Spikins and colleagues (2016) sought to rethink the role of AS and other alternative patterns of human cognition as a *positive* force that played a critical role in human societies and their ability to evolve and survive. Could AS be a different but equally important, and indeed critical and creative form, of human sociality (Spikins et al. 2016, 294)? Spikins and colleagues (2016) point out that in contemporary hunter-gatherer societies, particular forms of collaborative morality are highly valued; this is where people can bring things to society in the form of sharing the outcome of food gathering, care for individuals, and craft skills that do not rely necessarily on the ability to imagine another person's thoughts and motivations. Rather than empathetic understanding, they rely instead on committing to forms of rules and agreements in ways that people with AS are comfortable doing today. The emphasis on "social logic," rather than understanding complex emotional contexts, can enhance social reputation (Spikins et al. 2016, 295). This means that in societies where sharing food, for example, is a critical social rule, what is relied upon is an ability to follow those rules and to commit to them, not to imagine why other people might or might not do the same.

More than this, however, Spikins et al. (2016, 295–7) point out that people with AS can often have, by comparison to other people, quite extraordinary abilities with music, detail perception, focus, painting, memory, mathematics, and more. This, in turn, could have had significant implications for early human societies. The skill of remembering the details of animals, plants, or landscapes could have had major implications for the ability of groups to survive, especially as they spread into new regions or climates (Spikins et al. 2016, 302). Therefore, the different forms of social and other skills here need *not* be perceived as a lack. Instead, this is a *positive form of difference* that creates new possibilities for human communities in the past and present. Spikins and colleagues (2016, 300) support this point in reference to complex genetic evidence that shows that AS can be understood as a critical adaptive strategy in human beings. Rather than positioning it as less-than the "normal" human ability to communicate, which elevates and privileges humanist Man once again, we can instead reposition this way of thinking as one example of how *multiple* ways of thinking, all creating different ways of understanding the world, allowed human beings to flourish. Although Spikins and colleagues (2016) do not employ the approach to difference we have advocated here, their work acts as a superb example of what happens when instead of defining human beings as certain types, which differ negatively from the ideal, you explore how differences themselves can be generative forces in the world, allowing other ways of living to become possible.

A thousand different figurine genders

A recent study of figurines made and used during the emergence of the Teotihuacan state in Mexico (Hagerman 2018) provides a fitting example of how ideas from our theoretical toolkit might apply to a different archaeological case. Kiri Hagerman analyzed changing figurine styles in the Mexico Basin from 800 BCE to 600 CE (the late Middle Formative to the Classic periods). Hagerman considers how the representation of gender in figurines changed over the course of 1400 years, during which time the Teotihuacan state was formed. During this period, figurines were the most common depiction of people known to archaeologists; Hagerman tracks changes in figurine forms through time, looking at how they depicted people, e.g., clothing, jewelry, etc. Teotihuacan was "a multi-ethnic metropolis that ruled an eponymous expansive state from approximately 200–600 AD" (Hagerman 2018, 692). At its core, the metropolis consisted of a vast and impressive ceremonial and religious architecture with clear centralized planning; the city was also home to a large population living in multi-family compounds (Cowgill 2015) (see Figure 6.4).

The figurines under consideration are ceramic and were ubiquitous in the area from 1000 BCE to 1500 CE; scholars estimate that they were produced in the millions (Hagerman 2018, 695) (see Figure 6.5)! Figurines were handmade, molded, or a combination of the two; they were also likely decorated with paint that no longer survives. They were made in domestic contexts and in specialized workshops in Teotihuacan as well as in rural settlements. One workshop that produced molded figurines sat next to the Ciudadela (a state building), suggesting that some, but not all, figurine production involved state officials and elites (Hagerman 2018, 695). Figurines are primarily found fragmented, often in domestic spaces, courtyards, and architectural fills; they were occasionally placed in burials, but people likely used them primarily in domestic rituals that took place in shared courtyards with altars (Hagerman 2018, 695). Although archaeologists do not know precisely how people used these figurines, their production and use declined with the collapse

Figure 6.4 Teotihuacan, Mexico.
Image: David Horan.

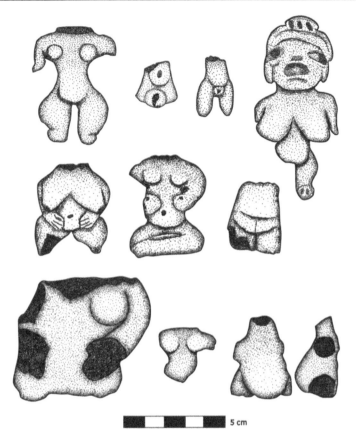

5 cm

Figure 6.5 Middle and Late Formative gynomorphic sexual attributes from Huixtoco (top row) and Axotlan (middle row), and Terminal Formative gyno-morphs from Teotihuacan (bottom row.) From Hagerman (2018, fig. 4).

Image: Kiri Hagerman.

of the Teotihuacan state. The ceramic figurines studied by Hagerman were, there-fore, a common part of life in the Basin of Mexico at the time. In summary, they persisted across thousands of years, were used in both rural and urban contexts, were made in domestic spaces and workshops, and were seemingly embedded in domestic rituals.

Our choice to consider figurines here is deliberate. This example combines ele-ments of our arguments about how categorizing types of objects links directly to the categorization of types of people. Archaeological engagements with figurines help to highlight what these twin processes share. As anthropomorphic representations of different types of bodies, figurines offer unique opportunities to address catego-ries of both objects and persons (e.g., Bailey 2005, 2013; Chapman and Gaydarska

2006; Nanoglou 2008). As archaeologists, we often ask *who* is represented and *why*, using figurines to think about different identities in the past. As noted, figurines are categorized as objects of archaeological study—their form can be used to interpret archaeological phases (Montoya 2001; Scott 2001; Valliant 1931)—and as representing types of people. For example, does this figurine represent a man or a woman, a warrior or a mother? These types of categorizations operate using the same processes of comparing similarities and differences, often focusing on what things or people *lack*. Our point though is broader than just that; instead of focusing on difference as a negative lack, we can alter our understandings and think more creatively by foregrounding difference as positive and productive.

Hagerman is interested in how the formation of states affected gender roles. She draws her data both from the urban center of Teotihuacan and from three sites in the more rural surrounds (Axotlan, Cerro Portezuelo, and Huixtoco), allowing her to think about how the state impacted rural and urban lives differently. She uses an assemblage theory framework (see Chapter 2) to break out of the typical typological approach, arguing that typology "necessarily privileges sameness over difference" (Hagerman 2018, 691). She employs existing typologies to date the 2,045 figurine fragments in her sample but then looks in more detail across typologies at the visual imagery of the figurines. She identifies masculine and feminine body parts (for example, breasts, pregnant abdomens, penises) and masculine and feminine aspects of dress. She then tracks the co-occurrence of these features through time.

Overall, Hagerman identifies a series of trends in the representation of masculine and feminine bodies through time. She argues that in earlier, pre-state periods, sexual attributes were commonly represented, but that this waned chronologically and was replaced by masculine and feminine clothing covering the bodies (Hagerman 2018, 703; Tables 1, 5, and 6). This is not a neat nor a clearly bounded transition, but a messy one that is smeared across the flow of time. She also observed that there were initially more feminine-gendered figurines, but from the Terminal Formative period onwards, masculine-gendered figurines dominated the record (Hagerman 2018, 706–8; Figure 10).

What is interesting here is that throughout the period of study, many figurines were simply *not* gendered in permanent ways that are obvious to archaeologists in the present (Hagerman 2018, Figure 10).[2] Although our tendency as archaeologists is to group the figurines by gender, their material forms actively resist these categories. For many figurines, archaeologists cannot tell which are masculine or feminine. Using a more traditional approach, we might categorize these figurines as "lacking" gender. Taking a more positive approach to difference, however, we could think about how their different forms created new possibilities. The decision not to give gendered features to these figurines was not an accident, a lack of skill or time, but a deliberate decision by their makers. The figurines resist our categorization in this way, but they open a world of possibilities; for example, perhaps gender did not matter so much in the rituals they were involved in. Other categories of identity might have come to the fore in such practices, or maybe the emphasis was on a collective, anonymous "every person" rather than specific gendered types.

If we consider the figurines from the Middle, Late, and Terminal Formative periods, when feminine sexual attributes were more commonly identified, there are still more intriguing patterns to consider. Hagerman (2018) identifies feminine bodies based on the presence of breasts, vulvas, pregnant abdomens, and pubic triangles. These features do not always co-occur, so, for example, one might have a figurine with breasts but no pubic triangle. Taking a classic typological approach, we might imagine an *idealized* feminine figurine and see many of the figurines as imperfect or incomplete—lacking breasts, lacking a vulva, etc. Alternatively, we might think about how the choice to represent a particular sexual characteristic was about creating difference; for example, a figurine with breasts is different from a figurine with breasts and a vulva. It depicts different things, so it can do different things. Perhaps these were different types of people, people at different moments in their lives or their days, or these figurines were able to carry out different roles in rituals.

Delving deeper into the data, Hagerman (2018, Table 3) shows that figurines which have a combination of sexual attributes were more common at a particular site (Huixtoco) during the Late Formative period. In a traditional analysis, we might ask why the other sites lacked these figurines that were "more fully realized." Alternatively, we can think about how different ideas about bodies and gender were being materialized in different places and in particular moments. Whether or not the makers chose to add sexual characteristics, and particular combinations of sexual characteristics, opened different possibilities.

As noted, over time, the production of figurines with sexual characteristics decreased, and there was an increased use of clothing and jewelry to decorate the figurines (Hagerman 2018, 699). From the Terminal Formative period onwards, clothing was more frequently represented, and a wider variety of styles emerged, particularly masculine dress. The addition of clothes provided new possibilities and opportunities for the differentiation of bodies. During the Classic period, for example, new types of masculine figurines emerged because of the possibilities created by the additions of clothing and jewelry (Hagerman 2018, 702). During this time, feminine figurines became increasingly standardized, and their form was relatively fixed for the following 300 years—appearing throughout with similar varieties of clothing and jewelry.

The contrast between handmade and molded figurines is also pertinent. Figurines from the Formative period were entirely handmade, whereas figurines from the Classic period were dominantly mold-made (Hagerman 2018, 695). Despite this, it was still common in the later periods to have handmade figurines that were decorated with molded heads and headdresses, making any simple division between handmade and mold-made unhelpful when trying to typologize or phase figurines. As an example, the bodies of some later feminine figurines literally disappeared; these figurines consisted only of clothes and an attached head or headdress (Hagerman 2018, 701). We might think about this as an absent body, but we can also think about this transition as indicating the importance of the outfits themselves and how they allowed different kinds of rituals to be carried out with figurines. Who was inside the clothes mattered less than the clothes themselves; it could be any kind of body—male, female, or something else.

We can use our theoretical approach to think about this transition in the way the figurines were being made, not as the development of a more complex technology that allowed mass production, but as a *development of differences that this transition made possible*. The increase in the use of jewelry and clothing on figurines emerges in tandem with the development of molded forms. Molds made it possible to elaborate the bodies of figurines in different ways and for differences in the figurines to be brought out in ways that were not observed with the handmade examples. This might help us to rethink the argument that we are shifting from a concern with bodily sexual difference towards a concern with socially and culturally created gender (Hagerman 2018, 698).

Scholars often argue that the arrival of state societies coincided with the subjugation and decreased importance of women (Engels 1972 [1884]; Gailey 1987; Joyce 2001). We could read the data in this study in a similar way; women were depicted more often before the state emerged, and over time, when they were represented, it was in increasingly standardized ways. By contrast, masculine figurines increased in numbers and elaboration over time. Yet, this is only one way to read the data and it relies on strict binary categorization of figurines and a concept of an ideal figurine body (each linked with the assumptions associated with humanist Man). This traditional approach puts the figurines into predefined categories rather than looking for the story that emerges from them. As Hagerman (2018, 707–8) highlights, the figurines resist a simple binary male/female categorization; they indicate gender was more complex and only one facet of identities at the time. Harkening back to one of Ford's main points in the 1950s, attempts to categorize these varied figurines as simply masculine or feminine says "more about the people doing the sorting than it does about the people who produced" the figurines (Hagerman 2018, 708). It tells us more about the potentials that difference introduced into the world than it does about pre-existing ideals.

Conclusions

The figurines from Teotihuacan show how, when we attend to the play of difference rather than the imposition of preordained types, we can begin to engage in much more interesting narratives about bodies, gender, and material culture. Rather than simply presuming a singular narrative of male empowerment and female disempowerment, we saw instead the interweaving potentials of multiple forms of dress, body parts, and acts of making. Differences become multiple, and differences become productive. Instead of types telling us about a past we have already organized into opposed categories of male and female, and a worryingly simple story of the former dominating the latter, we can instead tease out a richer world of past identities. Similarly, our example of autism and evolution showed how thinking of difference as positive, instead of difference as lack, allows a richer reading of evolutionary history. Rather than simply presuming that the categories of humans that will prove most evolutionarily successful reflect those categories lauded in society today, we can think about how different forms of cognition allow for different understandings of the world to emerge and with that, different possibilities for a species to grow and adapt.

These criticisms don't mean that we must completely reject typology. Hagerman's brilliant study of the figurines depends in part on her ability to draw on typologies to sort them chronologically. The work of Spikins and colleagues (2016) also depends upon sorting people into types (people with AS and people without, for example). Neither study, however, ranks these differences in a hierarchy or presumes that either side is produced and defined by what they lack. For archaeologists, the order that typologies provide can help pose questions, but it is often our ability to disentangle and think beyond those typologies that help us begin to answer the very questions that typologies help us to ask (cf. Agbe-Davies 2015; Tsoraki et al. 2023). Yet, we need to recognize that typology, although a useful heuristic tool, will always be limiting (as soon as we create a type, it closes off certain questions) and will always be partial (there are other ways of sorting anything into types). As intimated by Ford so many decades ago, typology is also a tool that emerges from an ongoing process, one involving the people in the past, the archaeologist in the present, and the materials that link them together. There is thus no final or absolute typology (sorry, Spaulding), just a constant set of shifting categories that can prove useful for some things (creating archaeological questions, sequencing finds, etc.) but not for others. Therefore, we need to maintain a flexible, fluid, and contingent approach to typology rather than demand that we "accurately" identify a particular pot, a particular monument, or a particular person in fixed and eternal ways.

What does this all mean when we think about the future—both of archaeology and of the world in general? For us, it means making room for types that are *multiple, shifting, and contingent*. It means recognizing that all things and all people are intersectional and, crucially, that the categories themselves shift and move. We should expect types to change through time and across social space; categories like race, gender, and sexuality will shift; indeed, the existence of these categories at all can come and go (Foucault 1978; Robb and Harris 2018). We find great value in approaching these differences as productive and emergent, not negative and damaging. New kinds of difference can come into the world and make new ways of understanding and thinking about our society, our species, and our existence possible in both the past and the future. None of this means that differences between people in either the present or the past were not treated negatively or used to disenfranchise people. Instead, it is to recognize that this negative difference is *secondary* to the kinds of positive difference we have worked with here. As new kinds of difference emerge, new ways of being human become possible. As we look at the past, by embracing the contingency of types and the positivity of difference, we can explore other ways of being human there, too (Barrett 2021). Difference as productive creates the possibility for a past that was full of complex and intersecting ways of existing, whether in the bodies and figurines of Teotihuacan or in the cognition of Paleolithic hunter-gatherers. Difference-as-productive creates a possibility for a future where such distinctions are celebrated as well.

Notes

1 This is what the philosopher of science Bruno Latour would call blackboxing, what Karl Marx would call alienation, or what Deleuze and Guattari call miraculation—these are all terms that can be used to describe how archaeologists obscure what makes our things the way they are when we reduce them to examples of an ideal type.
2 Some caveats are necessary here; the fragmented nature of the figurines means that more of them may have been gendered than can now be established and that male figurines may be underrepresented because fragments that are broken at the waist could have once been male, but we cannot now tell (Hagerman 2018, 706).

Chapter 7

How we know the past
Truth as relational and emergent

Introduction: building trust in the world of fake news

One of the questions that archaeologists often get from the public, from the media, and from students is about how they *really* know what happened in the past. Since archaeologists work with fragmented remains from hundreds, or even thousands, of years ago, this is a fair question. While digging on the Isle of Man and in Ardnamurchan, Scotland, respectively, Rachel and Ollie have both answered this question while speaking with police officers. In both places, when you find human remains, no matter how old you think they are, you must inform the police. Such discussions can be strange and disarming for an archaeologist. The police officer on the other end of the line asks questions like: "How do you know the remains date to the Bronze Age?", "Why do you think they are not recent?", and "What is your expertise to know this?". In such conversations, the delicacies of the relationships between different soil types are not usually of consequence, nor are the details of ceramic chronologies. The police want the "facts" so that they can write their reports; they aren't looking for an hour-long lecture on changing burial practices between 3000 and 1500 BCE. The conversation forces you to boil situations down to the nitty gritty—the burial was found with this kind of pottery, which we know dates to this period. I am the right person to tell you this because I am an expert. I am an expert because I did a Ph.D. on this topic, have published papers on it, and teach it at a university. As archaeologists, who often paint with nuanced brushes, incomplete data, and a certain amount of uncertainty, the directness of the police questioning can be uncomfortable. But their questions stand. How *do* we know things about the past? How can the police officer trust us? How do they know we are not murderers covering up a crime?

These concerns do not just impact archaeology and the pasts that we study. This is especially evident considering that the world we live in is increasingly concerned with what constitutes truth, post-truth, and even "fake news." There is a multiplicity of different narratives about the contemporary world, presented from different political and social positions. Similarly, there is a multiplicity of different narratives about the past. Just think of the proliferation of television programs and social media content that focus on ancient aliens, Knights Templar, and other

DOI: 10.4324/9781003244141-7

pseudo-scientific interpretations of the past. Social media, multiple news outlets, and the rise of the internet seem to have swept away the supposed certainties of older times, leaving modern society bereft of anchors to reality. People will question the right of an expert to speak, and they will argue that their own opinion is just as valid. Online, people will tell you that the world is flat, that vaccines will kill you, that Bill Gates wants to implant a chip in your arm, and these examples are just scratching the surface! Yet these multiple truths do not just circulate in the darker corners of the internet.

Take for example, January 20, 2017, when Donald J. Trump was sworn in as the 45th President of the United States of America (see Figure 7.1). The inauguration of an American president is a public event, traditionally held outside in the chilly January air of Washington D.C. The event itself went off without a hitch, but the day after, some commentators noted that the crowds for Trump's inauguration were far smaller than those that had been there in 2009 to witness the historic inauguration of the first Black president, Barack Obama. Trump had predicted the turnout would be "record-setting." The media widely reported that the crowds for Trump's inauguration were smaller than those for Obama (e.g., Wallace et al. 2017). This caused the White House to go on the offensive with the Press Secretary, Sean Spicer, declaring the inauguration audience to have been the biggest in history, referencing statistics for the number of metro journeys taken in Washington on the morning of the event. The media criticized Spicer and offered evidence to show

Figure 7.1 Donald Trump's inauguration.
Image: The White House, Public domain.

that he was wrong about metro ridership (e.g., Hunt 2017). Kellyanne Conway, a spokesperson for Trump and the White House, later went on to argue that the facts being offered by the media to counter Spicer's claims were false and that the administration had "alternative facts," a phrase now heavily associated with the Trump presidency. How do we know which "facts" to follow? How do we know whose version of events to trust? When multiple sources offer different interpretations of the same event, where do we begin?

The standard response here is to call for *objectivity*. What we need is a set of objective facts about the event. In such circumstances, many media commentators appeal to "common sense." Take a minute or two, and Google some photos of the two inauguration crowds (or see Rein 2017). You might take a photo of each and place them side by side. This might allow you to decide for yourself using these objective representations. Similarly, the radiocarbon dates, stratigraphy, and knowledge of expert archaeologists can be deployed to show "objectively" that a particular set of human remains date to the Bronze Age and not to recent times. If objectivity is such a simple solution, however, why is it increasingly under threat? Why is it that people believe the Earth is flat, vaccines are part of a global conspiracy, or aliens built the pyramids? Furthermore, is objectivity really such a great thing? Who gets to claim objectivity? More than this, is objectivity even truly possible?

Take another look at the inauguration photos you found. How do you know that the images are labeled correctly? Because that is how whoever posted the photos labeled the images! So, objectivity here is determined by whether you trust them or not. Here, we must recognize that in the context of this "truth-finding" mission, the power relations between them (the people who posted and labeled the photos) and you are not equal. Just as when the *Guardian* or the *Washington Post* declares something a fact, it carries more power than if *Take a Break Fate and Fortune*, the *National Enquirer,* or Jimmy, your dodgy neighbor, does. This is because objectivity and power are closely intertwined. There are, of course, ways for you to help verify if the images that you found are correctly labeled. You could conduct interviews with people who were at both inaugurations. You could look at a range of other sources and even check the metadata on the photos you found. If you do so, however, you'll find that truth doesn't lie in simple "objectivity" but in a complex set of relationships involving people, memories, data, imagery, representations, and events. Objectivity doesn't simply reside in the power of people to post on the internet, but in the relations between people at the inauguration, in the cameras that filmed Washington on those two days, in media organizations, and much more. Suddenly "truth" emerges in much more complex and interesting places, ones that require a more thorough investigation. Yet, this version of truth may be more robust than narrow and common-sense appeals to "the facts" or to "objectivity."

In this chapter, we explore how thinking relationally—that is, as we defined in Chapter 1, by mapping and attending to the relations that make something up— and thinking archaeologically can help build a more robust approach to truth. This includes truths about the past and truths about the problems we face in the present. We explore the extent to which scientific approaches can help us and how these must be situated within feminist, Indigenous, and other approaches. Our aim in this chapter is to respond to the comment with which we started our introduction: how can you ever *really* know? We want to show that through skill and ingenuity, archaeologists can build approaches to the past through which knowledge becomes increasingly secure. By embracing that the past, and our truths about it, are what we call "emergent," we can defend them in a much more secure way. While it may never be completely certain, this approach is potentially much more robust and ethical than a knowledge that claims objectivity based on power and authority could ever be. In turn, this provides us with critical tools for building truths in the present and challenging those around us who want to provide "alternative facts."

Setting the stage: objectivity and archaeology

How do we respond to the question presented at the start of this chapter? How *do* archaeologists know the past? Let's turn to an archaeological example from the Isle of Man to explore this question further. Imagine that you've been working away with your supervisor, digging a huge oval cut feature below a large mound. You're feeling excited because you think it might be the primary burial—the first event that defined the space as a burial site. As you get down to the base of the pit, you reveal an inhumation burial accompanied by 122 jet beads (see Figure 7.2). Your supervisor tells you that they are part of a kind of necklace called a "jet spacer

Figure 7.2 Emily Banfield records the beads of a jet necklace *in situ*.
Image: Rachel J. Crellin.

plate necklace" that dates to the Early Bronze Age. They show you a picture of a complete necklace on Google and explain that the material the necklace is probably made of, jet, is only really found in Whitby in Yorkshire, UK, nearly 200 miles away, including a journey across the Irish Sea. The necklace is beautifully decorated and exquisitely crafted. You are blown away! You turn to your supervisor and say, "Wow. The woman who wore this must have been important and powerful. I wonder if she was a female chief?" Here, your fellow student pipes up, noting, "It could be a man, though, right? Men wear jewelry. Why do you think it was a woman who owned the beads?".

A standard way to address this challenge is to turn to science, a way of providing facts about a given situation. Science is presented in the Western world as an arbiter of true knowledge. Yet, archaeology's relationship with the sciences is complicated. During the 1960s and 1970s, the processual turn (Binford 1962; Clarke 1973; Renfrew 1973b; Watson et al. 1974) sought to make archaeology both more anthropological and more scientific (Binford 1968, 270). By engaging with the sciences and employing the new range of developing scientific techniques, we could increase what we knew about the past. Consider how the emergence of the technology that measures carbon isotopes allowed the radiocarbon dating revolution (Bayliss 2009; Renfrew 1973b; Wylie 2020), which turned on its head much of what we knew about the sequence of the past. Archaeology adopted scientific techniques at this time as well as positivism, the thinking that informed them. Facts produced through the scientific method are presented as being objectively true. Our scientist, in their white lab coat, sets out with a hypothesis and a methodology with which to test it. That methodology has been carefully developed to effectively answer the question, and our scientist who applies it is an expert. To return to our burial, perhaps scientists, osteologists, in this case, can help resolve the issue of whether the remains are those of a male or a female. Will they uncover the objective truth of the matter?

Osteologists follow a standardized protocol for recording and sexing skeletons (Bass 1995; Brickley and McKinley 2004; Buikstra and Ubelaker 1994; White and Folkens 2005). To do this, they rely on systematic differences between male and female skeletons; these differences are a result of how male and female bodies grow, develop, and age differently (but see Geller 2005). Based on this sexual dimorphism, scientists can sex skeletal remains in the archaeological record as either male or female. The skull and the *Os Coxae* (pelvic bone) are the key skeletal elements that osteologists examine (White and Folkens 2005). Published studies examining the sex estimates of osteologists for known individuals indicate these methods are between 70–98% accurate and that they are more accurate when used in combination with one another (Inskip et al. 2019, Table 1). That there is a range of accuracy already tells us something about the objectivity of science—there are things about which our scientific methods cannot be completely certain. It is also notable that when the skull and the *Os Coxae* are studied together, the accuracy of studies increases; in other words, combining multiple lines of evidence produces stronger results.

So why exactly is there a degree of error in this methodology? The identification of sexual dimorphism is based on the study of reference collections with particular histories; in other words, we must ask whose bones were collected and used as references. Such questions are important because the specific histories of collecting, it turns out, have serious consequences for science and objectivity. This is because the human body is plastic, meaning that it changes through the life course in response to its surroundings (Sofaer 2006). It takes shape from histories of exercise, stress, disease, and activity. For example, war dead from Korea and the Balkans have been used in some reference collections, giving these collections a bias towards maleness and physical fitness (Inskip et al. 2019, 341). Similarly, reference collections are often modern, and it is unclear whether modern-day sexual dimorphism is the same as it was in pre-industrial societies (Inskip et al. 2019). It is also evident that sexual dimorphism varies between groups because of the influence of environmental factors; this means that a method that might work on one population to sex a skeleton might not work on another (Maat et al. 1997; MacLaughlin and Bruce 1990; Ubelaker and DeGaglia 2017; Walker 2005). In short, if reference collections are subject to particular biases, or are representative of specific kinds of populations, then our analyses are skewed in these ways too.

Feminist philosophers of science have been pointing to these kinds of issues for a long time now. As introduced in Chapter 1, they argue that science is not produced by neutral methods or neutral practitioners; it is instead produced in specific contexts, with biases, and by particular kinds of people (Harding 1991, 2004; Haraway 1988; see also Chapter 8, this book). Standpoint theory teaches us that we all work from a specific positionality and that we are all located *somewhere*. These factors directly impact our relationship with a given subject (Harding 1991, 2004 and papers therein; Wylie 2012). Similarly, Donna Haraway (1988) argued that we cannot write from either *nowhere* or *everywhere*; instead, we write and carry out science from particular locations that affect our methods and our results. This means, of course, that our scientist, with their reference collection shaped by twentieth-century collection practices, is doing science from a specific standpoint, complete with biases.

Turning back to our burial from the Isle of Man, the project osteologist who excavated the bones is about to disappoint us; they cannot tell if the individual was male or female. The soil on the Isle of Man is very acidic, so not all of the bones survived; those that have are in a very fragile state. The skull did not preserve, and the pelvis is ambiguous, meaning it could be from either a male or female. A decade ago, this might have been the end of the story, but the rise of aDNA research means that we now have other methods at our disposal to sex skeletons. If we could extract aDNA from the skeleton, then that might provide another line of evidence to help resolve our question. Some researchers argue that aDNA analyses are up to 100% accurate at sexing individuals (Daskalaki et al. 2011; Skoglund et al. 2013). In part, this has prompted the archaeologist Kristian Kristiansen (2014) to declare a third scientific revolution in archaeology. He argues that the strengths of aDNA analysis (alongside isotopes, big data, and quantitative modeling) mean that studies of what he terms "prehistory" could become as detailed as studies of modern material culture (Kristiansen 2014, 24). He argues that these techniques and methods give us better (stronger) information than ever before—even more objective facts.

Our feminist and Indigenous philosophers are not convinced, though. From their perspective, big data, aDNA, isotopes, and modeling are no less subject to biases than our standard osteological methods. These methods are still located and particular, meaning that they are subject to built-in biases. To correct for this, feminist and Indigenous thinkers argue that we must embrace the positionality of our science and combine as many viewpoints as possible; rather than seeking the singular objective facts, they look to combine many standpoints to produce *more objective* understandings and to always start from the standpoint of the marginalized (see for example, Harding 1991, 2004; Haraway 1988; TallBear 2013, 2014; this book, Chapter 1 and Chapter 8).

The osteologist is about to disappoint us again, though. There are no bones suitable for aDNA analysis. One of the site directors points out that there are a number of these jet necklaces from across Britain, and, in many cases, the osteological analysis suggests that they were associated with female bodies. Our osteologist is quick to question sexing based on grave goods (Stratton 2016). They ask when these assessments were carried out, arguing that older osteological assessments were often inaccurate and highly influenced by associated "gendered" grave goods (Gamble and Fowler 2013). If an osteologist in the 1970s found a sword, for example, they were perhaps more likely to look for and "find" more male traits in the skeleton. At the time that these osteological assessments were carried out, they were treated as rigorous science, but our osteologist today is not treating them this way. It seems that our science is contextual, or located in the time and place in which it was carried out. What were once considered "objective facts" or hard truths are no longer so reliable. None of this means that the skeleton with the jet beads is not female (in fact, there are many lines of evidence that suggest it could be), but preserving a level of equivocation allows us to remain aware that this is far from certain.

Objective facts, it seems, can change! What counts as objective, as science or as fact, is not universal. These things are born in what Michel Foucault (1977) termed a particular "regime of truth." His argument is that specific conditions make it possible to think in particular ways and establish specific forms of knowledge and truth about the world. Science, for him, is not a universalizing higher quest for knowledge outside of bias but a particular way of knowing the world located in specific times and places. Paralleling our earlier example, Foucault (1977, 2001) essentially demonstrates that facts are historically and contextually particular. There is a thread here that runs through Foucault's thinking, the postprocessual critiques, feminist standpoint theory, philosophy of science, and Indigenous approaches that shows that what counts as objective and what we call "a fact" is particular to a given context and not a universal truth. It is, of course, this kind of argument (rooted in postmodernism) that has been blamed for creating the context in which the Trump administration could appeal to "alternative facts." As demonstrated later in the chapter, however, this does not have to equate to simply pulling truths out of our imagination; beyond postmodernism, there exist methods for comparing different truth claims against one another in any given context. And, as we argue later, the archaeological toolkit has much to offer in this regard. As demonstrated thus far with our Isle of Man example, many archaeologists are familiar with using multiple lines of evidence and remain open to the fallibility of certain interpretations and inherited truths in the discipline.

On the one hand, there is a political argument for speculating that the remains in question are those of a woman—this could allow us to identify a powerful woman in the past, upset the model of male chiefly power, and present an interesting narrative that might question assumptions that people have about the past. On the other hand, there is also a political argument for speculating that men might have worn elaborate jewelry and that simply associating women with finely crafted and highly decorated objects is problematic (particularly given historical arguments that these might have been gifts to wives). Yet, there is still another side to this story—genetic and biological sex is not binary but a more complex spectrum with chimeric individuals and those who have unique chromosomal combinations (Geller 2005). This, of course, is to say nothing of the complex relationship between sex and gender and the wider complex patterns around gender emerging across Europe at the time (cf. Robb and Harris 2018). That we are even asking whether the skeleton is male or female is a product of our positionality—our location in the patriarchal societies of the twenty-first century, where sex and gender matter and, indeed, are matters of life and death. That we question whether male and female are the right identifiers at all is also a product of the society in which we live; other labels and other identifiers are also possible.

Theoretical tools: evidence and truth as relationally emergent

It follows that evidence and truths are not simply "out there" in the world awaiting discovery by the correct, most-scientific methodologies. With this, of course, we must remember that evidence and truths are also not simply made up out of thin air; everything has a context—a set of relationships through which truths and evidence emerge. This means that truth is produced relationally. Archaeologists and many other people in the world today subscribe to an empirical understanding of the world. This means that they base their understandings of the world on *what they experience* or *what they observe* rather than spontaneously making something up that feels right. Considering our earlier discussions, of course, we'll need to unpack what this means. Archaeologists and other empirical thinkers agree to base their interpretations on some type of evidence gathered in a way that is acceptable to the group, yet this does not mean that their evidence is completely independent of them and their sensibilities, interests, and needs. As we have seen with our skeleton associated with the jet necklace, archaeological evidence and acceptable archaeological methodologies are constantly changing in relation to other archaeologists, new technologies, different archaeological materials and sites, and the world in general.

If we accept that truth and evidence are relational, how do we compare different forms of data, different methodologies, and different truth claims to decide which ones are best? Is the skeleton that of a male or a female? Did humans or extraterrestrials make the pyramids? Before we get to these types of questions, we first need to dwell just a little bit longer on the notion of *relational emergence*. What exactly does this mean? Earlier, our example from the Isle of Man showed that the archaeological record wasn't simply out there waiting to be interpreted in a singular, correct way. Along the same lines, we could say that the archaeologist who might find and interpret that archaeological record also doesn't exist "out there" in the same way as they will once they encounter the archaeological record in question. As the two intersect, they emerge together—each of the elements involved (i.e., the archaeologists and the archaeological record) is subject to change *with* the other.

As an example, let's take the infamous mound-builder debates of nineteenth-century America. Settler colonists encountered large, sometimes enormous, earthen mounds in many parts of America—a place assumed by settlers to lack deep or complicated human histories prior to European presence (Feder 2017; Squier and Davis 1848; see also Thomas 1894). Initial responses to—and explanations of—these unexpected mounds ranged widely; for example, elves, the lost tribes of Israel, and ancient societies from Europe or Asia are just a few of the beings given credit for building the mounds. But here we see how mounds and settler colonists remade one another via relationships. That is, they *emerged* together. On the one hand, settler colonists carried with them a certain understanding of the world that attributed very little to the Indigenous peoples and the history of North America; they saw the continent as lacking in human history and "improvement." On the other hand, the mounds were traces left behind by earlier eras of Indigenous settlements. As the two came together, the settler colonists had to rethink the world they lived in, especially the land they were colonizing; but the mounds changed via these relationships too. They became signs of previous land modification, evidence that someone had been there before (someone other than the Indigenous peoples that settler colonists saw in the nineteenth century), and they demanded an explanation. The mounds went from traces of past lives to fodder for new discussions of the history of this land. Unsurprisingly, in many cases, settler colonists made mounds into evidence that supported their efforts to colonize.

Sure, you say, I can see how the nineteenth-century relationship between mounds and people *might* have changed the people and maybe even the mounds, but why call this an "emergence"? It's not as if the people and the mounds didn't exist before they met, right? Fair enough, but the term emergence helps us remind readers not to cling too tightly to an approach that uses basic (essential) lists of characteristics for different entities, like people or mounds. Remember our discussions of relationality in Chapter 1. To review, rather than relying upon ideas about the "essential" nature of things, we argued for a need to attend to the relations things have with the world around them and how these change through time. We say they "emerge" together because relationships create new possibilities and new qualities that did not exist before the relationship. A classic example comes at the molecular level. Atoms, let's say two hydrogen atoms and one oxygen atom, exhibit different qualities and tendencies apart from one another than they do when they come together to form water molecules. This is why we prefer the term "emergent." It forces the reader to rethink how different things are subject to transformation as they come into new relations with the world (cf. Fowler 2013a). As the assemblage thinkers discussed in Chapter 2 remind us, the whole is greater than the sum of its parts. You're still probably wondering what all of this has to do with facts and evidence. Maybe the mounds and the settler colonists emerged together in the nineteenth century from our vantage point, but those are matters of interpretation rather than hard scientific facts that stand alone and show exactly what happened, precisely who was to blame, etc. Let's expand this discussion with some new additions to our toolkit.

Using our toolkit: from fingerprints to the Sphinx

Fingerprints of truth

Let's take a break from skeletons and mounds and consider something more familiar to general audiences, something that is valued as an unflinching truth of the world—fingerprints from crime scenes. Archaeologist Zoë Crossland's (2018) writings on different forms of evidence in forensic science serve as an excellent example of the relational nature of even the hardest scientific facts and evidence.[1] Crossland notes that forensic scientists tend to write about dead bodies in ways akin to how archaeologists write about the archaeological record. They use phrases like "whispers of the dead" and "bones as witnesses" (Crossland 2018, 623); similarly, when explaining their work on court cases to the public, forensic scientists typically discuss human witnesses as less trustworthy and forensic data as relatively more reliable. In other words, like those archaeologists who argue for a static archaeological record "out there" ready to simply reveal the truth of the past, forensic scientists sometimes make it seem like dead bodies hold singular truths about crimes. As Crossland (2018, 622, our emphasis) describes, forensic science "presents the dead as testifying facts that not only *stand aside* from the stories told by the living but *have their own* representational power." Such a perspective glosses over the voices and interpretations of the scientists themselves. In such discussions, facts and evidence carry "a kind of animacy" (Crossland 2018, 622) where they hold responsibility for how they are mobilized in the world of the living. In some ways, this is like a ventriloquist insisting that their puppet speaks completely on its own. To explore how this animacy works, Crossland takes a relational approach that challenges the neat divides we often assume about the world, specifically between the categories of death/life, fact/interpretation, and human/nonhuman. If, following Crossland, facts do *not* actually speak for themselves, if the dead "can only have life through others" (Crossland 2018, 625), how do these truths work?

Crossland (2018, 627) uses fingerprinting as one of her examples, focusing on how fingerprints are sometimes treated as if they "attest to identity without the intervention of language." To put it another way, fingerprints are typically understood to stand in as reliable proof that someone's finger touched a surface at some point in the past, providing a static record on which to build forensic claims (Crossland 2018, 628–33). Courts often base their findings on fingerprints, and people have been convicted of crimes based on fingerprint matching, so they must be completely straight-forward, static, and reliable, right? Unfortunately, this isn't quite true. To begin, it is difficult to distinguish prints from other background noise on the surfaces from which they are collected. Also, fingerprints at crime scenes are hardly ever as perfect as ones taken in a controlled environment. To take a familiar example, if you set up fingerprint identification on your smartphone, the phone will request much more than one "impression" of your finger. Instead, to collect all the information that it needs to make the match almost every time you want to unlock your phone, it requires multiple prints from multiple angles. Thus, perhaps it isn't so surprising that there are examples of "false positives" in crime scene fingerprint matching. This is because relationships of similarity (where we match the print to the finger that supposedly made it) are relationally emergent, not just out there, waiting to speak the truth.

There are two related but distinct components of fingerprint identification (see Crossland 2021). The first is *recognizing similarity* between the unique ridges of someone's finger surface and the print found at a crime scene (Crossland 2018). Even with this first component, many things could go wrong. The print might be made on an unstable surface, there might be other prints on the surface, and things can happen to a print between the time it is made and the time it is recorded by the forensic team. Let's just assume this first component goes smoothly. We find evidence that this print looks like the pattern on someone's finger—it's just pattern matching where pattern A (the print) resembles pattern B (a pattern on a fingertip). This seems straightforward; anyone can match the pattern "with apparently little interpretation needed to determine that one image resembles the other" (Crossland 2018, 630). But, yet again, things are more complicated than that. This is because pattern matching always involves difference, meaning that pattern A and pattern B are *not* identical. The finger that made the print will always be different from the print it leaves behind in the dust. The print is made of ink or blood or sweat; it is flattened; it incorporates other surface features that it adheres to; and it can disguise or omit elements that are observed in the actual ridges of the finger. Sure, you say, but there must be guidelines and regulations to help determine how much variation is acceptable. If fingerprint identification is used in court cases and forensic science, the way science accepts or rejects a positive match must be a cut-and-dried universal methodology upon which all specialists agree. Again, not quite. For instance, scientists in the UK once used a minimum of 16 points of similarity to make a positive identification, whereas, in the US, experts would use features like pores, creases, and scars to make a match. What isn't defined is "the flexibility in what was defined as the same" (Crossland 2018, 631).

The second component of fingerprint identification is the most powerful; it is when we say that *this* specific finger made *this* specific print pattern, or, in other words, when we argue for a causal relationship between the two. While, as noted previously, basic pattern matching *can* be incorrect (it is just a similarity, not a 1–1 match), when we assume there is a causal relationship between a specific person's finger pad and a print, there is no room for error. Unfortunately, forensic finger-printing demonstrates this second component based almost entirely on the first component (identifying similarities). In this form of analysis, the two components are all mixed up, but that isn't always the case.

Consider, for example, a portrait hanging in an art gallery (cf. Crossland 2018, 632). Perhaps you don't recognize the person shown in the painting. Nonetheless, you clearly recognize a human form—eyes, a nose, etc. Here, the first component of identification is matching the depiction in paint to your experience interacting with people and depictions of people. There is a match, but you're still not sure who the painting is supposed to show. What do you do? You look down at the museum label for more information; there, neatly labeled below the image, is a name (let's say, "Jane Doe"). This is the vital second component of identification. It is a contextual clue; the copresence of a painting and label tells you that the paint-ing represents Jane Doe. This general type of copresence[2] is precisely what crime scene fingerprinting is looking to reconstruct, but crime scenes are never as contex-tualized as art galleries; something is always missing, namely the criminal and their fingers. Thus, crime scene fingerprint matching is like going to an art museum's portrait gallery and trying to determine who is who without reading the labels.

In short, what seems like a simple matching process in forensic fingerprinting, folds those two components into one another and confuses things. What seems, at first, to be a strong argument isn't so strong after all when we don't have a "smok-ing gun" like the museum label telling us who did this or that. When these two components are conflated, other types of information that might be influencing the interpreter (their positionality and their biases) are allowed to do work without us paying them much attention. Unfortunately, fingerprint specialists tend to deny the possibility that their fingerprint matches could be wrong or, at the very least, less reliable than they let on. Perhaps they don't want to lose their jobs—here, again, is an example of how their positionality in the world shapes how they see and use the patterns they observe; they, as fingerprint experts, emerge alongside the evidence and the truths they encounter and employ.

Dating the Sphinx

Enough about crime scenes; let's consider a more traditional archaeological exam-ple. For this one, we'll jump to a place and a time that almost any mention of the word "archaeology" conjures up in public imagination—Ancient Egypt. Let's think about the Great Sphinx of Giza (see Figure 7.3). Most Egyptologists and archaeologists argue that people made the Sphinx during the fourth dynasty, spe-cifically between 2520 and 2494 BCE, or approximately 4,500 years ago. Although there is no known method of deriving an absolute date for the Sphinx, specialists base these dates on a few different observations, some more reliable than others (Gauri et al. 1995, 119–20). These include the absence or presence of artifacts that offer relative dates for human activity on site, general landscape patterns (the monument sits among other monuments made at the time), and more tenuous arguments about the resemblance of the Sphinx and the pharaoh who ruled at that time. Archaeologists have found very few artifacts predating 2600 BCE in the general vicinity of the Sphinx, and there are no written records offering clues to the timing of the Sphinx's construction. Nonetheless, considering all the information they have at hand, Egyptologists and archaeologists were, and are, quite comfortable with these proposed dates.

In the 1990s, things became slightly more complicated, exacerbated by the firm hold that Ancient Egypt has over popular interest. It began in 1992 when a professor of science and mathematics, Robert Schoch, and some colleagues attempted to shake things up. They argued for a much older date than the conventionally accepted ranges. Instead of 4,500 years old, they asserted that the Sphinx was at least 7,000 years old. Since that time, this claim has led some interested members of the public, including what archaeologists sometimes refer to as "pseudo-scientists," to envision the Sphinx as constructed by the fictive civilization of Atlantis (made up over 2,000 years ago by the Greek philosopher, Plato). The proposed amendment to the dates of the Sphinx wasn't simply made up out of thin air, though; instead,

Figure 7.3 The Great Sphinx of Ghiza.
Image: Mabdalla, Public domain.

it was based on "the nature and degree of chemical and mechanical weathering which the limestone walls of the Sphinx Enclosure, the body of the Great Sphinx, and the limestone cores of the Sphinx and Valley Temples have experienced since becoming subaerially exposed" (Dobecki and Schoch 1992, 528). In other words, Schoch and his colleagues argued that the type and amount of wear on certain parts of the Sphinx demonstrated that it was *much* older than conventionally proposed. This interpretation was met with skepticism from the archaeological and Egyptological communities, but since this time, other researchers have proposed similar, if not equally as radical, adjustments to the dates based on similar lines of evidence, namely patterns of weathering. Eight years later, for instance, another geologist (Reader 2000) argued that weathering and erosion within the enclosure surrounding the Sphinx demonstrates a pre-fourth dynasty construction.

How are we to make sense of these competing claims? What is the truth? Is the Sphinx 4,500 years old, or is it significantly older? Let's think back to the relationality of fingerprint matching. How do these two cases compare? They have more in common than you might initially think. Previously, we outlined two components of fingerprint identification: pattern matching, where a fingerprint resembles the pattern on a fingertip, and establishing a causal connection, asserting that *this* print was made by *that* person's finger. Here, the pattern matching is between wear patterns on the Sphinx's limestone and wear patterns found on other stones in other places. This seems easy enough, and no one (to our knowledge) has argued that the wear patterns on the Sphinx did *not* result from exposure to the elements. So, just as one might match a print to a finger, archaeologists and other specialists analyzing the Sphinx match its specific wear patterns with other stone surfaces known to be weathered.

Next is the tricky part. In this case, it involves connecting wear patterns to a specific amount and duration of exposure to the elements. Of course, this depends on the history of rainfall in a place, the types of stone being impacted, general weather patterns (like humidity), and other contextual factors. As with the earlier examples of matching fingerprints and figuring out whose portrait you are looking at in the museum, this second component of the matching process has many more contextual possibilities to consider. It isn't straight forward, and so, unsurprisingly, this is where the disagreements emerge in the literature. Gauri and colleagues (1995), for example, do not deny the existence of the wear patterns under scrutiny but suggest an alternative cause that does not require the Sphinx to be any older than the currently accepted dates. Since there are more possible explanations than Schoch et al. recognize, Gauri et al. (1995, 121) suggest that "an absolute age cannot be assigned to the Sphinx on the bases of existing geological evidence." In other words, parts of the Sphinx are undoubtedly worn by exposure to the elements, but there isn't enough geological information to establish a fool-proof causal link, "the smoking gun," between the wear patterns and a very specific duration of exposure.

Then there is the matter of the other lines of evidence. Some Egyptologists and archaeologists (e.g., Wilkinson 2000) are open to refining the dates of the Sphinx, even if that means accepting that it is older than previously thought, but they rightly place the burden of proof on those arguing for older dates. Wilkinson notes that some of the geological wear-based arguments are not "inherently impossible" even though extant archaeological and Egyptological evidence does make them unlikely. Archaeological patterns become important here; Wilkinson notes that there is very little evidence of human activity in the area around the Sphinx before the fourth dynasty. He points out that archaeologists have found a grand total of four pre-fourth dynasty pottery vessels from the area. This isn't much, and on top of this, there is a rather long (600 years or so) break between these pots and the next archaeological indications of human activity in the area. Considering that the Sphinx and the surrounding landscape have been subject to intense archaeological excavations over the last century, this dearth of evidence doesn't seem to be the result of a sampling problem. There are many possible explanations for why archaeologists might not find durable material traces of human activity in a place where people lived and worked, but in this case, with monumental construction, it seems improbable that the only material trace one might find is the actual monument. Like many tenuous fingerprint identifications, recent interpretations of a much older Sphinx are shaky at best. But a relational approach to truth and evidence helps us better understand how to sort the competing truth claims in cases like this. Viewing these problems and the evidence and truths marshaled in competing claims *as relational* also reminds us of how science is shaped by the wider world in which it is practiced. Evidence and truths might congeal more easily for researchers when the personal gains increase, but researchers aren't the only ones affected. Making sensational claims that stoke the interests of those who believe in Atlantis might be a quick path to fame and possible fortune for a few people, but such claims also have implications for other people. In this case, we might consider the people of Egypt, whose ancestors built the monuments. As with the mound-builder example, we should take great care before we jump to new interpretations that threaten to take away credit for the blood, sweat, and tears of their ancestors, not to mention their technological prowess.

Conclusion

Where does this leave us? We have seen how truth is neither objectively out there, waiting to be found, nor simply made up. It emerges through work, through relationships wrought with power—those regimes of truth that Foucault (1977) identified—and from the positions of those doing the work. Approaching truth like this might seem frightening. If we give up on the idea of a singular truth out there, are we risking an anarchic emergence of "relativism," a postmodern echo-chamber, or the idea that anything goes? Are we giving in to Donald Trump's alternative facts? We will return to the question of relativism in Chapter 8, but the evidence we have examined in this chapter suggests otherwise. To determine the sex of a skeleton, we need access to lots of lines of evidence; we need to draw on studies of skeletal material, potentially including analysis of aDNA or new analytical techniques like peptide sexing; we also need to consider material culture, wider patterns of how bodies are treated, and much more. Crucially, we need to situate these things within a robust interrogation of our own perspectives and contexts. To understand the age of Egyptian monuments or the security of fingerprint identification, we must understand the relationships through which they emerge. Far from undermining claims to truth, these understandings allow us to be more robust. Imagine a building in front of you. Would it be more secure if it was built on multiple firm foundations or on a singular and shaky leg? If you claim that "all people buried with jet necklaces are female," you are one aDNA test away from having your whole understanding of Bronze Age gender collapse. If you explain that multiple lines of evidence tie specific sets of bodies and material culture together and that there is room in this for divergence and difference, then your arguments can withstand new evidence emerging. This doesn't mean we won't ever need to change our minds, but that the production of new truths will emerge again through multiple lines of evidence, not via singular discoveries.

What really is truth, then? We've circled around this issue for the whole of the chapter without ever addressing it. Truths are relationally emergent arguments about events and processes. They emerge from collaborative work by heterogenous assemblages, for example, our police officer, their fingerprint expert, the science of fingerprint analysis, the dusting powder, the criminal, and many others. With our archaeological examples, we must consider the archaeologist, the history of excavation, books of analysis, radiocarbon dates, pottery typologies, the materiality of monuments, and much more. They are always located, contextual, and situated; they always have the possibility of shifting. These heterogenous assemblages are not, however, simply made up. They emerge from work, and they become more secure when they are formed from multiple lines of evidence. There is value in saying when we do not know or when we are unsure of the truth of events. That does not mean, however, that we should not also be equally keen to point out what we *do* know and to reject what we know not to be true. Truths do not simply exist; they are built and rebuilt.

It is this relational nature of truth that engaging with archaeology highlights. Our multiple and partial evidence, collected over the course of centuries, encourages us to assemble multiple lines of evidence when we construct our facts. It forces us to see that things may not always be simple, straightforward, or obviously and clearly "true." The challenge of archaeology is to combine our many lines of partial, messy evidence from the sciences and the humanities successfully. Doing this requires that we identify and think about our biases and positionalities carefully. We need to understand how data from archaeological science are colored by the modern world we live in and how our positionalities in the world shape what we think was possible in the past. If you want to make the leap from our world to that of the Bronze Age as successfully as possible, you must understand your biases better than most. Sometimes this means confronting not only evidence that is partial and complex but evidence that comes from a world radically different from your own (Chapter 8). This unique combination allows archaeologists to generate sophisticated ways of critically creating robust and relational modes of truth. When a member of the public asks: "how do you really know?" it turns out that archaeologists have a better answer than almost anyone else.

If we turn back to the political place where we started this chapter, we can see how taking a relational approach to truth allows us to reject Trump's alternative facts. They aren't based on the emergence of multiple lines of complex intersecting evidence. They emerge as if truths could simply be willed into existence. We don't then have two competing truth claims, which are equally matched. We have one truth claim securely tied to multiple lines of evidence and another that floats freely. Both might claim to be objective, but both cannot claim to be equally as relationally emergent. Thus, taking an approach to truth modeled on the careful work of archaeologists can provide us with a far more robust way of dealing with problems like this. We can embrace both our own position and the complexity of the world without either demanding singular objectivity or simply shrugging our shoulders and saying, "we'll never really know for sure."

Notes

1 Although it refrains from using the specialized and sometimes esoteric terminology of Peircean semiotics, this case study draws heavily upon Peircean theory (for other archaeological examples, see Agbe-Davies 2015, 2017; Cipolla n.d.; Cipolla and Gallo 2021; Crossland 2014a, 2018; Harris and Cipolla 2017; Preucel 2006; Preucel and Bauer 2001; Swenson 2018; Watts 2008).

2 These two types of copresence do differ in important ways. The finger/fingerprint relation is physical, whereas the portrait/portrait label is much more social. In other words, we know to look for the label because someone either told us to do so or because we have experience visiting museums (Zoë Crossland, personal communication).

Chapter 8

The past as multiple

Positive difference, ontological difference

Introduction: living in a fraught world

Increasingly, we find that the world we live in is characterized by strife and opposition. When one encounters a person with a different view from their own, they are encouraged to utterly defeat that person, showing them how wrong they are. Or, more passively, they might post a biting meme on social media that clearly demonstrates (to people who see the world as they do) how their view is the only correct approach to reality. More frustrating than this, however, is the way that our differences are often packaged in clusters. In America, for example, if one supports small government, society often assumes that they are also pro-life, support gun rights, and are all for anti-trans legislation. The point is that once we become aware of an instance of difference, we are encouraged to assume or project all the rest and immediately stop listening. Such an approach leaves little room for the themes of this chapter: multiplicities and collaboration. What if we took a different tack? What would that world look like? In Chapter 7, we argued that to understand how to reconcile and deal with the complex and multiple truth claims we encounter in the present we are best off taking an archaeological and relational approach. This means not relying solely and unflinchingly on notions of expert authority and objectivity, which are all too easily undermined, nor simply accepting that everyone can construct their own truth. In turn, we must embrace, rather than deny, our own engagement in producing evidence and arguments and use those relations to strengthen our claims about which interpretations of the world are more secure than others.

In this chapter, we want to take this perspective further by asking how we can go beyond establishing our own knowledge and by thinking about situations where we encounter certain truth claims that can seem equally as jarring as those explored in Chapter 7. These claims come from members of under-represented groups in archaeology, like Indigenous peoples and other social collectives who suffer disproportionately from the structural inequalities of settler colonialism and late capitalism. In some cases, these claims are quite familiar to us. They might offer critiques of—and corrections to—the same systems of inequality and disadvantage that we live with, components of the world we share with others. Think back, for

DOI: 10.4324/9781003244141-8

example, to our discussions of undocumented migration and homelessness from Chapters 2 and 3; an undocumented migrant or a homeless person will undoubtedly have different experiences of, and perspectives on, the world we share with them. What would it mean if, as exemplified in the collaborative work at Turbo Island by Rachael Kiddey and John Schofield (2009, 2010, 2011), archaeologists opened themselves up to different perspectives and positionalities to rethink the past, present, and future? What does it mean when archaeologists work with underrepresented groups to rethink and reshape what archaeology is and how it works? What new ideas and critiques do previously excluded perspectives contribute to archaeology? In these cases, we can learn from taking different positionalities and different forms of situated knowledge seriously (Gould et al. 2020).

In other cases, however, the knowledges and truths we encounter seem radically different from the ones we hold so dearly. Reading an ethnography of an Indigenous society, for example, you might encounter a world where powerful people can turn into animals, where stones can be alive, or where the past and present operate alongside each other rather than in any kind of sequential order. These differences present a distinct set of challenges from the ones concerning homelessness or undocumented migrants discussed earlier. Initially, these claims might seem every bit as disconcerting as the idea that Earth might be flat; or every bit as wrong as the idea that ancient aliens built the pyramids. Yet, over the last few decades, some archaeologists and anthropologists have taken on a very different attitude in these situations (Alberti 2013, 2014; Alberti and Marshall 2009; Holbraad 2007; Wilkinson 2017). Rather than dismissing or ridiculing these claims, some argue that we need to take these ideas much more seriously than previous generations of archaeologists have. This means not just treating them respectfully but exploring what kinds of worlds, and what kinds of *ontologies*—to use the term favored by archaeologists and anthropologists—might exist for these claims to be just as well articulated and just as strong as those that align more closely with our reality. This poses a challenge for us: which claims do we take seriously, and which do we disregard?

Our aim in this chapter is to explore these questions in further detail, both to set out why archaeologists and anthropologists should engage with these different positionalities and ontologies (for a brief definition of ontology, see Chapter 1), how we might think them through, and what it might look like when we embrace these multiplicities. We begin by exploring examples of some differences—radical and otherwise—between Indigenous and archaeological positionalities in current-day Australia (David 2006; Hiscock and Faulkner 2006; Porr 2018). From there, we turn to a broader discussion of situated knowledge and the need to rethink and reshape disciplines like archaeology and anthropology. We draw inspiration from the writings of Indigenous feminist Kim Tallbear (2013), looking closely at her experiences working with scientists who study Indigenous DNA and thinking critically about the types of difference these perspectives beget. Next, we turn to our theoretical toolbox, introducing two crucial tools for this chapter: first, posthumanist-inspired discussions of difference as a positive force, introduced previously in Chapter 6; and second, recent archaeological and anthropological discussions of ontology (sometimes labeled "the new animism" or "perspectiv-ism"). These together allow us to think of the past as what we will term a "mul-tiplicity," which is something that is always more than one but less than many (Deleuze 1991). What does it mean to open ourselves up to different positionalities and different forms of objectivity? Kathleen Sterling's (2015) work provides a clear answer to this question, offering a Black Feminist reframing of the European Paleolithic. What does it mean to conduct archaeological research collaboratively, with multiple different positionalities shaping the research process? The collabora-tive work of Dana Lepofsky and colleagues (2017) on the northwest coast of North America provides key insights here, demonstrating how collaboration remakes the archaeological discipline for a much wider segment of society by drawing on dif-ferent forms of knowledge and expertise, even knowledges that are radically dif-ferent from those traditionally held in archaeology (see also Gould et al. 2020 for an excellent example from northeastern North America). For us, these multiplici-ties, the ways that these different positionalities and worlds come together in these examples, offer valuable insights into other collaborations that we need in the world today, namely political collaborations that, at this moment, seem unbridge-able or irreconcilable. Collaborative archaeologies, which embrace—and refuse to deny—ontological difference (cf. Cipolla et al. 2019), provide critical lessons for how we can engage with contemporary problems. They ask us to learn how to be "diplomatic," as Bruno Latour (2013, 13) would put it, and to forge connections across barriers that at first might seem impermeable. Collaborative archaeologies, in other words, can offer us methods and tools for addressing contemporary dis-putes in new ways.

Setting the stage: positionalities and worlds coming together

Let us begin by exploring some examples of the challenges that Indigenous posi-tionalities and concepts (see Deloria 1997; Steeves 2015, 2021; Wilson 2020) pose for traditional archaeological approaches. One place where these challenges are especially noticeable is in Australia, a settler colony where, for a host of reasons, Indigenous sensibilities and concepts often clash with Western approaches and views. The philosopher Simone Bignall (2014) discusses an example of a more practical "collision" and power imbalance between settler-colonial and Indigenous peoples in Australia. She writes of a house that she once lived in on the traditional lands of the Kaurna people (southern Australia). While living in the house, Bignall learned that it sat on a Kaurna burial site. As she noted (Bignall 2014, 341):

> The burial represents an entire world of traditions . . . which became practically forbidden on this site when the land was seized from the traditional owners. . . . And yet this world persists—not only as past 'heritage', but as a present and living connection . . . and its protection is the objective of Australian Indigenous peoples' ongoing efforts of resistance to the elimination and assimilation of their societies.

Here we are reminded of forms of difference that aren't necessarily radical. They involve recognizing the positionality of peoples who suffer from the ongoing inequities of settler colonialism and capitalism, worlds that settler colonists (and westerners) tend to know, but not necessarily from the same perspective as Indigenous Australians. As we will discuss, archaeologists and anthropologists are increasingly recognizing what they can learn from taking those perspectives and positionalities seriously. Moreover, as members of under-represented groups become professional archaeologists, they are contributing valuable new insights and reshaping the discipline accordingly. Some, following early appeals of feminist archaeologists like Janet Spector (1993), argue that a discipline shaped by multiple positionalities—in this case, settler-colonists and Indigenous peoples of Australia—are better and stronger ways of knowing the world.

Yet, Bignall's example also raises questions about very different knowledge systems and realities clashing. A related example comes from the study of shell mounds in northern Australia (Hiscock and Faulkner 2006). These mounds vary in scale, with some that are more than 10,000 cubic meters in volume (Hiscock and Faulkner 2006). Aboriginal groups sometimes include these shell features in their understandings of the world. In certain areas, like central Arnhem Land, Aboriginal peoples link the larger of these mounds to creation events that took place in "the Dreaming" (Hiscock and Faulkner 2006, 214), that is, within a conception of time in which the past and present are interwoven. Elsewhere, stories associate the shell mounds with specific forms of ritual practice. In both cases, some archaeologists have drawn on these Indigenous narratives and insights to help them interpret the sites.

Archaeologists Peter Hiscock and Patrick Faulker (2006) object to this. For them, all shell mounds are at least 600–800 years old and were produced in a variety of different social, economic, and ecological environments than the ones that exist in the present (Hiscock and Faulkner 2006, 216). Rather than explaining these archaeological landscapes through contemporary Aboriginal narratives, they argue that archaeologists can track the emergence of Aboriginal narratives about shell mounds in parallel with archaeological work. Here we must pay attention to the weight placed on different knowledge forms. They describe, for example, how archaeological evidence showed that a mound that Aboriginal peoples once saw as natural was made by humans; this archaeological finding was then incorporated into Aboriginal understandings (Hiscock and Faulkner 2006, 215). So, according to the authors, rather than use Indigenous knowledge to explain archaeological patterns, *archaeological patterns should be used to explain Indigenous perspectives.* In a related fashion, archaeologist Bruno David (2006) has warned against using contemporary Aboriginal understandings to understand the distant past because doing so renders Aboriginal peoples as outside of history and as eternal in a manner that denies them their full position within the wider human race (see McGhee 2008 for a similar North American critique; discussed in Cipolla and Quinn 2016).

Such arguments treat Indigenous knowledge as "less than," as flawed understandings of the world that must be explained in terms of the (western) archaeologists' sense of reality. The Dreaming does not operate, as Martin Porr (2018) has set out, as an equivalent version of "the (western) past" that archaeologists work with. It cannot be fixed in time, and rather than being an external chronological measure, the Dreaming and the time it embodies emerges through relationships (Porr 2018, 397; Rose 2004). Thus, time, history, Dreaming, the past, and the present do not, for Aboriginal peoples, exist as objective measures, but are emergent qualities. Places, like shell mounds, are thus not created at some point "in the past" and then understood "in the present" but are rather constantly emerging. While accurately dating shell mounds might show, *archaeologically*, that they were built 800 years ago, one might wonder whether that has any impact on Aboriginal understandings, especially since they have very different ontological concepts of time and temporality. Indeed, does declaring this knowledge to be right and Aboriginal claims to be wrong help us take Indigenous knowledge seriously? Or are we returning here to ideas of objectivity and singular truth that we framed as problematic in the previous chapter? Are we simply saying that archaeologists know how the world *really* works, and Indigenous people do not? As some archaeologists and anthropologists have argued, this kind of argument not only returns us to the issues we encountered in Chapter 7, but it also acts as a moment of "recolonization," where we demand, having destroyed Indigenous lifeways across the globe, that Indigenous peoples also recognize that Western systems of knowledge are the only correct ways to know the world (Alberti and Marshall 2009; Holbraad 2007; Viveiros de Castro 1998; see also Bignall 2014; Watts 2013).

If, as Foucault (1977) argued and as we saw in Chapter 7, truth and power are interlinked, then how do we reconcile different truths in a world where power isn't equal and where that power imbalance is a direct result of colonialism? Taking Indigenous knowledge seriously means this chapter's theoretical approach needs to address moments in which archaeological sensibilities and knowledge clash with other sensibilities and knowledge. How do we approach these moments of ontological encounter, of ontological difference, without either saying archaeologists or Indigenous peoples are wrong? We will return to this example, and in doing so, we will present alternative ways of doing archaeology that require no such singular claims but, instead, embrace multiple forms of knowledge along with other important insights, guidance, and expertise that comes from outside traditional archaeological realms.

The need for new perspectives, knowledges, ontologies

The work of Kim Tallbear is an excellent place to begin exploring multiplicities and collaborations further; her work provides helpful ways to think about different forms of situated knowledge in our discipline. Tallbear (2013) is a Dakota anthropologist who studied how scientists extract, study, and use Indigenous DNA. This positioning is, in itself, very different from traditional forms of anthropology, discussed later in the chapter. Here, an Indigenous person explored the world of western science, including how it produces truths by studying "Others." As Tallbear worked on her book *Native American DNA: Tribal Belonging and the False*

Promise of Genetic Science (2013), she questioned the unbalanced (and largely White) institution of science. In 2011, she wrote a blog post on this topic, focusing specifically on her experiences attending a conference held by the *Society for the Advancement of Chicanos and Native Americans in Science*. Tallbear argued that to improve science, scientists themselves needed to become more open-minded about the need for change; more than this, however, they needed to recognize that all scientists practice their discipline from a *specific place in the world*—what Donna Haraway (1988) referred to as "situated knowledge." As discussed previously, this means that science needs to be practiced by a much wider field of practitioners if it is to become something that is useful and, more importantly, less harmful to under-represented groups like Chicanos and Native peoples.

What happens when you create forms of science that are multiple? That is, what would science look like if it treated differences (and different positionalities) as strengths? What would the study of DNA look like if it took Indigenous perspectives seriously, making space for multiple ontologies to coexist and learn about the world in tandem? For example, Tallbear (2011, 4) discussed how Indigenous DNA scientists have an interest in innovating new methods that avoid doing violence to Indigenous communities, their values, and systems of belief, writing: "Native Americans have the incentive to develop research methods that are less destructive of bone and that are more respectful to the being whose remains are being studied (they are not viewed as simply lifeless bone)." Such an approach could lead to very new and different forms of scientific inquiry. Although scientists interested in Indigenous DNA technically work *with* Indigenous communities, Tallbear (2011, 5) recognized "a lack of real investment in the flourishing of the indigenous communities whose DNA was required for study." This is what Tallbear (2014) calls a "reciprocal" approach to working with communities, where the researcher agrees to use their expertise and funding to help the community in some way in exchange for data for the scientist's research endeavors—a tidy transaction. This research formula shows the same old scientific (often colonialist) traditions being perpetuated with the addition of some new surface dressing in the form of collaborative, community-based, or even decolonizing language. The traditional ontology of science ultimately prevails, paying homage to Indigenous perspectives but ultimately doing what is right for science even if it violates central components of Indigenous worlds—where deceased ancestors might be present and powerful.

As Tallbear (2014) began to question her allegiance to the projects of non-Indigenous scientists who work with Indigenous DNA, she developed a new approach to the problem. She wanted to work with a community whose goals she shared, so she developed a project working with Indigenous scientists. Her innovative approach challenges the researcher/researched dualism so prevalent in extractive sciences like DNA work and archaeology. Tallbear (2014) argued that, regardless of their background, researchers must *care* for their subjects and, in doing so, work toward democratizing knowledge production. She sought situated knowledge from the perspective of marginalized communities. As she notes, feminist objectivity is not scientifically distanced but grounded in specific places and communities for which the researcher cares. Tallbear does not simply study communities; she inhabits them. From an archaeological standpoint, this might entail caring for the lands on which we walk and work.

Theoretical toolkit: positive difference and radical alterity

What theoretical tools are required to rethink the different ways that people engage with the world? The starting point here is positive difference, introduced in Chapter 6. Drawing on posthumanist feminism and its engagement with Gilles Deleuze (2004), we argued that a great deal of western thinking approaches difference *negatively* through hierarchical comparison (Braidotti 2011, 2013, 2022). This is exactly what we saw previously when Hiscock and Faulkner (2006) treated the differences between archaeological and Indigenous knowledges as ones where Indigenous people "lack" the things that archaeologists know. In Chapter 6, we thought about how, in the production of typologies, we compare our specific Beaker pot or barbed and tanged arrowhead to an idealized Beaker or arrowhead that does not really exist. In this process, we focus on what our actual Beaker or arrowhead *lacks*. We think about how different it is by focusing on a presumed absence. Thinkers like Rosi Braidotti (2011, 2013, 2022) have used this critique of difference to critically approach how humanism holds up the White western Man as the ideal human (see Chapter 2, specifically Figure 2.4 for an image of the Vitruvian Man) and how all other forms of humanity are compared to this and found lacking and thereby less human. This is what happens when we compare Aboriginal knowledge and archaeological knowledge negatively. In contrast to this, Braidotti argues that we should see difference as a productive force. Rather than one kind of human or one kind of knowledge, lacking something that the other has, the encounter between different people or different knowledges can be productive. Indeed, within this perspective, difference is the very driving force of the world itself (Deleuze 2004). Rather than seeing difference as the thing that emerges when we compare two things, which always seems to produce a sense of lack, difference is the force that produces two things in the beginning.

How can we think through this positive force of difference? In many anthropological encounters, you can experience worlds that can seem very strange and very different indeed, ones where shamans become jaguars or stones are alive. One way to approach the kinds of knowledge we encounter is to think about it as cultural difference. We each grow up in a particular culture, society, and geography at a certain moment in time; this specific context creates and shapes us as individuals. It shapes how we see, describe, and experience the world around us and the specific ways that we dwell in the world. Classic ethnographies often involve our anthropologist going to live with a specific group and immersing themselves within that culture to come to understand it in relation to their own. They might, for example, record the different kinds of kinship relations between people to learn the term that the culture they are studying uses for cousin, or indeed how sibling relationships are understood and described. From this perspective, the difference between their own culture and the one they are studying is *cultural difference*. The job of the anthropologist is to explain different cultural systems to us and to translate them into our own western way of understanding the world. The ability to hold and compare the differences between two cultures and not to demand that they are the same in the end is often referred to as cultural relativism.

Yet, this general approach is not quite as equitable as it might seem. Despite recognizing that different people hold different points of view about the world, it still separates those people, and their cultures, from the world around them. In other words, it depends on the idea that there is one world out there that is the same for everyone, but different people simply have different ways of describing it. This serves to squash and erase the real differences between cultures and how they understand and approach the world. Underlying many such approaches are assumptions that, although different understandings are possible, one form of knowledge—Western science—is superior to the others. Thus, if an Indigenous person tells you that they emerged from the Dreaming or that a particular rock is alive, we can both accept that we have different beliefs but also know that, in the end (thanks to Western science), their version of reality doesn't hold up. In other words, as democratic as cultural relativism seems, it holds up an ideal and treats differences negatively.

Indigenous Studies scholar Vanessa Watts (2013) (Haudenosaunee and Anishnaabe) writes evocatively about Indigenous ontologies, noting that Earth is alive, is feminine, and is ancestral for Haudenosaunee and Anishnaabe peoples. Moreover, she recounts the specific process of how, for Haudenosaunee and Anishnaabe peoples, the world was created. This began with a being known as Sky Woman falling from a hole in the sky (see Figure 8.1). Watts (2013, 22, parentheses added) notes that,

> Our [Haudenosaunee and Anishnaabe] understandings of the world are often viewed as mythic by "modern" society, while our stories are considered to be an alternative mode of understanding and interpretation rather than "real" events.

A cultural relativist would certainly recognize the importance of this account of world creation but would only take this recognition so far, ultimately appealing to "Western" scientific accounts (like geology and physics) to tell a more accurate story. How else might we approach these differences?

Let us turn here to one of the more famous examples we have already touched on. What happens when an Indigenous person in South America makes the claim that powerful animals, including some jaguars, and powerful people, like shamans, can turn into one another? That is, what do we do when they tell us that these beings can transform their bodily forms (Viveiros de Castro 1998)? As the anthropologist most famous for engaging in this debate, Eduardo Viveiros de Castro (2014) has shown, the issue that arises when we are confronted with these moments is one of radical difference, or *alterity*. The claim that some humans and

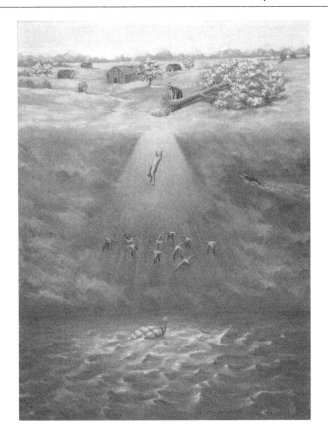

Figure 8.1 Painting of Sky Woman by Ernest Smith (Tonowanda Seneca Nation).
Image: Ernest Smith, Public domain.

animals can change their bodies isn't just an example of difference of degree (like the difference between a tall person and a short person), it is an *ontological* difference, a difference in kind. To appreciate the force of the Indigenous claim, what is required, Viveiros de Castro (2014) argues, is a moment of *equivocation*, to hold that alterity in place without demanding that we commit to resolving the differences between their world (where shamans and jaguars can shift bodies) and ours (where they cannot). When these differences encounter each other, the Western tendency is to want to clearly translate the claims Indigenous peoples make, both literally—we translate the language, often into English—and conceptually—we try to make their concepts fit ours. Viveiros de Castro (2014, 83), however, argues that "translation is always betrayal." Thus, the need for what he calls equivocation. This is still a moment of translation, but one that refuses to deny the uncertainties and the incommensurability of the terms at play. This is a moment that strives to take the knowledge *on its own terms*.

As a second example, we turn to the work of archaeologist Darryl Wilkinson (2017), who studies how thinkers in the present struggle with the claims made by non-western groups in the past. Amongst the Inka, for example, Wilkinson notes how certain kinds of stone could act like human beings (see Chapter 8 provocation image). They had personalities, could become tired, could get married, and so on. In this sense, as western thinkers have described it, stones were people. This is a classic moment of alterity, two things (stones and people) which Western knowledge thinks of as radically different are aligned. Wilkinson (2017, 301–2), however, points out the slippages that come in here. Note how we have given you the English translations rather than the Inkan terms. The Inkan term for animate non-humans, including these stones, is *Wak'a*. *Wak'as* had many of the same characteristics as the Inka term for person, *runa*, but were not identical. Furthermore, *runa*, as the term for person, does not map directly onto the term for human. Yet more issues arise: the Inkan term *rumi*, is normally translated as stone but does not easily capture all the same meanings as the English term. Thus, while it is the case that for the Inka some *rumi* (stones) could be *Wak'as* (animate non-humans) which held some of the same characteristics as *runa* (people), each of the terms in brackets are translations, which miss much of what Inkan people were actually saying. In effect, the notion that, for the Inka, stones could be people isn't an Inkan claim; it is a western claim (Wilkinson 2017, 303). The Inkan claim is that *rumi* could be *Wak'as*. Rather than rendering their claims as metaphors about the real world, it is the English translation that is a metaphor, the best we can do to understand what they were saying. This inverts the traditional approaches to Indigenous knowledge we saw earlier. Instead of assuming that we know what the real world is and that Indigenous groups use symbols or metaphors to describe it, Wilkinson (2017) shows how it is our translation that creates the metaphors, not the other way around. To return to the Amazon, the ability of the shaman and jaguar to change, thus, does not require us to abandon our basic understandings of biology and physics but rather to understand that the terms jaguar, shaman, body, and change all refer to very different concepts, ones that operate within very different sets of relations.

This "ontological turn" (Holbraad and Pedersen 2017) thus makes difference not about one group having less of an understanding than another, or lacking something (for example, say, scientific views of the world) that the other has, but rather a productive moment of encounter. This is the kind of positive difference that Braidotti (2011, 2013, 2022) wants. What does this mean when we go back to the shell mounds in Australia and consider their relationship to the Dreaming and Aboriginal communities that we encountered earlier in the chapter? How do we reconcile one claim—that these are entirely separate from the worlds and concerns of contemporary Indigenous people, as a linear concept of time relied on by archaeologists would suggest—with another—that past and present are coterminous and emergent together? The answer that the ontological turn offers, is that by refusing to insist these two descriptions match up, by staying with the moment of equivocation that we have identified, we can explore how these mounds can be both in the past *and* in the world of the Dreaming (Deleuze and Parnet 2002). This is not the same as saying the mounds can be anything. Instead, we can see these mounds neither as simply one thing (either past or present) or absolutely *any*thing. Rather they are an entity that has more than one but less than many sets of relations, meanings, and associations. This is what some philosophers would call a *multiplicity* (Deleuze 1991, 2004). As we saw earlier, this embraces how a single thing (the past; the world) is both neither one nor many but always a complex amalgam of intersecting components and perspectives. With this in mind, we can see how both the archaeological and the Indigenous perspectives have much to teach us about how we can understand the complexity of the worlds we encounter.

These theoretical tools of positive difference and radical alterity are important; they allow us *to think through multiplicities*. Yet we still have a few issues left to work out. First, how does this work in practice? How can archaeologists take these multiplicities of understanding, or an emphasis on positive difference, and understand the past differently? Second, how might this work, not just in our understanding of the past, but in our collaborations, where we work with, alongside, and for people who hold parallel or even radically different understandings to ours? For answers to these questions, we turn to our main case studies, going from Black Feminist thought about Paleolithic Europe to collaborative Indigenous histories of landscape management on the northwest coast of North America.

Using our toolkit: multiplicities, different standpoints, different ways of working

Rethinking Neanderthals using Black Feminism

Our first example of a multiplicity comes from Paleolithic Europe, specifically from new perspectives on the relationships and interactions between Neanderthals and anatomically modern humans (hereafter AMH). This topic represents a very old point of interest in the discipline of archaeology. Many archaeological sites have been excavated to help archaeologists tell better, more accurate accounts of this rather mysterious part of the human past. Archaeological and anthropological understandings of Neanderthals have changed greatly over the course of these disciplines' histories (Doronicheva et al. 2019; Gabucio et al. 2018; Groucutt 2014; Henry et al. 2014; Scerri and Will 2023; Spinapolice 2020; Vaquero et al. 2001; Will et al. 2019). In some cases, this is due to new archaeological discoveries, new sites that tell different parts of the story, and, in other cases, this is due to new technological advancements, such as the ability to extract and interpret various types of DNA from Neanderthal remains.

Here, we focus on another form of novelty—that is, different perspectives and sensibilities or *different standpoints*—from which to consider these archaeological patterns and how these can create positive difference. More specifically, we are interested in how archaeologist Kathleen Sterling (2015) rethought these patterns from a Black Feminist perspective. One's immediate reaction to this juxtaposition (Black Feminism versus Neanderthal-AMH interactions) might be to question the fit. After all, Black Feminism emerged as a solution to twentieth-century problems;

what can that possibly have to do with Neanderthals and AMHs living tens of thousands of years ago in the continent that we now call Europe? We must remember that the goal here is not to match up our theory and our perspective with those of the past peoples we study but rather to learn from different vantage points that allow new understandings of archaeological patterning. The argument is that these historically under-represented perspectives in the discipline of archaeology will offer novel (and objective) insights. In other words, multiplicity here yields better, more well-rounded disciplines.

Let us consider Sterling's work more closely. She noted how archaeological evidence shows that Neanderthals and AMHs coexisted alongside one another for a significant period. More than this, however, aDNA research now shows that the two groups interbred (Slon et al. 2018). We also know that there were similarities in both appearance and behavior between the two groups, but also key distinctions. Sterling (2015, 107) noted how most of the literature on this topic assumed that technological change diffused from AMHs to Neanderthals and that the AMHs were ultimately able to outcompete Neanderthals. Similarly, she discusses how violence is often assumed to have broken out between the two groups and that AMHs are typically assumed to be the obvious victors, perhaps even sometimes taking Neanderthal women into their possession in the process. Social evolutionary, progressive, and linear approaches to change are clearly at play in these traditional narratives and understandings (cf. Chapter 2). Here, Neanderthals were assumed obsolete and wiped out by AMHs because AMHs are framed as simply superior—they were assumed to have better technologies, more developed cognitive capabilities, and a greater capacity for art. In other words, these traditional narratives see the AMHs that lived concurrently with Neanderthals as *more human* than Neanderthals. We can see a mirror of this argument in other times and places as more "advanced" and "sophisticated" peoples violently triumphed over Others (seen as "less than").

Black Feminist perspectives, being hyper-aware of these sorts of assumptions and the damage that they do, offer new and valuable insights into these histories. Sterling argues (2015, 105–6) that traditional archaeological narratives of Neanderthals (read primitive) and AMHs (read human) are racially coded and are thus in vital need of rethinking. She reviews archaeological literature to show that traditional approaches overlooked important clues that were sometimes prominent parts of the archaeological record. There were assumptions that AMHs developed blade-based tools and ivory and animal bone artifacts, but at the same time, there was ample evidence that Neanderthal sites predating AMHs included examples of these technologies (Sterling 2015, 107–8). Sterling also describes recent research on a collapsed shelter made from mammoth bones in present-day Ukraine (Demay et al. 2011). Because the site is so old, it could only have been made and occupied by Neanderthals. Yet it includes evidence for many of the practices and technologies that were traditionally assumed to be the sole domain of AMHs; these include evidence of symbolic use of red ochre and non-butchery related striations (possibly decorative) found on animal bones. Combining this evidence with recent genetic findings, Sterling argues that interactions between Neanderthals and AMHs were not all aggressive and violent, nor did they all end with AMHs wiping out Neanderthals. Since humans today share a small percentage of Neanderthal DNA, this suggests to Sterling that "hybrid" Neanderthal-AMH children were cared for by their families and communities. In short, the evidence suggests that Neanderthals and AMHs were not so different after all and that, in some cases, the two interacted positively. Even though the archaeological evidence suggested otherwise, many archaeologists before Sterling simply laminated their expectations over the archaeological records. Black Feminist perspectives thus ask new and important questions and provide useful ways to reconnect and rethink evidence and what it means. This isn't the case of making something up that feels good; it is about creating more sound and more complete understandings of the past. In other words, this example of multiplicity—people of different backgrounds and sensibilities practicing and redefining archaeology—is transformative; it draws on and makes differences that are positive rather than negative. It makes for a better understanding of human pasts.

Creating multiplicity on the northwest coast of North America

Our second example of an archaeological multiplicity takes a related but different approach; what happens when archaeological projects are built by representatives of multiple different groups and thus embrace multiple knowledges? For this example, we look to the northwest coast of North America, where Dana Lepofsky and her colleagues (2017) study landscapes using a combination of archaeological tools and Indigenous knowledge systems. As with many Indigenous landscape management histories that left subtle or unexpected archaeological traces, human-environmental dynamics on the northwest coast have historically gone undetected by the Euro-colonial gaze. As Jeff Oliver (2007) has documented, the father of American anthropology, Franz Boas, was no exception. Describing a trip along the Fraser River in 1896, Boas (1896, 229, quoted in Oliver 2007, 3) wrote:

> The overwhelming solitude and stillness on the shores, the monotony of the dark pines and cedars, or the channels and of the roaring cascade beget a longing for the sight of human work, of human habitation, that swallows the admiration of the magnificent scenery.

As Oliver's work began to reveal, Boas simply did not have the conceptual tools to see that he was describing a heavily anthropogenically-modified place (with a long history of human-environmental interactions); as with Sterling's work summarized earlier, Eurocentric orientations (in this case, of "human work" and "human habitation") simply did not work for this place and its history. This parallels how European colonists encountering Australia for the first time interpreted a heavily managed landscape as entirely "natural" (see Chapters 2 and 9).

Lepofsky and colleagues (2017) conducted collaborative research on landscapes of the northwest coast of North America that offer new tools and frameworks for seeing and understanding what Boas could not (see Figure 8.2). A key part of these new tools and frameworks is collaboration with different First Nations of the region. As outlined in their work together (Lepofsky et al. 2017, 450), communities chose to participate in these collaborative projects for a variety of reasons. Some participated to assert the value of their knowledge systems and understandings of their histories and the land. Others became involved in the work to share their knowledge and combine it with other forms of knowledge. Finally, some gravitated toward the collaboration because they recognized that the different collaborators shared a common concern for the land they live upon and its future, a general theme that we will return to in Chapter 9.

One of the places that the researchers learned about was the Hauyet watershed (Figure 8.2). The team used multiple lines of evidence to better understand this landscape. They compiled Indigenous place names and stories, including origin

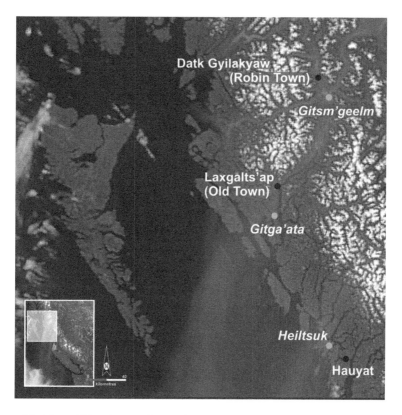

Figure 8.2 Map of Northwest Coast showing key landscapes studied (black dots) collaboratively with three communities (grey dots).

Image: Dana Lepofsky (Lepofsky et al. 2017, 450).

stories, associated with the watershed from local knowledge holders. They also conducted an archaeological survey, recording an "intensely occupied and managed landscape" (Lepofsky et al. 2017, 452) that included monumental stone and wood fish traps and clam gardens, and a 6,000-year-old multi-tiered settlement, what the researchers refer to as a "persistent place." These research practices combined different forms of knowledge that might otherwise clash or attempt to cancel one another out. But the goal was not to prove one group wrong and the other right (cf. our opening examples), but rather to construct an ontological space where both groups could respectfully work and learn from one another and from the land. As mentioned, one of the motivations for doing the work and bringing multiple peoples together was a mutual concern for the land they all lived upon.

This work involves multiple ontologies (cf. Harris and Robb 2012). For example, the authors included a photo (see Figure 8.3) of what many researchers might think of as three large stones, but the image is captioned as, "A father, mother, and son who were turned to stone during the flooding of Hauyat" (Lepofsky et al. 2017, 453). Like some of the examples discussed in the first half of the chapter, in Heiltsuk origin stories, stones are ancestors, in this case, former living beings that were turned to stone. Here we are reminded of Watts' (2013) discussion of Earth as alive, as feminine, as ancestral to humans. As with the reactions to Indigenous

Figure 8.3 A chief, his wife, and son who were turned to stone during the flooding of Hauyat.

Image: Dana Lepofsky (Lepofsky et al. 2017, 453), photo by Julia Jackley.

truth claims that Watts (2013) discusses, it is more than likely that at least some of the researchers involved in the project *did not* understand the world in this way; for them, perhaps stone is stone and ancestors are people, and the two don't share an ancestral connection. Rather than halt the project to debate if this were true or not, however, the research continued. It forged a space of inquiry not only where these seemingly incompatible truths could coexist but where they build off one another in a positive way.

Conclusion

As explored throughout this chapter, archaeological multiplicities can take various forms. This sometimes entails reassessing old archaeological problems from angles that were historically excluded from the archaeological discipline. With Kathleen Sterling's (2015) work, for example, we learned about how a Black Feminist perspective has been used to productively rethink the complicated relations between Neanderthals and AMHs in present-day Europe. In other cases, multiplicities involve creating new ways of doing archaeology, working together to create new modes of thinking and doing. With the work of Lepofsky and her colleagues, we saw how Indigenous knowledge and sensibilities combine with archaeological toolkits to reveal human-environmental histories that even Franz Boas was incapable of seeing. In these examples, the multiplicities we considered didn't always consist of radical differences in truth claims or realities, but some certainly did. We learned that it is possible to design and conduct archaeological research in which stone is multiple things for different participants (see also Cipolla 2018). Does this mean Lepofsky et al.'s (2017) project is simply another case of good old anthropological relativism? We don't think so. Relativism in anthropology is not typically employed with a mind for *changing* the mode of inquiry; this is why it is different from the collaborative approaches and ontological considerations discussed throughout this chapter. In other words, deferring to cultural relativism in ethnography (stone is an ancestor for that society) rarely leads to changing the methods for how one recognizes, collects, and interprets data. This is because of the "one world" hierarchy of cultural relativism introduced earlier, which operates on what we refer to as negative differences. We feel that something else is going on in the examples and concepts explored in this chapter. They speak to different methodologies "on the ground," as it were, but they also speak to the ontological concerns at the heart of our discussion. By embracing positive difference, moments of alterity, and ontological difference, we can create multiplicities that do not simply place one way of knowing above another.

At the beginning of this chapter, we differentiated our discussion from Chapter 7's analysis of relational truths. In the previous chapter, we looked at claims about the numbers of attendees at a certain presidential inauguration. We suggested that the strongest way to resist those claims was to develop a relational approach to truth. In contrast, in this chapter, we did not attempt to resist alternative claims about the world. Instead, we advocated for developing multiplicities that dwell on the positive differences they can create. So, it seems that there are some claims that we should be resisting and others that should be taken seriously. How do we tell the difference? In a world shorn of easy answers, the reality is that this question can only be answered with specifics, in particular moments.

Approaching truth as emergent and relational, which we saw in the last chapter, and embracing the need to equivocate and avoid insisting upon fixed translation, which we explored here, provides a starting point. When a Haudenosaunee and Anishnaabe woman tells us about how the world was formed, this claim sits in a very different web of relationships of history, power, suffering, wisdom, and knowledge than the claims we saw in Chapter 7. The approaches in this chapter and the last ask us to hold up knowledges and examine the relations they dwell within, the claims they make, and our relations with them. This means archaeologists can work with Indigenous groups in sympathetic but not naive ways.

When an Amazonian person says that a shaman can turn into a jaguar, this is not the same as when a White British person claims to be indigenous and to have unique access to the past of that country. Each of these claims emerges from different relational constellations, and each operates within different flows of power. One refuses easy translation, and the other benefits from it. Whereas a cultural relativist approach would argue that there are different understandings of the same world, an ontological one allows us to explore how different worlds meet and collide and to hold those differences up for examination. Alfredo González-Ruibal (2019), for example, has explored the difficulties that could arise from ignoring that Indigenous people can be complicit in acts of violence or oppression or might conceive of the world in ways that are not just different from western ones (like the Dreaming), but more deeply problematic. This might be because they endorse, or actively carry out, violence, engage in collaboration with predatory capitalist companies, or are happy to destroy rather than preserve the ancient past (González-Ruibal 2019). Similarly, Liv Nilsson Stutz (2018) has worried about the treatment of Indigenous ideas in ways that essentialize the diversity of these groups and cut them off from history. What we have argued for in the last two chapters leads to neither of these outcomes. Instead, the ideas outlined earlier call for engaged relational approaches that work to build multiplicities of knowledge but that remain critical, that remain in a position where we can recognize that not all collaborations will succeed and that some are destined to fail. If collaboration begins and one party sees or hears something that they feel is unacceptable (like a human rights violation), they, of course, have the right to walk away and to speak out against such injustices. Collaborations are not everlasting or totalizing; they involve differences and similarities, and when they are successful, they create new spaces in which ontological differences can coexist and push research (and problem-solving) in new and valuable directions. In our view, the ideas discussed throughout this chapter on how to listen, hear, and take people seriously, concern more than the study of the past; they include vital lessons on how to work across lines of difference, and to imagine new futures together. It is here that archaeological multiplicities can speak to the wider issues of a divided world. They can provide models of collaboration that can allow us to speak well of others (Latour 2013), but not to embrace those positions uncritically. They can allow us to explore difference positively, and they help us to create space for new ways of thinking and doing. They start on the ground, and like all archaeology, in the moment of encounter. One question here remains unanswered: how does this debate relate to issues of decolonization, a word you might have expected to encounter in this chapter before now? The answer is complicated and one we return to in the final chapter of this book.

Chapter 9

Archaeology and the Anthropocene

Futurity and affect

Introduction: tensions of the Anthropocene

The current world is a complicated place. Our planet is warming; the human population is increasing; industrialization is reshaping the landscape; goods flow over ever greater distances. Some of us live longer and better lives than ever before, while the distribution of wealth and resources is becoming ever more uneven (cf. Chapter 3). Scientists analyze, the media reports, and increasing numbers of people protest, calling for climate justice (see Figure 9.1). The changes caused by humans to planet Earth's many different systems are now so significant that we are told we are living in a new geological epoch: *the Anthropocene* (Crutzen and Stoermer 2000).

Anthropocene research is inherently interdisciplinary; geologists work alongside anthropologists, scientists, and humanities scholars, while political scientists and lawyers work alongside biologists and meteorologists (Edgeworth 2014, 74; see also DeLoria's 1997 discussion of the importance of interdisciplinary research). In fact, Jason Kelly (2014) argues that the diversity of research and the fragmentary nature of the discourse have led to the emergence of multiple Anthropocenes. Anthropocene research thus tends to disrupt traditional disciplinary approaches, urging scholars to think differently (Campbell 2021; Domanska 2014; Pétursdóttir 2017); as an example, geologists who study a time scale bewildering even to archaeologists—4.5 billion years—are searching for a stratigraphic marker for a period that will be chronologically tiny from their perspective. One place where the diversity of Anthropocene research is most obvious is in debates over when precisely it began (Balter 2013; Graves-Brown 2014). Did it begin with the advent of farming (Growdy and Krall 2013), deforestation 8,000 years ago (Ruddiman 2003), the proliferation of tools and technology (Zalasiewicz et al. 2014), the colonization of the Americas (Davis and Todd 2017), the appearance of concrete in our stratigraphic layers (Simonetti and Edgeworth 2022), or with the invention of the steam engine (Crutzen 2006)? Indeed, the term Anthropocene constitutes an assemblage of researchers crisscrossing subjects, time periods, and scales of analysis. All of this seems new and exciting.

DOI: 10.4324/9781003244141-9

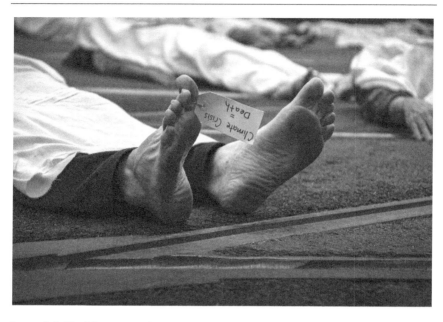

Figure 9.1 Healthcare workers die-in at the front of the Victoria Parliament,
Melbourne, Australia. From Day 1 of Extinction Rebellion's Autumn
Rebellion 2021.

Image: Matt Hrkac from Geelong/Melbourne, Australia, CC BY 2.0 license (https://crea
tivecommons.org/licenses/by/2.0).

Yet, much of this work tends to preserve an old relic of modernist thought; it
often rests upon a dualism between culture and nature, one of the problematic
oppositions noted in Chapter 1. We can take the definition as our prime example.
The Anthropocene is typically thought of as the period marked by human (read cultural) impact on planet Earth (read nature) (Pétursdóttir 2017, 180, 2020, 93). On
the one hand, Anthropocene research challenges dualistic thinking when it demonstrates just how entangled humans are with planet Earth. On the other hand, however, most approaches to this new geological period continue to be anthropocentric
(Kelly 2014, 92); that is, they privilege human beings in very specific ways (Chapter 1). Geological thinking makes humans appear small within the overall history
of Earth, yet the concept of the Anthropocene gives them an outsized impact as the
drivers of a whole proposed geological period—culture ruling over (and sealed off
from) nature. As Þóra Pétursdóttir (2020, 88) highlights, the Anthropocene pro-
vokes difficult questions about agency as it serves to simultaneously centralize and
decentralize the role of human beings.

In this chapter, we think about the contribution of archaeology to the study of the
Anthropocene and climate crisis more broadly. We consider three sets of proposed
solutions: first, rewilding; second, the idea of returning to an older and simpler
way of life; and third, the belief that human ingenuity will innovate a solution to

the climate crisis. We go on to explore how ecofeminist and particular elements of Indigenous thinking might offer us a critical foundation for our thinking before introducing our theoretical tools: the concepts of futurity and affect. Finally, we use the example of waste to further explore these themes and concepts. This chapter argues that it is by attending to the world as archaeologists—by thinking about time, affect, and relationality in posthumanist ways—that we can generate an ethics of care that might sustain our world into the future.

Setting the stage: working our way out of the problem?

Archaeologists often point to the contemporary relevance of their discipline by suggesting that we can learn from the past to help us face contemporary problems (Chapter 1). The tensions outlined earlier around the Anthropocene are rife with possibilities here. For example, some archaeologists use the study of the past to highlight the elasticity and adaptability of the human species (e.g., Cooper and Peros 2010; Sabloff 2008; see discussion of this as an archaeological response to the Anthropocene in Pétursdóttir 2017). We know the climate has changed in the past, so we can use archaeology to see how communities adapted and to gauge their level of success. As an example, Jago Cooper and Matthew Peros (2010) consider how humans responded to changing sea levels, rainfall, and hurricanes in the pre-Columbian Caribbean. Working specifically with data from Cuba, they explore how communities changed their settlement locations, household architecture, and food procurement strategies in relation to environmental change. Cooper and Peros (2010) found that the faunal remains from pre-Columbian Cuba suggest that people had diverse diets that involved multiple environmental zones, with food moving across significant distances. They argue that this made communities more resilient, both in terms of food sources and social relations (Cooper and Peros 2010, 1230). Their work highlights the complexity of ecological relationships involving humans while emphasizing the challenges of using the past to meaningfully provide strategies for future climate change. This lesson from the past is difficult to translate into our world; moving food across great distances in pre-Columbian Cuba is different from doing so in our present world; it involves a different set of ecological relations and has different scales of effect. Questions thus remain as to precisely how we can learn from the archaeological past and adjust our relationship with the world accordingly.

Rewilding provides another popular, though poorly defined (Schulte to Bühne et al. 2022), response to the climate crisis. The aim of rewilding is often to increase biodiversity by letting "nature" take its course with minimal human interference. Rewilding efforts sometimes produce intriguing results. The reintroduction of beavers into rivers in Devon, UK, for instance, appears to provide evidence that beaver management of waterways can help mitigate flooding (Brazier et al. 2020). On the other hand, a project to rewild an area in the Netherlands, called Oostvaarders-plassen, proved more controversial and less successful (Lorimer 2015, chapter 5). Some of the animals that had been introduced, such as red deer, Knik horses, and heck cattle, had to be slaughtered because they began to starve. With a lack of natural predators, like wolves, the numbers of these species increased rapidly. A series of bad winters followed, making it difficult for these species to sustain themselves on the land. Local people became outraged, with some protestors breaking laws to throw bales of hay to the starving animals (Barkham 2018). These approaches are intriguing from a posthumanist perspective; if we let non-human animals return to the habitats that they once occupied, this could lead to an increase in biodiversity and mitigation of some of the effects of the climate crisis, but this tampering also often comes with unintended consequences.

The concept of rewilding presumes that we can return to a "before time" when humans were *not* shaping the environment. This premise is complicated since there are multiple ways that people relate to ecosystems. Archaeological evidence shows this diversity, including examples where people had complicated and subtle relations of care with natural environments (see, for example, in Australia, Bowman 1998; Gammage 2012; Roberts et al. 2021). These relationships *do* impact environments, but they leave only faint traces. Thus, landscapes that appear to be "wild" might be the product of careful landscape management strategies that are less exploitative (Chapter 8). Pétursdóttir's (2020) work with drift deposits on the uninhabited coastlines of Iceland and Norway also demonstrates that simply having humans leave a landscape will not stop human influence on that landscape; drift deposits continue to accumulate in rewilded coastlines. In short, rewilding suggests that non-humans, particularly plants and animals, might hold the solution to our problems if we humans simply got out of the way. It turns out that this might be more challenging than it first appeared (see Figure 9.2).

There are parallels between rewilding arguments and related calls to a return to a "simpler time," more generally. If we could live in a way that had less impact on the planet, as the narrative goes, then the environment might have a chance to recover. Here again, the call is to return to a past with fewer human impacts. Such a project operates on a slightly different scale than that of calls to rewild, which look to plant and animal life as solutions to our problem. Here, instead of leaving the plants and animals alone, it is the humans that must actively strive to go back in time and adopt the practices of their (romanticized) predecessors. In both arguments, however, there is an underlying assumption that it would be possible to return to an earlier way of life. Even if this were possible, to what time should we return? Since there is little consensus on when the problem(s) began (as we touched on earlier in the chapter), there is also little consensus on what period contains the solution. Before capitalism? Before the start of farming? Even if we could reach a consensus, how precisely would we turn back time? If, for example, we move to the woods, begin growing and gathering our own food, and stop using fossil fuels, then airplanes, power stations, and oil companies would all still exist. None of this is to say that living a simpler life might not be good for the planet, just that the idea of returning to a time before the present—"turning back the clock"—is not possible.

Gilles Deleuze (2004, 50–1) explores this challenge in *Difference and Repetition*, where he dwells on the idea of the eternal return from the philosopher

Figure 9.2 A rubber duck from a rubber duck race on the river Liffey in Ireland in 2006 washed up on the shores of the Isle of Man in 2022.

Image: Kevin Rothwell, Duck number 26845, Derbyhaven, Isle of Man, CC BY-SA 2.0 license (https://creativecommons.org/licenses/by-sa/2.0/).

Friedrich Nietzsche—the idea that you might be visited in the night by a demon who offered to take you back to live your life again and again. How would you respond to the demon? Would you cry in horror or jump for joy? Deleuze (2004), with his emphasis on becoming over being and the constantly changing nature of the world, points out that you could not live that same life again. It would be different every single time, meaning that you would not be the same person, and the conditions of your life would differ. Thus, for Deleuze, we cannot return to a "simpler time" and simply shed all the things that have got us to this point; we roll into the future with an ocean full of microplastics and drift (cf. Pétursdóttir 2020) (see Figure 9.2), an atmosphere full of carbon, communities addicted to highly processed fast foods, and with the knowledge that we can extract oil from rocks and use it to power all manner of things. Our solutions need to account for all these things rather than simply wishing them away. Invoking a simpler life thus places emphasis on human action as both the cause and the solution to our problems while pursuing the impossible task of returning to another time.

Others put all their faith in yet-to-be-invented (or fully developed) technology as the solution to our Anthropocene problems. As the narrative goes, humans created the Anthropocene and all its messy consequences, thus, humans will be able to tidy up after themselves too. Just as humans have invented technologies to make food transportable, protect people from viruses, or capture renewable energy, we will, once again, invent something new that solves our problems. There is no doubt that innovation and technology will be key aspects of our future approaches to the climate crisis (IPCC report AR6 2023, 34–5, sections C6 and C7). This is not simply a belief that more solar panels, wind turbines, or electric vehicles will solve things, but a faith in technologies that do not yet exist. Here, we might pause to think. Our ingenious problem-solving has not always been wholly for the good. From plastics to antibiotics, many of our most innovative problem-solving solutions often beget their own problems, whether that is an ocean full of microplastics or bacteria that evade our best medicines. While the emphasis in this kind of thinking is on an unspecified future (unlike calls to rewild or to return to a "simpler life"), the same kind of dualistic thinking informs it. Whereas in the examples given earlier, nature was coming to the rescue, here, human culture and technology will provide us a way out of the environment that we are embedded in and, most importantly, provide us with a way to master our changing climate (cf. Crossland 2014b, 125).

Archaeology has lots to say about the climate crisis and the emergence of the Anthropocene (Mitchell 2008), and there are certainly lessons it can teach us, but our argument in this book is that our discipline is not just a source of "cautionary tales," but also a provocative way to challenge us to think differently (see, for example, Pétursdóttir's (2020, 182) call for archaeology to be a "jolt to the imagination" regarding the Anthropocene). Some of the key solutions that are being implemented and experimented with as we write are—from our theoretical viewpoint, at least—not best placed to deal with the scale of our problems. Rewilding suggests that if we remove humans from the equation, then we can solve the climate crisis. Returning to a "simpler life" suggests that if humans could simply go back to living in a different way, then our problems would be solved. The call to unknown technological solutions argues we will invent our way out of the climate crisis, and that technology is our savior. These may all be good things to do: more beavers, fewer flights, and more solar panels are all good moves to make. Alone, though, they are based on shaky thinking that separate humans and the environment from each other and suggest that one side of the equation will solve the problem; leave it to the deer, the wild boar, and the eagles or wait for the scientists to solve it. Our solutions should include deer, wild boar, eagles, and scientists as parts of heterogeneous assemblages, but they need to be oriented to the future, not to a return to an idealized and unreachable past.

Setting the stage: turning to feminism as a way out?

The solutions presented so far leave us thinking about and understanding the world in a dualistic and anthropocentric way. Are there ways we could approach the climate crisis and the Anthropocene differently by changing our theoretical outset?

One response is ecofeminism, a varied set of critiques and approaches that share concerns over two broad problems: human exploitation and desecration of the environment and the structural inequalities and violence that women face in different societies. Scholars often trace the intellectual roots of ecofeminism to the writings of Françoise d'Eaubonne (Gates 1996), but the movement also emerged through grassroots activism and protest (activities and struggles that were not necessarily connected with academic disciplines). Crucially, for ecofeminists, mistreatments of both planet Earth and women are closely related. From this perspective, the devaluation of women and the degradation of Earth (Gates 1996, 8) are distinct expressions of the same problem—the arbitrary hierarchy that places a certain type of human at its apex, with everyone and everything else valued below them (as *less than*). As Rosi Braidotti (2022, 74) puts it, "Patriarchal culture has confused the human with the heterosexual male." For Vanessa Watts (2013, 24), these Eurocentric knowledge systems also elevate humankind "outside or above the natural world." These critiques bear some resemblance to our earlier discussions of humanist Man (see Chapter 2), but we hasten to note that not all ecofeminists define themselves as posthumanists. Let's dwell just a little more on this connection that ecofeminists draw between the mistreatment of the planet and the mistreatment of women. How exactly do they connect these two problems?

For some, this comparison probably calls to mind the phrase "Mother Earth," which is often used metaphorically to liken the planet's life-giving qualities to that of women. In this regard, one could look to the history of human-environmental interactions, particularly those associated with the last few hundred years of colonialism and capitalism, and find clear cases where people extracted resources from environments and landscapes with little to no regard for the consequences (Chapter 3); as examples, consider recent debates around fracking or where we began the book—concerns about oil pipelines polluting the environment (Chapter 1). These mistreatments threaten to harm Earth's life-giving and sustaining qualities. Yet, some might argue that we *must* frack; we *must* install new oil pipelines. For them, these environmental threats are necessities for providing for Earth's ever-expanding human population (of over eight billion at the time of writing). Ecofeminism points to the connections in this example between exploiting the environment and population growth, which tie into the ways that many societies objectify women as vessels for childbearing. One only needs to think of America's recent overturning of Roe versus Wade, which eliminated abortion as a federal right. As Gates (1996, 9) explained, "Overpopulation is ruining both humanity and the earth, for the earth is treated with the same disregard as are women." Yet, ecofeminists note that women often take the lead when it comes to caring for Earth and protecting it from environmental threats (Braidotti 2022, 79).

Like some of our critiques of approaches to the Anthropocene outlined in the first part of this chapter, ecofeminists point to the harmful role that Cartesian dualisms play in these problems (Jelinski 2005, 275; see also Gaard 1997; El-Kamel Bakari 2015). According to them, dualisms that oppose men, culture, rationality, and spirit on the one hand, with women, nature, emotion, and matter, on the other, sit at the heart of these struggles. As noted by Braidotti (2022, 74), such dualisms are both arbitrary and Eurocentric. These perspectives share much in common with posthumanism, which, according to Ferrando (2019; see also Cipolla 2021; Cipolla et al. 2021), offers three key critiques of humanism: 1) its privileging of only certain kinds of humans (in this case, men); 2) its privileging of humanity (in this case, as a species that can extract from any environment regardless of the consequences); and 3) its dualistic modes of seeing and being in the world (in this case, a system that opposes nature to culture, men to women, etc.). Crucially, for Alaimo and Hekman (2008), ecofeminist critique also brings feminism into critical dialogue with the material world—a realm that many forms of feminism, with their traditional focus on social construction, avoid or engage with only on a limited basis. This, too, aligns with elements of posthumanism and new materialism.

Yet, as demonstrated by the history of the feminist movement and its various waves (especially third-wave feminism and beyond), ecofeminism must be considered in specific social and cultural contexts rather than treated as a universal approach. For example, Gaard (2014, 92) points out how our current ecological crisis was not created proportionally by all nations and peoples (Crossland 2014b, 125; Gaard 2014, 92; Yusoff 2018). Instead, it is the wealthiest nations that disproportionately pollute and impact environments most, compared to the world's poorest nations that often suffer the most from climate change. As Kathryn Yusoff highlights, the "White Anthropocene" is built on the extraction and destruction of Black resources, bodies, and labor. Here, the work of Indigenous feminists is important to consider. Gina Starblanket (2017, 30–1), for example, writes evocatively about this issue. They note how, as colonists stole Indigenous land, they laminated over diverse Indigenous gender systems, forcing them into binary frames (of men versus women), limiting what Indigenous women could do, and restricting their access to land; according to Watts (2013) and others, Indigenous knowledges (for Watts, "Place-Thought") are embedded in landscapes. Restricted access to specific landscapes thus clearly resulted in ruptures in the flow of specialized Indigenous knowledges—forms of place-based knowing in which many Indigenous women played crucial roles. Prior to colonialism, many Indigenous peoples in what we now call North America used matrilineal kinship systems, meaning that members of these societies traced their lineages through their female ancestors and relatives (see also Watts 2013); in other words, women were often powerful and important in these societies.

Yet, things began to change with colonialism. As Starblanket (2017, 30) describes:

> Gendered divisions were reinforced in the work of missionaries and in the labour programs carried out in Canadian residential schools, which aimed to train boys for physical labour such as agriculture and woodworking, while training woman for domestic work such as sewing and doing laundry.

These colonial institutions also attempted to sever ties between Indigenous women and their lands—a sacred relationship, according to Joyce Green (2017; see also

Watts 2013). All of this is not to mention the problem of missing and murdered Indigenous women and girls (Bourgeois 2017), a uniquely North American crisis. Since colonialism began in North America, thousands of Indigenous women and girls have been taken and murdered, almost certainly by Euro-colonial peoples. More than this, however, there is a strong correlation between where oil or mining companies develop land and where Indigenous women and girls often go missing (Grable 2021). Again, we are reminded of the link between environmental exploitation and the violence of settler colonialism, specifically as experienced by Indigenous women and girls. Here, it's important to note that by turning to feminism and Indigenous thinking, we are not asking women or Indigenous communities to solve the atrocities done to them or to the environment; instead, we humbly look for alternative ways of thinking, for different perspectives, that might help us to rethink the problems we face concerning our collective futures.

Theoretical toolkit: futurity and affect

To achieve the goals of this chapter and present a post-anthropocentric critique of the Anthropocene that reconceptualizes the natural world and revisits our interconnectedness with it, we require a few more specialized theoretical tools, some of which build on the ecofeminist and Indigenous critiques discussed earlier. Some of the tools connect back to concepts introduced in previous chapters, while others represent relatively new conceptual tools for this book. We begin with archaeological discussions of futurity. This provides us with critical tools for thinking about how archaeology can contribute to challenging dominant concepts of the Anthropocene. We then return to more familiar ground by exploring new materialist and posthumanist perspectives on affect.

As already argued in this book, even though archaeologists rarely discuss it explicitly, they have clear connections with the future (see Crossland 2014b; Reilly 2019 and associated papers); they engage in archaeological research to learn about past worlds that they will partially reconstruct and/or interpret in the *future*. They do this with the hope that, in the future, their archaeological findings might have value for other people. When people think about and plan for possible futures, we typically associate that with the term *futurity*. Although the two terms share a clear connection, futurity and the future are not the same. Futurity is epistemological—specific ways that people speculate on and attempt to give shape to future happenings (compare with our discussion of prefiguration in Chapter 4). As we all know, when we plan for the future with specific ideas in mind, those futures don't always unfold as we predicted. The theme of this chapter—the Anthropocene—is perhaps one of the greatest reminders of this uncertainty. Figures who played key roles in shaping the world that we currently live in, take the famous industrialist Henry Ford as an example, likely did not anticipate our current ecological crisis. In many ways, Ford resembles our earlier discussion of faith in technology. He believed in human progress and technological advancement, operating on what we might now label as a false hope that humans were so advanced that they would come up with solutions to any future environmental challenges or unintended outcomes of, say, mass-producing motor vehicles with combustion engines. In other cases, people might not try to predict a specific future but instead, imagine new possibilities based on certain aspects of how the world works in the present. This is best exemplified in the science fiction genre, which applies aspects of how the world works in the present to imagine radically different futures. Thus, science fiction is not *pure* fiction. Additionally, works of science fiction might inspire readers to think of the world and the future in new and exciting ways and thus inspire them to take action to realize those potential futures.

For archaeologists, discussions of futurity typically take one of three main approaches (see papers in Reilly 2019). First, archaeologists sometimes think about how past people envisioned their own futures. Second, archaeologists occasionally use archaeological perspectives on the past and present in attempts to shape the future. Archaeologist Kent Lightfoot (2013) provides a striking example of one such project. He worked with Indigenous peoples and ecologists in northern California to study past practices of controlled burning and hypothesized how this information sheds light on a contemporary problem, namely California firestorms. Lightfoot and his team found that Indigenous burning practices regularly reduced fuel loads that have gone unchecked since Spanish and Russian colonialism restricted Indigenous access to California landscapes. Third and finally, some archaeologists speculate on what archaeology will become in the future (Rizvi 2019; Witmore 2019; Wurst 2019).

In this book, we are primarily interested in the second group of future-oriented archaeologies, those that attempt to rethink the future based on archaeological findings. Yet, we take a slightly different approach that looks not only at specific patterns recovered from the archaeological record but also at how archaeologists think and work in general. To rethink the Anthropocene, we must rethink our categories and our notions of causality. As emphasized by various ecofeminist and Indigenous critiques, this begins with non-dualistic ways of thinking and doing (see also Harris and Cipolla 2017). This entails questioning dualistic ways of thinking about the world that oppose nature and culture, women and men, or materials and ideas, and attempting to replace them with relational approaches (see Chapters 3 and 7) that recognize the messiness of the world. Henry Ford, for example, acted in the world as if culture and nature were two distinct and opposed realms. In his world, culture would always triumph over nature; technology would always give humans a way to fix any potential environmental problems. In hindsight, we now see that the two were anything but separate. Ford produced cultural products (cars) that were made of "natural" materials like minerals mined from deep underground; his factories were built in specific places where forests were cleared, streams and rivers polluted, and human populations amassed to work. More than this, however, Ford's cars burned oil and gasoline, giving off emissions—namely carbon dioxide—that helped produce the greenhouse effect, slowly warming global temperatures. Owning and driving a vehicle is thus caught up in a tangled web of relations to "nature," especially shrinking polar ice.

If we take a post-dualistic approach to such problems, we quickly realize how difficult it becomes to attribute causality to single people or events (Crellin 2020).

For Braidotti (2022, 76), a strength of ecofeminism is its emphasis on the "relational force that binds all living systems," a force that is typically cleaved apart by dualistic approaches and searches for singular forces of causality and agency. Sure, Henry Ford made differences; his agency certainly helped to create the problems we now face, but blaming him doesn't solve them. In fact, only blaming him (and other people like him) ignores many important parts of the problem, such as carbon dioxide and its properties (see our discussion of blame in Chapter 5). This is where the concept of *affect* comes in handy. Affect can mean many different things, but one version of the concept presents an alternative to the thorny issue of agency and causality in archaeology by taking a relational, non-dualistic, and post-anthropocentric view of the world. This version of affect concerns how bodies (broadly defined) press into one another (Crellin and Harris 2021; Crellin et al. 2021, chapter 2) and emerge together (see Chapter 7 for more discussion of emergence). You can think of how two people, dancing together, guide each other's movements with subtle changes in direction or pressure from one hand to another. Alternatively, think about when you walk into a gym, and your body is overwhelmed by the heat, the sounds, and the smells produced by the exercising bodies around you. Affect in these contexts is not just about human bodies either. The friction of wheels on the tarmac sends vibrations through the seat on the bus you are sitting on, just as your body adds to the pressure of the bus on that tarmac and slowly increases the fraying of the fabric of the seat you are sitting on. Affect leads us to consider how bodies, both human and non-human, emerge alongside each other, how they shape and guide the movements of which each is capable, just as the sea shapes how a human body needs to move to swim through it, movements of the swimmer and the water responding to one another (Deleuze 1997, 24). Here we must consider much more than industrialists like Ford if we are going to grapple meaningfully with the Anthropocene. In fact, with affect in mind, we might want to rethink the naming of the Anthropocene altogether; that name, privileging *anthropos* or people, suggests that people are the ultimate cause of the ecological problems that we face. There is no doubt that people played an important role in creating the problems we face, but they didn't act alone. As we saw in Chapter 5's discussion of violence, while it might be appropriate to "blame" individuals for their actions, this offers little in terms of tools to address how to fix an issue or much in the way of historical explanation.

Using our theory tools: thinking through waste

To explore these issues and approaches in more detail, we want to consider one of the most common archaeological materials of study: waste. Archaeology finds great value in the things that people sought to discard. The irony here is that the things we think we have disposed of are, of course, far from gone; they continue to have effects long after their disposal, as Pétursdóttir's (2017, 2020) work on drift demonstrates so elegantly. The site of Potterne, in Wiltshire, UK, provides an example of a monumental deposition of waste dating to the Late Bronze Age and Early Iron Age (Lawson 2000). The site includes a buried deposit covering 3.5 hectares up to 1.4 meters deep in places (Lawson 2000, 13). It is so large that it effectively blends into the landscape, giving the appearance of a natural topographic feature (Madg-wick et al. 2012, 130). Included in the deposit was a vast ceramic assemblage and a smaller amount of metalwork and worked stone. In addition, there were masses of faunal remains; for example, excavations of 1% of the midden produced over 130,000 bone fragments (Locker 2000), including caprines, pigs, and cattle thought to be the remains of periodic feasting events. Analysis of the plant remains shows that the rich compost-like nature of the deposit encouraged the growth of specific kinds of vegetation on the surface (McCobb et al. 2003, 1270), indicating that this was no "disappeared" or neutral deposit of waste. It went on to shape the landscape and the kinds of plants that grew there; it had particular effects even after the waste was buried. Thinking at the non-human scale, we can consider how bacteria and fungi in amongst the midden material transformed the boundaries of things, an assemblage greater than the sum of its parts. Multiple affects, and scales of affect, are at play here.

Thinking about Potterne as a site of compost brings us to the work of Donna Haraway (2015, 2016). In response to the climate crisis and the current "trouble" we find ourselves in Haraway asks us to think of ourselves as "compost." Blurring the boundaries between human and non-human, across species and at different tem-poralities, we can think about how compost is both the medium in which species can become and the medium into which we can break down as bodies return to the earth. She urges us to think of ourselves as entangled with the rest of the world:

> Critters—human and not—become-with each other, compose and decompose each other, in every scale and register of time and stuff in sympoietic tangling, in ecological evolutionary developmental earthly worlding and unworlding.
>
> (Haraway 2016, 97)

We can think of Potterne as compost—the feasting events through which commu-nities came together and literally became communities and the decomposition of matter to produce the medium for new life across species. Potterne is both waste and medium for the future.

What happens, though, when that material we want to get rid of is not so pro-ductive for new life? Nuclear waste as a material offers a fascinating resource for archaeologists to think about. It was created in the past but lasts into the present and creates challenges for the future (Holtorf 2019, 4). Yet, this future doesn't just run to the end of the year, the decade, or even the century. It requires us to think of a future on an *archaeological timescale*. Indeed, Cornelius Holtorf (2019, 2) argues that nuclear waste bears many similarities to cultural heritage—we must manage it, it requires care, and it impacts future communities. In a sense, both nuclear waste and heritage help shape and create certain kinds of futures (cf. Harrison 2020). This suggests that archaeologists might be able to draw on their own theoretical resources to think through some of the issues that nuclear waste poses. Through this exercise, we will identify how thinking like an archaeologist, and using our theoret-ical tools, can help us with a broader range of issues that the Anthropocene raises.

Nuclear waste, like Anthropocene research, bridges all kinds of disciplines and concerns. It draws on the power of atoms themselves but situates that force in clear cultural contexts—the production of power and the challenges this causes. It denies any easy separation into nature or culture or into the sciences or the humanities (Holtorf 2019). Like the other elements from the Anthropocene, from carbon in the atmosphere to plastics in the seas, its material presence has provoked an archaeological engagement (e.g., Dawney et al. 2017; Harrison et al. 2020; Holtorf 2019; Holtorf and Höberg 2014, 2015; Joyce 2020; Wollentz 2020). Yet nuclear waste is different; it is immediately deadly, with the capacity to kill animals, plants, and human beings if they are exposed to it (for up to the next 100,000 years). It is this timescale that connects this material to archaeology; it presents a very specific contemporary challenge. Locking up the waste for a year or a decade is one thing, but how can we be certain that the people in 50,000 years will remember that nuclear waste is dangerous or that it is buried in a particular location? How can we understand this idea of "nuclear memory" (Keating and Storm 2023)? This is a clear example of contemporary futurity—how we imagine the future today—and one that really matters. What kind of people do we imagine will exist then? Will they speak or read any contemporary languages? What technology will they have? The only disciplines that really think about change at this scale are geology and archaeology, and so perhaps it is no surprise that archaeology has been engaged in these issues.

The most noticeable example of the use of archaeology is in the design of a nuclear waste facility in New Mexico. As the archaeologist Rosemary Joyce (2020) has set out, two teams were tasked with designing the outward-facing elements of the Waste Isolation Pilot Project (or WIPP). The aim was to design elements that might survive well beyond written human records and warn future visitors of the dangers contained within. One team drew explicitly on archaeological sites to aid their work (Joyce 2020, 8). They saw Stonehenge, the Neolithic monument in Wiltshire, UK, and the mounds at Cahokia, in Illinois, USA, as examples of how architectural features could survive for millennia, transmitting knowledge down through the ages. Yet, as Joyce (2020) sets out, these examples rested on rather dubious understandings of the archaeology of these sites. It will probably come as no surprise to any actual archaeologist, but the notion that archaeological sites simply transmit their messages through the ages is far from straightforward (consider our discussion of the Sphinx in Chapter 7). Instead, for the past to transmit any meaning at all, it requires active engagement (Joyce 2020, 114). The material doesn't encode meaning, rather, meaning emerges in the conjunctions of people and things together (cf. Cipolla n.d.). As many archaeologists have remarked, these sites seem likely to attract investigation and excavation (as Stonehenge and Cahokia have done) rather than put people off as places of risk and danger.

There *are*, however, helpful lessons that archaeologists can share with people studying and working with nuclear waste. The first is that, as the past shows us, the future will be different than the present. Stonehenge is not the same site today it was in 1500 BCE, and in 1500 BCE, it was very different to how it was in 3000 BCE.

While this might seem depressing, it stresses the power of the future to generate change. We might now scoff at the innocence of Henry Ford building cars with no idea of the climate crisis he would help produce, but equally our current malaise and dithering (cf. Haraway 2015), and the sense that cataclysm is inevitable, is no more certain or justified. Narratives of eternal progress and narratives of inevitable decline are equally as unconvincing. Neither technological saviors nor environmental collapses are guaranteed. The only thing that is certain is change itself. An archaeological approach that draws on the past, but orientates to the future, cannot help but recognize this.

Change is something the nuclear waste itself understands, as it shifts and decays, interacting with the material properties of the sites where it is located, yet this happens at very different rates. Some isotopes will decay quickly, and others will take much longer. Sites for depositing nuclear waste are built in places that are highly geologically stable; the aim is to avoid placing them in a location where an earthquake might open them up to the environment. Thinking about nuclear waste can thus draw on another archaeological skill, that is, thinking about how landscapes involve multiple, overlapping kinds of time (Harris 2021b; Lucas 2021). Visit any archaeological site, and you become attuned to the different temporalities around you: the sound of trowels scraping at that very moment, the distant pasts emerging into the light of the present, the discussions of memories of campfire songs the night before, the shade being cast down from the hill scored by ice flows millennia old, and the wall built only a century ago. So, dealing with nuclear waste and the wider challenge of the Anthropocene needs an archaeological mentality that embraces the multi-scalar nature of time, conceptualizes past, present, and future as both laid out in order and folded together, and thinks of a world where the past—whether archaeological feature or toxic nuclear waste—can be re-encountered both deliberately and unexpectedly. The message from archaeological sites is not the one that the designers of WIPP thought—that they endure statically and pass on eternal meanings—but rather something quite different: that they constantly change, transform, and fold multiple layers of time within them.

If archaeological engagements with futurity and time offer important intellectual tools to wrestle with nuclear waste, our discipline also allows us to think through this dangerous materiality in other dimensions as well, especially when we incorporate the ideas of affect introduced earlier. One of the fundamental questions raised by approaches to nuclear waste is not just how to communicate with human beings about dangers over huge timescales but *what kinds of human beings* might be around to receive these communications. Throughout this book, we have drawn on posthumanism to question the idea of humanist Man. We have tried to unpick the notion that a single united concept of the human can act as an umbrella for all the wonderful variations our species displays. Of course, if this is true for the 300,000 years for which *Homo sapiens* have occupied the globe, then it is equally true looking at humans over the next 100,000 years. Our engagement with posthumanism throughout this book has taught us that we cannot rest on the notion that there is a single "something," an "essence," if you like, that defines us. An emphasis on affect, however, offers something different. As we saw earlier, ideas of affect ask us to reflect on how bodies press into one another, and how they change one another. Rather than concentrating on what bodies *are* or what they *have*, thinking about affect makes us concentrate on bodies' capacities for acting and feeling, on what bodies can, or could, *do* (O'Dell and Harris 2022). Rather than thinking about human beings as a particular kind of animal defined by a check-list of attributes, then, thinking through affect creates an open approach to what it means to be human, one that celebrates the different relations and connections we can forge (cf. Dawney et al. 2017, 114).

Leila Dawney and colleagues have considered how this approach to humanity relates to how we think about and consider nuclear waste (Dawney et al. 2017). By thinking through how specific materials and bodies come together, they explore how we can think about a sense of commonality and a duty of care across such huge timespans without falling back on an eternal, transcendent, and exclusionary vision of Man. When we think through both nuclear waste and the materials that are needed to contain it, we are inevitably drawn to the qualities of those materials and the effects they have on each other. These include how, at sites like the waste repository of ONKALO in Finland, the material properties of everything from the gneiss bedrock in which it is built to the bentonite clay poured in by the makers prevent isotopes like Uranium 238 from leaching out into the world. These different non-human bodies—stone, clay, nuclear waste—bring certain capacities to bear. They have their own affects and their own capacities, which emerge in relation to one another. Human bodies in the future will also have their own capacities to act and to be acted upon, to affect and to be affected. Just as when we look back as archaeologists and think of human bodies in the past, when we look forward, we can imagine their capacity to move, to feel, and to engage with the world. These are not fixed eternal properties but capacities that we can postulate. This is the same as when we write about the past, creating connections with past humans and writing about what their bodies could do by exploring the worlds they occupied. What anchors both our understanding of the past and the future are the materials that humans live within. These are the non-humans that help guide and shape them, that affect them, and are affected by them. In this case, these materials include the stones that protect and enclose the waste, as well as the waste itself. Just as we saw when we considered how archaeologists build concepts of truth out of multiple connections in Chapter 7, here we can conceptualize how archaeologists thinking of future humans can build maps of the different capacities they might have and use these to foster relations of care for the people of the future (Dawney et al. 2017, 125). This can help us develop a relation of care that challenges us in the world of the Anthropocene today.

From Potterne to the WIPP and ONKALO, archaeology helps us to think about the future and, specifically, a future shaped by climate crisis. Archaeology can help us think about how humans will remain sites of affective potential and about how specific bodies and certain kinds of materials bring connections into being. Archaeology shows us that even the things we think we have disposed of do not really disappear—they are part of the compost from which the future emerges (cf. Tsing 2015). Finally, archaeology shows us how the future, like the past, is never certain and how any trajectory can change and shift through time. All of this might seem unsettling for attempts to generate a singular solution to marking the locations of nuclear waste, working out what to do with our ocean full of drift, or how to get rid of our waste materials; instead, perhaps, it is radically hopeful. Change and risk are always present, but it is unlikely by hiding away from our past that we will be able to change our future. Rather, it is by embracing the thoroughly emergent quality of a humanity that is forged not by an ideal checklist but by understanding the question, "what can a human body do?" that we can create a space where a conversation with our future does not depend on a shared notion of humanist Man that rules out so many members of our species, past, present, and future (Dawney et al. 2017, 120). Fundamentally, by approaching the future as archaeologists of the present—not imagined archaeologists of the future—we can begin to think through how this complex material puzzle can be safely engaged with, both today and tomorrow.

Conclusion

Facing the future creates a problem for the settler colonist and for former colonizing societies of Euro-America. Climate crisis rears its head. The Anthropocene positions human beings as both agents of geological transformation and ever closer to being victims of environmental destruction. Yet, in the face of these challenges, we seem utterly inadequate. Rows rage over statues, refugees driven from their homes (by those very processes we refuse to confront) are turned away, wars rage, and yet we remain acquiescent. As Walter Benjamin (2003, 394) noted, the spirit of radical resistance is much more likely to be motivated by ideas of enchained ancestors than liberated grandchildren. So, pushing over a statue of a slave owner raises far more media revulsion than a proposal to open a new coal mine. Clearly, our ways of thinking need to change. For "mainstream subjects," the climate crisis is a moment of despair as we confront our frailty, yet for others, that moment of despair has been ongoing for centuries; Black, Indigenous, LGBTQI+, and other communities, for example, have lived through violent processes that aimed to destroy them (Braidotti 2022, 27). In the face of despair, we keep going, we turn anger into activism, and we do the work.

   As ecofeminists have shown us, new ways of thinking cannot rest on old divisions of nature and culture. Nor, as Indigenous thinkers emphasize, can they simply impose a one-size version of humanity onto the world. Such approaches, such failures to get outside of the ways we have been taught to think, will never really undo the traps that our traditions and our concepts create for us. They will, in the end, lead us back to an inevitable logic where our only hope is that somehow something—AI, new technology, capitalism—can save us, despite all the evidence that this logic (and faith) is what has brought about our potential demise.

   Here archaeology can offer a different way forward, and not just as a model of the past to learn from or as a call to an older or simpler way of life. Instead, archaeology can lead us to a way of approaching the future that suggests other ways of thinking might have something to offer. Archaeology demands that we think about time as multi-scalar; in our day jobs, we need to move from the moment that a pit was dug via the histories of a site's occupation to the patterns of process that shaped a society or an economy or a way of life over a millennium or more. As we saw with nuclear waste, such an approach moves us away from seeing a singular time and moves us toward embracing the multiple temporalities of which the world is made. With the wider challenges of the Anthropocene, this means we can think both about the small-scale moments of change we can make every day and the wider transformations that need to happen simultaneously; the former, no longer unachievable, the latter, no longer pointless.

This draws on the inevitability of change that archaeology shows us to be the one real thing on which we can rely (Crellin 2020). Just as narratives of progress that underlay thinking from the Victorian era through the twentieth century are overly simplistic, so narratives today of inevitable decline present a single trajectory that cannot, from an archaeological perspective, be taken seriously. This means the future is open, that it can still be changed, and, as Zoë Crossland (2014b, 127) has argued, that it needs as much attention as the material conditions we inherit. Finally, when we take an archaeological perspective, one that rejects simple ideas of eternal humanist Man, we can find a new way of connecting with the humans who lived in the past and, importantly for the Anthropocene, the humans of the future, too. Approaching human beings as a site of possibility, of potential, always emerging through and alongside all kinds of non-human allies, allows us to think through the worlds of the future and the work we can do to make those worlds as hospitable and caring as possible. A vision of futurity written with an archaeological eye can help us see a future for humanity, a future for the people yet to come, without anthropocentrism, and that might be the only future we can hope to realize.

Chapter 10

Building an archaeology for today and tomorrow

A conclusion

Introduction

Ask an archaeologist to define their discipline, and you will get a host of answers, but most will tell you that it has something to do with the past and something to do with material things. Most, probably all, archaeologists hope that their work isn't *just* self-indulgence. Whether they believe that preserving the past, in situ or as a record, is good in and of itself, whether they extoll the way archaeology boosts tourism, or whether they believe archaeology can be a therapeutic practice for the traumatized, most practicing archaeologists don't think of their discipline as solipsistic navel-gazing. For us, archaeology can be, and is, good because of all those things. But we also think that archaeology has something else to offer. Archaeology roots around in every corner of the globe and in all periods, stretching from the first use of stone tools to the production of junk in space and the construction of nuclear waste repositories. It brings together complex ideas from philosophy, on the one hand, with physics, on the other, along with every other discipline in between. It asks us to attempt to think about worlds that were radically different from our own and to build understandings of them from the fractions that remain behind. It is a discipline that asks you to look at, and attend to, the humblest materials—broken pottery sherds, abandoned clay pipes, fragmented animal bones, flakes of flint—and to think about why they matter and what they tell us. At the same time, archaeology asks us to shed our assumptions about what it means to be human, about what counts as "normal," and about what the possibilities of a past world might be. In this book, we suggest that, by drawing on contemporary theoretical trends in posthumanist feminism, new materialism, and more, we can use archaeology to say something new not just about the past but about the place of humans and nonhumans in worlds past, present, and future.

In this final chapter, we offer a summary of how our core chapters (Chapters 2–9) engage with the key themes of this book and how they explore why thinking like an archaeologist can help us reorient to the challenges that we face in the present and will face in the future. In each case, we focus on how the conjunction of objects *and* concepts, materials *and* theory, allows us to think in new ways. Following the summaries, we conclude the book by turning to two critical issues:

DOI: 10.4324/9781003244141-10

first, the role of our bête noire in this volume, humanist Man; and second, how our arguments for a more-than-human archaeology connect with broader calls, both in archaeology and in the wider world, to decolonize.

Object lessons

In each of the previous chapters, we argued that one can productively rethink contemporary issues and problems by engaging with them using archaeological tools. For us, what makes these tools archaeological is that they are one part theoretical—they draw on specific theoretical concepts and critiques—and one part material—they draw on objects, architecture, landscapes, and the *stuff* that surrounds us. As archaeologists, our skills lie in thinking through how things, theories, histories, and memories connect and shape our abilities to understand the world. In this book, we interwove things and theory to think through contemporary problems.

In Chapter 2, we explored how movement is understood in different ways in both the past and the present. We tried to understand a particular problem: why is it that movement for some people is celebrated, and for others it is decried, denied, and transformed into an all too often fatal exercise? The key object featured in Chapter 2's case study is the landscape of the Sonoran Desert. Drawing on Jason De León's (2015) work, we thought about how the heat of the desert, its form, and its material qualities shaped movement and killed some of those that moved through it. We looked at the material culture that marked the bodies of those who traversed it, the black clothes they wear, and the black water bottles from which they drink. To understand how this works, we drew on assemblage theory, which emphasizes how all things, human beings included, emerge in specific sets of relationships, both material and meaningful. The material components bring certain properties—the black clothes are said to hide the migrant while making their bodies hotter and more likely to succumb to the heat—and certain meanings—for border patrol agencies, dark clothing marks people as potential migrants. By starting with more than humans and by refusing to be *anthropocentric,* we were able to think through these acts of movement differently. A second, related, theoretical tool was key here. Alongside being post-anthropocentric and recognizing the role of non-humans in *all* forms of human movement, we drew on concepts from posthumanism to critique the notion of humanist "Man." Standard humanist ideals raise a specific version of humanity up to a pinnacle and then compare all others to that; from this perspective, it is little wonder that the bodies of those who are not the ideal—White, male, heterosexual, able-bodied, and so on—find their movements monitored, limited, and curtailed, often fatally. In bringing together the objects of the desert and the materials that move across it, with concepts of assemblage theory and posthumanism, we can begin to see why movements in the past and present are conceptualized so differently and why some forms are celebrated while others prove deadly.

In Chapter 3, we introduced readers to the site of Turbo Island in Bristol, UK, a place where the homeless community of the city gathered and, thus, a place where archaeologists Rachael Kiddey and John Schofield (2009, 2010, 2011) organized excavations in collaboration with homeless colleagues. In November 2022, archaeologist Brodhie Molloy told us that she had seen a video on TikTok showing that Turbo Island was being concreted over. This part of the city, abandoned by capitalism and deemed useful only as a site for a billboard, had seen increased "anti-social" behavior, thought to be related to changes in drug dealing (Bennett 2022). Fences were erected to block access, but people pulled them down and lit fires, which spread to the billboard. How did we end up in this situation? The owners, with support from the police and local residents, decided to modify the site in ways that reduced its potential for "anti-social" behavior (Bennett 2022); this included concreting over the area, giving it a sloping form, and installing anti-homeless benching. To the homeless community, however, this supposed location of anti-social behavior was an important part of their landscape and community—a place with a specific homeless heritage. In short, from these perspectives, Turbo Island was not a non-place to be erased and covered over.[1] The history of Turbo Island captures the ideas laid out in Chapter 3. We argued that capitalism was best approached as a set of flows; money, commodities, people, and materials flow in and out of different parts of the city (cf. Deleuze and Guattari 2013). Where these flows fail, spaces abandoned by mainstream capitalism emerge, in turn, creating spaces for people who have been left behind by capitalism, like homeless people. As with our argument in Chapter 3, rather than turn to the Marxist idea of ideology to explain why the owners of Turbo Island chose to concrete over the site, we can use the Deleuzo-Guattarian concept of desire. The owners were not duped into changing the site; they wanted it changed. Equally, the homeless community was not duped into thinking this place was important to them. These different communities are viewed in very different ways structured by the figure of humanist Man. In Chapter 3, we considered how those left behind by capitalism come to be cast as outside of society and distanced from the "norm."

Rather than conceive of leaders only as humans that *do* things to other humans, Chapter 4 prompted new questions about leadership and power. Beginning with the notion that *leaders make you part of their projects*, it charted a path for a more-than-human reframing that inspires us to think differently about the present and the future. There exist important alternatives to dusty narratives of the "silverback" leader who wrests control of the group. For us, power always involves *both potestas* (the negative and repressive aspects of power) and *potentia* (the positive and productive ones). This claim is not the same as neoliberal arguments about how everyone can change the world or become powerful leaders if they only choose to do so; here, we must remember the structural inequalities highlighted in Chapter 3. Just because someone wants to be a leader or wants to have more power, that doesn't guarantee success. This is because leadership and power, like many things discussed in this book, are relational. They depend on much more than human will and intention. Considerations of leadership and power must therefore consider non-humans, such as Bronze Age knife-daggers, burial mounds, and statues. Taking a case study from Bronze Age Britain, we argued that certain barrows and knife-daggers, like certain humans, draw people into their projects, leading the way. We discussed non-humans likely inspiring people to bury their dead in particular ways. The knife-dagger's potential *potestas* is obvious—it is a weapon that can do damage and help the silverback take control. Yet, its possible *potentia* is also important to consider—it can do things that were not possible before its existence, such as metaphorically performing a cut between the living and the dead in a ritual or ceremony. Here, leadership is not the sole domain of the human, nor is power monopolized by certain forms of human that exert their will on the rest of the group.

In some ways developing thematically from our knife-dagger in Chapter 4, Chapter 5 turned to violence and explored how it manifests historically. Setting aside unhelpful debates about the origins of violence or whether it is endemic to human beings or not, we explored the historically emergent way violence works. To do this, rather than drawing a hard and fast line between humans and non-humans, we set out how a post-anthropocentric account of violence demonstrates how non-humans can carry out and receive violence and help provoke violence in differing contexts. Archaeologists like Pamela Graves (2008) showed us how specific non-humans can be targeted for violence in specific ways and at specific times. Through Gilles Deleuze's (2004) concepts of the virtual and the actual, we explored how much more complicated violence is than the simple act itself. Violence isn't just the moment you get punched or stabbed; it lies in the threat of violence that accompanies a stranger waving a knife or a gun. This also gives us a means to understand how violence varies depending on who you are and how the potential, or the virtual capacity, for violence to occur changes depending on the context. The potential for violence is different for a woman walking through a dark street than it is for a man, or for a Black man engaging with a police officer than it is for a White woman. Our major case study looked at how understanding violence as both virtual and actual can offer a very different understanding of why the Indigenous Californian settlement of Puhú was attacked in the nineteenth century. Drawing on Nathan Acebo's (2020) analysis, we saw how it was not the actual actions of the villagers that provoked violent repression but the way their success, their *thriveance*, produced new virtual capacities to resist colonialism. This, in turn, shifted the relations with settler colonists, helping to actualize the Euro-colonial capacity for devastating violence. Throughout this chapter, we sought to show that making space for different ways of thinking about violence—about why it is carried out, by whom and to whom, how it involves non-humans and is both virtual as well as actual—doesn't stop us "blaming" individuals for their actions. What it does, though, is challenge us to recognize the historical complexity that explaining violence calls for. To understand why violence happens in the past, why it happens today, and why it might happen in the future, this more nuanced and archaeological understanding is essential.

In Chapter 6, we addressed difference. We developed our argument rooted in the masses of material culture that archaeologists find, organize, clean, study, and care for through their work. How do we tell different objects apart? How do we group them together? We considered one of the most basic acts of archaeology: the process of typologizing, which relies on comparison. We asked how we could rethink these acts of comparison that traditionally create an ideal and label everything that differs from that ideal as *less than*. By building the connections between processes of typologizing objects and those of classifying people, we aimed to highlight how the process of comparison is never neutral and is, all too often, highly damaging. When we compare, we often create an ideal, from the ideal arrowhead to the ideal Beaker pot. From there, it is only a short distance to the ideal human—humanist Man. To demonstrate this further, we turned to our material—anthropomorphic figurines from Teotihuacan in Mexico. On the one hand, these fragments of figurines must be sorted so they can be studied; on the other hand, that act typically focuses on the classification of bodies as male or female. We used Kiri Hagerman's (2018) analysis of these figurines as the basis for our discussion. We drew on the Deleuzian concept of difference and Rosi Braidotti's (2022) emphasis on positive difference that flows from that. Difference in this way of thinking is not about *lack* from an ideal but instead about how difference is productive. By shifting our focus from what one thing lacks, we instead emphasized how the differences between objects or people make new things possible. The differences between things are not bad, rather, they are foundational; difference is what drives our world and produces diversity.

Chapter 7 considered truth claims, asking, first, how archaeologists know the past and, second, how thinking archaeologically makes sense in an increasingly "post-truth" world. To address these challenges, we turned to the science of fingerprint matching. The often-invisible traces of sweat and dirt that our fingertips leave upon the surfaces we touch in our daily lives have the power to sway jurors and send people to jail. But even this "objective" form of pattern matching is not independent of the expert who makes the match, nor as clear-cut as many might think. Zoë Crossland's (2018) brilliant analysis of this process shows the many interpretive leaps inherent within it. Fingerprint matching includes gaps and imperfections, and approaches to "dealing" with these ambiguities are standardized differently between countries. Theoretically, this means that the "truth" of fingerprint matching differs from one country to the next! Moreover, as feminist scholars like Donna Haraway remind us, a particular fingerprint analyst's place in the world (their positionality) also determines how they define and practice objectivity, how they make interpretive leaps, and more. For us, this does *not* mean that we can simply disregard arguments that use evidence or that we should ignore appeals to a material world that exists independently from our minds and thoughts. Instead, we argued that we must approach truth claims as relationally emergent. In other words, we argued for an approach that looks critically at the connections between analyst and analyzed and between different forms of contextualized evidence. When considered as relationally emergent, different truths can be compared and sorted into stronger versus weaker claims. This process is highly familiar to archaeologists, many of whom assemble pasts using multiple lines of evidence, recognizing the limitations of their methods and data and, less frequently, recognizing their positionalities in the world.

In Chapter 8, we extended the line of questioning from Chapter 7 but took it in a different direction. Instead of considering claims that the Earth is flat, for example, and scrutinizing how we could possibly sort different truth claims as stronger versus weaker, we focused on how we might learn from—and work with—people who have different experiences, knowledges, and ontologies than ours. This type of collaboration and learning seems like it is on the decline in the twenty-first century when much of the western world feels increasingly fraught and polarized. On a daily, if not hourly, basis, the social media feeds and news headlines that we encounter seem to scream to us, "If you're not with us, you're against us!" What does archaeology (and the broader world) become if we embrace multiplicity and open ourselves up to historically marginalized perspectives, such as those of Black Feminists or Indigenous peoples? What if, as we discussed in Chapter 8, we become more open-minded when we are told that Figure 8.3 shows a photograph of a chief and his family who turned to stone during a flood? More than this, what if we work to create a discipline that doesn't fixate on whether the photograph shows a chief and his family or a collection of stones but rather prioritizes creating ways of doing archaeology where both knowledge systems and ontologies can coexist while learning from one another and from the lands that they work upon? Posthumanist discussions of positive difference (see also Chapter 6) and anthropological and archaeological discussions of the ontological turn and radical alterity joined together with the archaeological examples we considered, showing the strength of embracing multiplicity and the insights that thinking archaeologically might offer the wider world.

Perhaps the most profound of the challenges facing people today and tomorrow reared its head in Chapter 9: the Anthropocene. We looked at how many understandings of this new geological epoch rest on underexplored tensions which divide humans from the world, and culture from nature, even as they seek to explain the impact that our species has had on the planet. Similarly, the proposed solutions, from technological wizardry to rewilding, rely on outdated, idealized, and dualistic notions that we can get back to the past, return to nature, or that, magically, our culture and our intellect will create a solution. In place of this, we looked at how ecofeminist and Indigenous thinkers present alternative ways of conceptualizing how humans are always and forever caught up in the world and how this represents a much more honest starting point for any debate about how to face these challenges. Indigenous thinkers also remind us, once again, of the importance of difference—differences in who we are and differences in the impact we have made on the planet. We then looked at how archaeological approaches to futurity and affect could add to these approaches. These offer important tools to help provide ways into the problems we face without reaching for a mythologized past or a miracle future. Our case study on waste, and nuclear waste specifically, looked at how attending to these materials as archaeologists can help. Waste poses specific challenges to the future, like forms of heritage, it endures and asks questions of how people in the future will respond. Nuclear waste makes this especially potent because of how long it lasts and how dangerous it is. Our approach suggested that rather than worrying about how to communicate meaning long into the future (which archaeology shows is a rather hopeless endeavor), we are better off thinking about how materials and humans *affect* each other. How might human bodies in the future be affected by the materials we leave behind, and what can we do to develop a relationship of care today toward those future bodies? Archaeologists are well placed to appreciate how materials and humans change through time, both together and apart, and to deploy this to work with those changes rather than to try and fix a meaning, or fix what it is to be human, in the past, the present, or the future. Perhaps surprisingly, this acceptance of change brings with it a message of hope. While we cannot be certain what the future will bring, we can be confident it will not be the same as today; the future remains open—it can be realized differently.

Working with, against, and around humanist Man

In many of the chapters summarized here, we oppose our ways of thinking to the character of humanist Man. He is a leitmotif, and you might feel that he appears to be the scapegoat for many of the problems explored throughout the book. From structuring how we think about homelessness and migration to shaping who is more or less likely to be a leader or the presumed victim or perpetrator of violence, humanist Man seems to play a role in much of the injustice going on across the world. On one level, of course, this character is a gross simplification of ours—a strawman to burn down or a windmill to tilt at. Scholars who study the complexities of humanism itself would flag how, in its early stages, humanism's goal was not to universalize or codify a single concept of humanity; instead, it began as a means of undermining all-encompassing religious claims, opening them to critique for the first time in a long time (Tully 2008, 104–5). This form of classical humanism sought to rewrite the rulebook of how we could conceptualize and understand human existence (Tully 2008, 141). Yet increasingly, humanism has diverted from the radical possibilities of this initial model, moving away from questions about the underlying rules of how things work. Instead, an alternative set of boundaries has been drawn around a figure of Man, no longer given by God but now set by the standards of a small, privileged sub-section of our own species. As Michel Foucault (1988, 15) put it, "What I am afraid of about humanism is that it presents a certain form of ethics as a universal model for any kind of freedom." It is this universalizing essentialism we have coded as humanist Man in this book, and it is this critical, and increasingly dominant, element of humanist thought that our posthumanist approach seeks to critique.

The character of humanist Man is deployed in several different ways. We can use humanist Man as a tool to identify the shortcomings of our thinking, writing, and researching. By considering how thoughts and actions in our world are often unthinkingly structured by this ideal, we can use it to effectively "check ourselves." Does, for example, the argument we are making, the way we are working, or how we are thinking frame and present some forms of humanity as better than others? Are our arguments shaped by an ideal figure, and do they cast difference as negative rather than positive (see Chapter 6)? Have we accidentally imposed this modernist, negative, and damaging framework onto the past when it has no place?

We can also use humanist Man as an emancipatory tool. This is done by working to create a world that is no longer shaped in his image, rejecting universalizing and essentialist models of humanity, making space for others, and appreciating our manifold differences—not as a negative lack, but instead as productive forces. We aim for a world where humanist Man is no longer the yardstick, the measure, or the ideal. We can work each day, in tiny steps, to make that world come about. We aim to produce a world where different forms of humanity, different kinds of dwelling, and different types of knowledge are valued, where what defines the human is not fixed but *always in motion.*

This does not mean, however, that posthumanism as a theoretical approach, or humanist Man as a character, has nothing to say to times and places where there was no equality. Posthumanism is not (only) about a future utopia where we are all valued for our differences; it is a critical theoretical tool. For those studying worlds where people were not treated as equals, where slavery existed, or where some humans were seen as less-than, posthumanism still provides a critical edge. Eva Mol's (2023) recent work exploring Roman slavery and ontology from a posthumanist perspective demonstrates this neatly. By recalling the character of humanist Man and taking a posthumanist perspective, we can think about the processes through which people are Othered, their differences are made to be negative, and how—through material, symbolic, and discursive action—certain forms of people are systematically and structurally devalued. We can use the flat ontology that posthumanism begins with as a heuristic device here: start with a world where we do not presume to know the differences between humans and other-than-humans in advance and look for the archaeological evidence that points to particular kinds of human, or specific animals, or rocks, for example, being elevated above others. We can think about the specifics of our archaeological evidence and use it to build understandings of past worlds that are radically different to ours—where the ontological pyramid might have cows at the top, or pregnant women, or where some types of humans are valued less than pots, currency, or animals.

Humanist Man is not about a set of fixed identity categories. The kinds of posthumanist feminist approaches that we draw upon in this book wholeheartedly reject notions of fixed identity categories and focus instead on how we are always changing and thus moving in and out of categories. No one is a middle-aged man forever. This is not an exercise that puts people in a set hierarchy of disadvantage (or difference) for all their lives. Rather we can think about the different aspects of our identities as in motion. We might become more-or-less able-bodied through time. As our relations with capitalism change, we might find ourselves unfortunate enough to be experiencing homelessness. We may equally find ourselves lucky enough to gain more education. The fraught and toxic debates about the lives of trans people show that as we shift categories, how we are treated also shifts. In specific circumstances, we might find ourselves to be nearer or further from the idealized version of humanity. This makes our relationship to humanist Man partly a matter of situatedness; a person can take the central, powerful, authoritative identity in relation to one set of people or in one context, but find themselves isolated, disempowered, and disenfranchised in another.

Non-human materials form key components in the world of humanist Man. Humanist Man is not just a concept. It is made real, material, and structurally intransient every day through thousands of actions and processes: it is the non-human swimsuit or burka that flags particular bodies as more or less distant from the ideal; it is particular forms of bathrooms and buses that make people more or less able-bodied in certain situations; and it is extractive capitalism that turns certain forms of non-human (e.g., oil, gas, and water) and certain kinds of bodies (e.g., missing and murdered Indigenous women and girls) into disposable resources that can be turned into capital. Our posthumanist and new materialist approaches demonstrate the power of the non-human and the frailty of it—some non-humans uphold and sustain systems of inequality, and others are extracted and destroyed carelessly. Just as human subjects are varied and changing in their nature, never universal or essentialized, so are non-humans. Contrary to some claims, posthumanist and new materialist approaches could never be apolitical. They are political to their core and form a key part of any ethical moves we might make to build better worlds of today and tomorrow. This is why the move to post-anthropocentrism is not just an ontological shift but an essentially ethical one as well.

Decolonization and more-than-human archaeologies

A desert. A homeless encampment. A knife-dagger. A fallen monument. A figurine. A fingerprint. A *Wak'a*. A decaying house in the wake of a nuclear disaster.

These are the things we choose to think with as we look to the past, the present, and the future, and as our discussion shows, these things are always enmeshed in politics. We argue that with fresh and increased attention to what these things are, what these things do, and the differences that they make in the world, new and helpful orientations to the problems of today and tomorrow emerge. Throughout the book, though, we also emphasized our concerns about what some readers will gloss as "human issues," peoples' struggles involving migration, homelessness, inequality, violence, racism, alternative facts, collaboration, and climate crisis. Except for the climate crisis, many readers might conceive of these issues as "purely human" matters. Unfortunately, the world we live in tends to divide its problems as if we must focus on one thing or the other. Is it things that we are concerned with, or is it humans? This is precisely the problem that we have been trying to pick apart in the last nine chapters. As many thinkers before us have noted, it isn't one or the other; it is almost always both. To affect real change, we must dwell upon the complicated relationships, dependencies, and affordances that cut through and obliterate distinctions like "human" versus "non-human." To begin thinking about our world and the world of the future in new ways, it is necessary to reject the binary, reductionist, and transcendent thinking (see previous chapters) inherent in the question posed earlier. In other words, concern over social issues (or "human" matters) always involves non-humans and non-living matter. This means that concerns over humanist Man are intimately wrapped up with concerns about anthropocentrism. Here, we explore this connection one last time as a means of conclusion.

Within the discipline of archaeology, most practitioners aren't writing about migration, homelessness, or crime scenes. Instead of writing more on these topics, let us take an issue that should be familiar to many of our readers—calls to decolonize our discipline and the world more broadly (e.g., Atalay 2006a; Smith 2012; Steeves 2015, 2021; Tuck and Yang 2012; Wilson 2020). Decolonization efforts have long been a part of archaeologies practiced in certain parts of the world (e.g., Australia), but they have exploded and morphed into global concerns over the last three years. The murder of George Floyd on May 25, 2020, and the civic unrest that followed (Flewellen et al. 2021; Franklin et al. 2020; Questions Worth Asking Symposium 2023), forced many to reckon with calls for decolonization (and for social justice, more broadly). We discussed adjacent issues in Chapter 8, but it is necessary here to provide some additional context.

Archaeological discussions of decolonization emerged around a few key issues that resonate with many of the themes explored throughout this book. For the sake of brevity, we limit our discussion to four general points. First, most archaeologists bear a striking resemblance to the character of humanist Man. In other words, most archaeologists are White, western, cis-gendered, and able-bodied. Many, especially in senior positions, are also men. Second, archaeologists often study pasts that are not their own, building careers by writing about some other group's archaeological heritage. Third, archaeology has historically done a bad job of incorporating descendant community knowledge and expertise and an even worse job of respecting descendant community sensitivities and needs. We offered an example of this in Chapter 5, with our discussion of Zuni Ahayu:da (War gods) and Zuni perspectives on the violence of traditional museum and archaeological collecting practices. Fourth, descendant communities face a multitude of structural disadvantages (cf. Chapter 3), including disadvantages that make becoming an archaeologist or attending a university impossible for some. In a nutshell, decolonization asks that archaeologists address these inequities, carefully consider new and different forms of knowledge, and make space for under-represented groups to reshape or even remake archaeology as they see fit (cf. discussion of situated knowledge in Chapter 8).

What if we were to respond to these critiques by bifurcating the world into humans and non-humans? For us and for many readers, this isn't truly possible, but let's consider it briefly, nonetheless. Let's think back to our opening example from Chapter 1, the #noDAPL movement (Estes 2019), and consider a hypothetical example. Envision an archaeologist working on ancestral Oceti Sakowin Oyate (also called the Sioux Nation) lands who decides that they want to decolonize their archaeological practices. They are starting late since they are already working on the land, but what options do they have?

One thing they could do, a deceptively simple option, is to stop digging archaeological sites and writing about the archaeology in that area. This solution partially addresses the second point, but to understand the situation better, we would need to look to the non-human world; for example, such a decision has a host of financial and professional (read material) implications since the archaeologist works at a university. Another option might be to approach representatives of the Oceti Sakowin Oyate Nation, asking them for feedback, questioning them about their understandings of the past, or asking how their nation could use archaeology to address its own interests and concerns. This solution partially addresses the second and third points, but again, as we look further into the issues, non-humans show up again. The archaeologist gives gifts of tobacco to the community representatives, walks across landscapes as they discuss the archaeology, and holds archaeological materials as they converse. The university has also sent a photographer to capture some images of these discussions for the new DEIJ (Diversity, Equity, Inclusion, and Justice) section of their website! Non-humans abound here.

Perhaps a different perspective will help—one that is set to address some of the other concerns listed earlier. What about the university's perspective? Let's suppose the university found some extra funding to hire a member of the Oceti Sakowin Oyate Nation who will conduct research on their own lands and teach archaeology courses. The funding comes from a large oil company or another corporation that has a history of extractive and environmentally destructive practices. This solution partially addresses the first three points, but since no material changes were made at the university (e.g., to the ways that tenure cases are judged), the new faculty member struggles and ultimately ends up leaving the university. All of this is not to mention the oil company in the background, still doing what oil companies do while meeting some of its philanthropic goals. The point here with these over-the-top hypotheticals is that it is difficult (if not impossible) to come up with a way around our four key issues when we only make decolonization a "human" matter.

What is the alternative? Remember, contrary to popular belief (even in some archaeological circles) it isn't a matter of simply eliminating the trowels, sifter screens, or the boxes used to uncover, pack, and transport archaeological materials away from Indigenous lands. The alternative that we propose involves assemblages—relational constellations of humans and non-humans working together and doing things that each could not do on their own. If you want to change institutions, if you want to dismantle structural inequality, those things require paying non-humans their due. We can cease work in the area. We can talk with descendant communities. We can diversify the faculty. But none of those things eliminates the institutional problems listed. The first point—that archaeology overrepresents and underrepresents certain categories of people—requires careful attention to everything from wealth distributions, healthcare, access to clean water, histories of colonialism, and the inter-generational trauma that settler colonialism perpetuates.

Thus far, though, this is likely an uncontroversial and possibly banal argument for most readers. "Yes, of course, non-human things are important!" say the people who spend their careers toiling in the dirt to find minute material traces of past human lives. But this is not the end of the argument. For us, the dangers lie in assuming that, at all times and in all places, humans are fundamentally different and separate from the worlds in which they dwell. Some might call this stance "human exceptionalism" (paralleling Alfred Gell's (1998) influential approach, where humans are primary, and everything else is secondary, see Harris and Cipolla 2017). This type of transcendent, universalized, and commonsensical approach is exactly what we've been scrutinizing in the previous nine chapters. With this challenge in mind, let's consider repatriation, a key component of many decolonization efforts. Do we want a model that breaks down all repatriation cases in terms of primary (human) and secondary (non-human) agents? Such an approach would overlook many instances where repatriated ancestral objects hold power and memory for their Indigenous groups, allowing those groups to do things they literally could not do apart from those non-human things. This is clear in the many examples where museum objects prompt new forms of learning, cultural revitalization, and more in their ancestral communities (e.g., Bruchac 2018; Colwell 2017; Magnani et al. 2018; Smith et al. 2016). Here, labels of primary versus secondary hold little weight or meaning.

Let's say our hypothetical archaeology department from above makes their diversity hire (using the oil company's money). The oil company leverages this bit of philanthropy with the press to draw attention away from the fact that, in the background, the company is also helping fund a new pipeline. The line goes in without a hitch but later ruptures and pollutes the groundwater for entire towns along its route. In this case, again, oil and water occupy a special position in their relations to humans. As the #noDAPL protestors insist, water is life. Breaking the problem down into primary and secondary, or human and non-human, doesn't get us very far. In doing this, we might identify the oil company's CEO as the main culprit behind this evil. The company dismisses them promptly and does the requisite media blitz about it, but the structure of the company and its extractive practices are allowed to continue. Same problem, different human. Or, more accurately, same assemblage, different "primary" agent in the lead. For us, any call for social justice or decolonization is a call for more-than-human approaches that move beyond the anthropocentrism that characterizes much of our world.

The Indigenous peoples driving the #noDAPL protests are very clear on the importance of relationships and of more-than-human worlds. As Kim Tallbear (2017, 87) noted, "Indigenous standpoints accord greater animacy to nonhumans, including nonorganisms, such as stones and places, which help form (indigenous) peoples as humans constituted in much more complex ways than in simply human biological terms." This raises the issue of cultural appropriation. The theories we've outlined throughout the book resemble some Indigenous worldviews and ontologies (e.g., Deloria 2001, 2012; Tallbear 2017; Todd 2016). Is this yet another example of appropriation? Have we employed our privileges to take credit for the thinking and brilliance of disenfranchised and colonized peoples? Tallbear (2017; see also Chapter 8) provides an excellent discussion of this general question in considering how new materialism compares with different Indigenous standpoints and knowledges. She argues that new materialism isn't so new, pointing out that it replicates many aspects of Indigenous metaphysics found in the writings of iconic thinkers like Vine Deloria Junior (e.g., 1997, 2001, 2012). Yet, she also notes some distinctions. The new materialist thinkers she cites take a "secular" materialist view of the world, whereas she is much more comfortable "enfolding spirits and souls into descriptions of the beingness of nonhumans" (Tallbear 2017, 191). She ultimately ascribes this distinction to the different statuses of knowledge and belief. Crucially, she (Tallbear 2017, 193, our parenthetical) notes:

> Now that theorists in a range of fields are seeking to dismantle those hierarchies (between nature and culture, human and non-human), we should remember that not everyone needs to summon a new analytical framework or needs to renew a commitment to "the vitality of [so-called] things." Indigenous standpoints that never constructed hierarchies in quite the same way can and should be at the forefront of this new ethnographic and theoretical work. We can converse with the existing work and bring additional insights.

We agree with this sentiment, but given our positionality as authors, we are hesitant to frame Indigenous thought as the solutions to the problems of our world and to the problems of the intellectual genealogies of the discipline we practice. Archaeologists come from many different backgrounds. For those of us trained in the dominant philosophical and theoretical schools, we can gain much from reading minor traditions of western thinking. From Braidotti to Deleuze, these thinkers offer us a means of escape from our uncritical habits of thought (Colebrook 2020, 347). Clearly, such escape will not be needed for our Indigenous colleagues already working outside the central tradition. In relation to Indigenous thought itself, it is not our (the authors') place to take ideas that are located in a specific location and attempt to universalize them; to do so would be another act of extraction (Crellin et al. 2021). This is not to say that Indigenous thought has nothing to offer or that White, western, archaeologists do not have much to learn from reading the work of, and listening to, our Indigenous colleagues. This means engaging with Indigenous ideas both with an attitude of care—care for the ideas and for those who teach us and care for the contexts in which they emerge. For us, as emphasized in Chapter 8, we gain the most when we emphasize how ideas come together as multiplicities— by working with different peoples and conversing across different ontologies. For these reasons, we also agree with Tallbear that new materialism is not precisely the same as certain Indigenous forms of metaphysics. We want to hold those differences, and sustain that multiplicity, all while attempting to avoid appropriation.

Conclusion: water is life, and archaeology has *something* to do with it

This book began by juxtaposing the seemingly clinical and ivory tower world of archaeology and archaeological theory to the world of the #noDAPL movement, an assemblage that includes protestors, riot squads, blood, sweat, police dogs, water cannons, and so much more. What does archaeology and archaeological theory have to do with it? In a word, the answer that this book argues is "much." There is great potential here, but to maximize that potential, we need to embrace new and different perspectives. We must think of archaeology as more than a "discipline of things" (Olsen et al. 2012), archaeology as more than political action or activism (e.g., Atalay et al. 2014; McGuire 2008), and think critically about how these two slogans intersect and mutate together.

Whilst archaeology can offer us "solutions" from the past or offer us lessons from which we can learn, whether in terms of adapting to climate change or running barefoot, that is *not* where the discipline's most powerful contribution lies. Archaeology teaches us how to build stories, narratives, and three-dimensional visions of worlds that used to be, worlds that are, and worlds that can be. Sliding deftly between the boundaries of other disciplines, archaeology drags your hands into the mud and your imagination up to the stars. By demanding we seek and create powerful new ways to understand the complex assemblages of humans and non-humans we investigate, archaeology challenges us to think differently, to imagine differently. When we combine that process with the powerful intellectual tools at our disposal, archaeology offers up a methodology for tackling all kinds of problems, not just those we have traditionally wrestled with ("why did people start farming?"), but those that challenge us in the present today ("how can we imagine better forms of leadership?").

Archaeology can make a unique contribution to these conversations because it requires us to think about more-than-human worlds. Much of the effort in archaeology has come in trying to bend and fix our data to make it match up to expectations: if only we had people to talk to like social anthropologists, if only we had texts to read like historians. The reality, though, is that archaeology's partial, fractured, and broken materials can train those who encounter it to allow humans and non-humans, materials and theories, methodologies and philosophies, to come together in ways that celebrate the different things that each of them bring to the table. The archaeology that humans write about echoes through the materials we encounter much more directly. Rather than a flaw, this virtue trains an archaeologist to see how the boundary between human and non-human shifts and varies and emerges contextually. Archaeology, for too long, has tried to bend itself to meet the standards of subjects which grandly position themselves as the equivalent of humanist Man, the Royal Sciences, as Deleuze and Guattari (2004, 405) call them. By embracing our more-than-human status as a nomadic subject, moving through time and space, archaeology can reveal itself as better placed than most to develop the tools needed to reconceptualize the issues we face today. Our problems are always both human and material, and our solutions will be too.

There are many ways to build better worlds both today and tomorrow. This book touches on a range of issues that we, the authors, feel strongly about. There is no single thing that we can do that will fix all of our problems. Moreover, most of the decisions one could make about trying to build a better world have complex and often unpredictable consequences. We can shift attitudes towards migrants and homeless people so they are seen as fully human, respected, and treated with dignity, but this will involve making more good homes for people to live in and putting in place specific and complex support mechanisms to allow people to thrive as they move to new places. Similarly, we can reduce our use of fossil fuels, but this requires us to develop better batteries to store energy, and this will undoubtedly come with unintended and unanticipated consequences. There are no simple solutions or easy fixes, but there are always ways to build better worlds. For us, the key to this is thinking about a radical form of caring, not just for the people we love or the people who look like us, but caring respectfully for those who are very different from us and extending that care to non-humans too. Animals, plants, places, weather systems, and nuclear waste all require care. As Braidotti (2020) highlights, we are all in this together—including the humans and non-humans that share planet Earth in this moment, as well as those yet to come. But we are *not* all the same, and we do not need to become the same or to be treated as if we are the same, to care for others and to value their contributions. Instead, we revel in the wonderful diversity of matter that shares our world and see the differences within it as productive forces. This, of course, makes care very complicated. Who and what we care for and how we choose to do it is complicated. Care is always an act of power—it comes both with *potentia* and *potestas*.

In the end, this is not a book of solutions, a how-to manual on what to do with the challenges we face. It is a book, though, that suggests that the first step to dealing with our contemporary problems is *not* to continue business as usual and *not* to think in terms of business as usual. To deal with the problems of today and tomorrow, our first step needs to be to attend to the differences around us, the complex and emergent powers that shape our world, and the roles of humans and non-humans in all of that. And that means thinking like an archaeologist.

Note

1 A similar process happened at another key site from Kiddey's research, referred to as the Bear Pit.

References cited

Acebo, N.P. 2020. *Re-Assembling Radical Indigenous Autonomy in the Alta California Hinterlands: Survivance at Puhú*. Unpublished Ph.D. Dissertation, Anthropology Department, Stanford University.

Agbe-Davies, A.S. 2015. *Tobacco, Pipes, and Race: Little Tubes of Mighty Power*. New York: Routledge.

Agbe-Davies, A.S. 2017. How to Do Things with Things, or, Are Blue Beads Good to Think? *Semiotic Review* 4, https://www.semioticreview.com/ojs/index.php/sr/article/view/12. Accessed June 21, 2023.

Alaimo, S., and S. Hekman. 2008. Introduction: Emerging Models of Materiality in Feminist Theory. In S. Alaimo and S. Hekman, eds., *Material Feminisms*. Pp. 1–19. Bloomington: Indiana University Press.

Alberti, B. 2013. Archaeology and Ontologies of Scale: The Case of Miniaturisation in First-Millennium Northwest Argentina. In B. Alberti, A.M. Jones, and J. Pollard, eds., *Archaeology After Interpretation: Returning Materials to Archaeological Theory*. Pp. 43–58. Walnut Creek, CA: Left Coast Press.

Alberti, B. 2014. Designing Body-Pots in the Formative La Candelaria Culture, Northwest Argentina. In E. Hallam and T. Ingold, eds., *Making and Growing: Anthropological Studies of Organisms and Artefacts*. Pp. 107–25. London: Ashgate.

Alberti, B., S. Fowles, M. Holbraad, Y. Marshall, and C. Witmore. 2011. "Worlds Otherwise": Archaeology, Anthropology, and Ontological Difference. *Current Anthropology* 52: 896–912.

Alberti, B., and Y. Marshall. 2009. Animating Archaeology: Local Theories and Conceptually Open-ended Methodologies. *Cambridge Archaeological Journal* 19: 144–56.

Aldred, O. 2021. *The Archaeology of Movement*. London: Routledge.

Allard, A., and C.N. Cipolla. 2021. Failure and Colonialism in the North American Fur Trade: The View from Riverine Assemblages. *Historical Archaeology* 55: 110–26.

Angelbeck, B., L. Borck, and M. Sanger. 2018. Anarchist Theory and Archaeology. In *Encyclopedia of Global Archaeology*. New York: Springer, https://doi.org/10.1007/978-3-319-51726-1_2627-1.

Angelbeck, B., and C. Grier. 2012. Anarchism and the Archaeology of Anarchic Societies: Resistance to Centralization in the Coast Salish Region of the Pacific Northwest Coast. *Current Anthropology* 53: 547–87.

Angelbeck, B., and J. Jones. 2018. Direct Actions and Archaeology: The Lil'wat Peoples Movement to Protect Archaeological Sites. *Journal of Contemporary Archaeology* 5: 213–32.

Appleby, J. 2013. Temporality and the Transition to Cremation in the Late Third Millennium to Mid Second Millennium BC in Britain. *Cambridge Archaeological Journal* 23: 83–97.

Arbeláez, A., and E. Mulholland. 2016. Interrupted Journeys: Drawings by Refugees at the Kara Tepe Camp, Lesvos, Greece. *Journal of Contemporary Archaeology* 3: 233–44.

Atalay, S. 2006a. Indigenous Archaeology as Decolonizing Practice. *American Indian Quarterly* 30: 280–310.

Atalay, S. 2006b. No Sense of the Struggle: Creating a Context for Survivance at the NMAI. *American Indian Quarterly* 30: 597–618.

Atalay, S. 2019. Can Archaeology Help Decolonize the Way Institutions Think? How Community-Based Research Is Transforming the Archaeology Training Toolbox and Helping to Transform Institutions. *Archaeologies* 15: 514–35.

Atalay, S., L.R. Clauss, R.H. McGuire, and J.R. Welch, eds. 2014. *Transforming Archaeology: Activist Practices and Prospects*. New York: Routledge.

Bailey, D.W. 2005. *Prehistoric Figurines: Representation and Corporeality in the Neolithic*. London: Routledge.

Bailey, D.W. 2013. Figurines, Corporeality, and the Origins of the Gendered Body. In D. Bolger, ed., *A Companion to Gender Prehistory*. Pp. 244–64. Chichester: Wiley-Blackwell.

Bailey, D.W., A. Cochrane, and J. Zambelli. 2010. *Unearthed: A Comparative Study of Jomon Dogu and Neolithic Figurines*. Norwich: Sainsbuty Centre for Visual Arts.

Balter, M. 2013. Archaeologists Say the 'Anthropocene' Is Here—But It Began Long Ago. *Science* 340: 261–2.

Bandy, M. 2013. Tiwanaku Origins and the Early Development: The Political and Moral Economy of a Hospitality State. In A. Vranich and C. Stanish, eds., *Visions of Tiwanaku*. Pp. 135–50. Los Angeles: Cotsen Institute of Archaeology.

Barad, K. 2007. *Meeting the Universe Halfway: Quantum Physics and the Entanglement of Matter and Meaning*. Durham, NC: Duke University Press.

Barkham, P. 2018. Dutch Rewilding Experiment Sparks Backlash as Thousands of Animals Starve. *The Guardian*, April 27, 2018, https://www.theguardian.com/environment/2018/apr/27/dutch-rewilding-experiment-backfires-as-thousands-of-animals-starve. Accessed June 21, 2023.

Baron-Cohen, S. 2009. Autism: The Empathizing–Systemizing (E-S) Theory. *Annals of the New York Academy of Sciences* 1156: 68–80.

Barras, C. 2019. Story of Most Murderous People of All Time Revealed in Ancient DNA. *New Scientist*, March 27, 2019, https://www.newscientist.com/article/mg24132230-200-story-of-most-murderous-people-of-all-time-revealed-in-ancient-dna/. Accessed June 9, 2023.

Barrett, J.C. 2021. *Archaeology and Its Discontents: Why Archaeology Matters*. London: Routledge.

Barton, C., ed. 2021. *Trowels in the Trenches: Archaeology as Social Activism*. Gainesville: University of Florida Press.

Bass, W. 1995. *Human Osteology: A Laboratory and Field Manual*, 4th ed. Columbia: Missouri Archaeological Society.

Battle-Baptiste, W. 2011. *Black Feminist Archaeology*. New York: Routledge.

Bayliss, A. 2009. Rolling Out Revolution: Using Radiocarbon Dating in Archaeology. *Radiocarbon* 51: 123–47.

Bayoumi, M. 2022. They Are "Civilised" and "Look Like Us": The Racist Coverage of Ukraine. *The Guardian*, February 3, 2023, https://www.theguardian.com/commentisfree/2022/mar/02/civilised-european-look-like-us-racist-coverage-ukraine. Accessed April 21, 2023.

Becker, S.K. 2017. Community Labor and Laboring Communities Within the Tiwanaku State (C.E. 500–1100). *Archaeological Papers of the American Anthropological Association* 28: 38–53.

Becker, S.K. 2020. Why Heterarchy? A View from the Tiwanaku State's (AD 500–1100) Labor Force. *American Anthropologist* 122: 934–9.

Benjamin, W. 2003. On the Concept of History. In W. Benjamin, H. Eiland, and M.W. Jennings, eds., *Selected Writings, Volume 4, 1938–1940*. Pp. 389–411. Cambridge, MA: Harvard University Press.

Bennett, B. 2022. Turbo Island: What's Actually Going on?! *Peoples Republic of Stokes Croft* https://prsc.org.uk/turbo-island-whats-actually-going-on/. Accessed June 24, 2023.

Bennett, J. 2010. *Vibrant Matter: A Political Economy of Things*. Durham: Duke University Press.

Bernbeck R. 2018. An Emerging Archaeology of the Nazi Era. *Annual Review of Anthropology* 47: 361–76.

Bickle, P. 2013. Of Time and the House: The Early Neolithic Communities of the Paris Basin and Their Domestic Architecture. In D. Hofmann and J. Smyth, eds., *Tracking the Neolithic House in Europe*. Pp. 151–81. New York: Springer.

Bickle, P. 2020. Thinking Gender Differently: New Approaches to Identity Difference in the Central European Neolithic. *Cambridge Archaeological Journal* 30: 201–18.

Bickle, P., and A. Whittle. 2013. *The First Farmers of Central Europe: Diversity in LBK Lifeways*. Oxford: Oxbow.

Bignall, S. 2014. The Collaborative Struggle for Exocolonialism. *Settler Colonial Studies* 4: 340–56.

Binford, L. 1962. Archaeology as Anthropology. *American Antiquity* 28: 217–25.

Binford, L. 1968. Some Comments on Historical Versus Processual Archaeology. *Southwestern Journal of Anthropology* 24: 267–75.

Binford, S.R., and L.R. Binford. 1969. Stone Tools as Human Behavior. *Scientific American* 220: 70–84.

Blom, D.E. 2005. Embodying Borders: Human Body Modification and Diversity in Tiwanaku Society. *Journal of Anthropological Archaeology* 24: 1–24.

Bloxam, A., and M. Parker Pearson. 2022. Funerary Diversity and Cultural Continuity: The British Beaker Phenomenon Beyond the Stereotype. *Proceedings of the Prehistoric Society* 88: 261–84.

Boas, F. 1896. The Indians of British Columbia. *Journal of the American Geographical Society* 28: 229–43.

Bollongino, R., O. Nehlich, M.P. Richards, J. Orschiedt, M.G. Thomas, C. Sell, Z. Falkošova, A. Powell, and J. Burger. 2013. 2000 Years of Parallel Societies in Stone Age Central Europe. *Science* 342: 479–81.

Borake, T.L. 2019. Anarchist Action. Social Organization and Dynamics in Southern Scandinavia from the Iron Age to the Middle Ages. *Archaeological Dialogues* 26: 61–73.

Borck, L. 2018. Constructing the Future History: Prefiguration as Historical Epistemology and the Chrono Politics of Archaeology. *Journal of Contemporary Archaeology* 5: 213–302.

Bordes, F., and D. Sonneville-Bordes. 1970. The Significance of Variability in Paleolithic Assemblages. *World Archaeology* 2: 61–73.

Bourgeois, R. 2017. Perpetual State of Violence: An Indigenous Feminist Anti-Oppression Inquiry into Missing and Murdered Indigenous Women and Girls. In J. Green, ed., *Making Space for Indigenous Feminisms*. Pp. 253–73. Black Point, Nova Scotia: Fernwood.

Bowman, D. 1998. The Impact of Aboriginal Landscape Burning on the Australian Biota. *The New Phytologist* 140: 385–410.

Brace, S., Y. Diekmann, T.J. Booth, L. van Dorp, Z. Faltyskova, N. Rohland, S. Mallick, I. Olalde, M. Ferry, M. Michel, J. Oppenheimer, N. Broomandkhoshbacht, K. Stewardson, R. Martiniano, S. Walsh, M. Kayser, S. Charlton, G. Hellenthal, I. Armit, R. Schulting, O.E. Craig, A. Sheridan, M. Parker Pearson, C. Stringer, D. Reich, M.G. Thomas, and I. Barnes. 2019. Ancient Genomes Indicate Population Replacement in Early Neolithic Britain. *Nature Ecology & Evolution* 3: 765–71.

Bradley, R. 2002. *The Past in Prehistoric Societies*. London: Routledge.

Braidotti, R. 2011. *Nomadic Subjects: Embodiment and Sexual Difference in Contemporary Feminist Theory*. New York: Columbia University Press.

Braidotti, R. 2013. *The Posthuman*. Cambridge: Polity Press.

Braidotti, R. 2019. A Theoretical Framework for the Critical Posthumanities. *Theory, Culture and Society* 36: 31–61.

Braidotti, R. 2020. "We" Are in *This* Together, But We Are Not One and the Same. *Journal of Bioethical Inquiry* 17: 465–9.

Braidotti, R. 2022. *Posthuman Feminism*. London: Polity Press.

Brazier, R.E., M. Elliott, E. Andison, R.E. Auster, S. Bridgewater, P. Burgess, J. Chant, H. Graham, E. Knott, A.K. Puttock, P. Samsum, and A. Vowels. 2020. *River Otter Beaver Trial: Science and Evidence Report*. Devon: Devon Wildlife Trust, https://www.devonwildlifetrust.org/what-we-do/our-projects/river-otter-beaver-trial. Accessed June 22, 2023.

Breithoff, E., and R. Harrison. 2018. From Ark to Bank: Extinction, Proxies, and Biocapitals in Ex-situ Biodiversity Conservation Practices. *International Journal of Heritage Studies* 26: 37–55.

Breithoff, E., and R. Harrison. 2020. Making Futures in End Times: Rethinking Nature Conservation in the Anthropocene. In R. Harrison and C. Sterling, eds., *Deterritorializing the Future: Heritage in, of and After the Anthropocene*. Pp. 155–87. London: Open Humanities Press.

Brew, J.O. 1971. The Use and Abuse of Taxonomy. In J. Deetz, ed., *Man's Imprint from the Past: Readings in the Methods of Archaeology*. Pp. 73–107. Boston: Little Brown.

Brickley, M., and J.I. McKinley, eds. 2004. *Guidelines to the Standards for Recording Human Remains*, IFA Paper No. 7. Southampton and Reading: British Association of Biological Anthropology and Osteoarchaeology and the Institute of Field Archaeologists.

Bruchac, M. 2018. *Savage Kin: Indigenous Informants and American Anthropologists*. Tucson: University of Arizona Press.

Brück, J. 2019. *Personifying Prehistory: Relational Ontologies in Bronze Age Britain*. Oxford: Oxford University Press.

Brumfiel, E. 1995. Heterarchy and the Analysis of Complex Societies: Comments. *Archaeological Papers of the American Anthropological Association, Special Issue: Heterarchy and the Analysis of Complex Societies* 6: 125–31.

Buchli, V., and G. Lucas, eds. 2001. *Archaeologies of the Contemporary Past*. New York: Routledge.

Buikstra, J.E., and D.H. Ubelaker. 1994. *Standards for Data Collection from Human Remains*. Fayetteville: Arkansas Archaeological Survey.

Campbell, P.B. 2021. The Anthropocene, Hyperobjects and the Archaeology of the Future Past. *Antiquity* 95: 1315–30.

Carman, J. 1997. Introduction: Approaches to Violence. In J. Carman, ed., *Material Harm: Archaeological Studies of War and Violence*. Pp. 1–23. Glasgow: Cruithne Press.

Carter, R., and O.J.T. Harris. 2020. The End of Normal Politics: Assemblages, Nonhumans and International Relations. In J. Castro Pereira and A. Saramago, eds., *Non-Human Nature in World Politics*. Pp. 13–31. New York: Springer.

Chapman, J., and B. Gaydarska. 2006. *Parts and Wholes: Fragmentation in a Prehistoric Context*. Oxford: Oxbow.

Chapman, R. 2023. *Archaeological Theory: The Basics*. London: Routledge.

Cipolla, C.N. 2013. *Becoming Brothertown: Native American Ethnogenesis and Endurance in the Modern World*. Tucson: University of Arizona Press.

Cipolla, C.N. 2017. Indigenous People and Foreign Objects: Rethinking Consumption in American Archaeology. In C.N. Cipolla, ed., *Foreign Objects*. Pp. 1–25. Tucson: University of Arizona Press.

Cipolla, C.N. 2018. Earth Flows and Lively Stone. What Difference Does 'Vibrant' Matter Make? *Archaeological Dialogues* 25: 49–70.

Cipolla, C.N. 2019. Taming the Ontological Wolves: Learning from Iroquoian Effigy Objects. *American Anthropologist* 121: 613–27.

Cipolla, C.N. 2021. Posthuman Potentials: Considering Collaborative Indigenous Archaeology. *Cambridge Archaeological Journal* 31: 509–14.

Cipolla, C.N. n.d. When Smoking Pipes Grow Fins: Revisiting the Matter-Meaning Dualism in Archaeology. *Current Anthropology*.

Cipolla, C.N., and A. Allard. 2019. Recognizing River Power: Watery Views of Ontario's Fur Trade. *Journal of Archaeological Method and Theory* 26: 1084–105.

Cipolla, C.N., R.J. Crellin, and O.J.T. Harris. 2021. Posthuman Archaeologies, Archaeological Posthumanisms. *Journal of Posthumanism* 1: 5–21.

Cipolla, C.N., and T. Gallo. 2021. Can Birdstones Sing? Rethinking Material-Semiotic Approaches in Contemporary Archaeological Theory. *World Archaeology* 52: 463–83.

Cipolla, C.N., and J. Quinn. 2016. Field School Archaeology the Mohegan Way: Reflections on Twenty Years of Community-Based Research and Teaching. *Journal of Community Archaeology and Heritage* 3: 118–34.

Cipolla, C.N., J. Quinn, and J. Levy. 2019. Theory in Collaborative Indigenous Archaeology: Insights from Mohegan. *American Antiquity* 84: 127–42.

Clarke, D.L. 1973. Archaeology: The Loss of Innocence. *Antiquity* 47: 6–18.

Clastres, P. 1977. *Societies Against the State*. Oxford: Blackwell.

Cobb, H., and R.J. Crellin. 2022. Affirmation and Action: A Posthumanist Feminist Archaeology. *Cambridge Archaeological Journal* 32: 265–79.

Cobb, H., and K. Croucher. 2020. *Assembling Archaeology: Teaching, Practice and Research*. Oxford: Oxford University Press.

Cobb, H., O.J.T. Harris, C. Jones, and P. Richardson. 2012. Reconsidering Practice & Theory: An Introduction. In H. Cobb, O.J.T. Harris, C. Jones, and P. Richardson, eds., *Reconsidering Archaeological Fieldwork: Exploring the On-Site Relationship Between Theory & Practice*. Pp. 1–14. New York: Springer.

Colebrook, C. 2020. Extinction, Deterritorialisation and End times: Peak Deleuze. *Deleuze and Guattari Studies* 14: 327–48.

Colwell, C. 2017. *Plundered Skulls and Stolen Spirits: Inside the Fight to Reclaim Native America's Culture*. Chicago: University of Chicago Press.

Conneller, C. 2011. *An Archaeology of Materials: Substantial Transformations in Early Prehistoric Europe*. New York: Routledge.

Coole, D., and S. Frost, eds. 2010. *New Materialisms: Ontology, Agency, and Politics*. Durham: Duke University Press.

Cooper, J., and M. Peros. 2010. The Archaeology of Climate Change in the Caribbean. *Journal of Archaeological Science* 37: 1226–32.

Couture, N.C., and K. Sampeck. 2003. Putuni: A History of Palace Architecture at Tiwanaku. In A.L. Kolata, ed., *Tiwanaku and Its Hinterland: Archaeology and Paleoecology of an Andean Civilization*, volume 2. Pp. 226–63. Washington, DC: Smithsonian Institute Press.

Cowgill, G.L. 2015. *Ancient Teotihuacan: Early Urbanism in Central Mexico.* Cambridge: Cambridge University Press.

Crea, G., A. Dafnis, J. Hallam, R. Kiddey, and J. Schofield. 2014. Turbo Island, Bristol: Excavating a Contemporary Homeless Place. *Post-Medieval Archaeology* 48: 133–50.

Crellin, R.J. 2017. Changing Assemblages: Vibrant Matter in Burial Assemblages. *Cambridge Archaeological Journal* 27: 111–25.

Crellin, R.J. 2020. *Change and Archaeology.* New York: Routledge.

Crellin, R.J., C.N. Cipolla, L.M. Montgomery, O.J.T. Harris, and S.V. Moore. 2021. *Archaeological Theory in Dialogue: Situating Relations, Ontology, Posthumanism, and Indigenous Paradigms.* London: Routledge.

Crellin, R.J., and O.J.T. Harris. 2020. Beyond Binaries: Interrogating Ancient DNA. *Archaeological Dialogues* 27: 37–56.

Crellin, R.J., and O.J.T. Harris. 2021. What Difference Does Posthumanism Make? *Cambridge Archaeological Journal* 31: 469–75.

Cronon, W. 1983. *Changes in the Land: Indians, Colonists, and the Ecology of New England.* New York: Hill and Wang.

Crossland, Z. 2014a. *Ancestral Encounters in Highland Madagascar.* Cambridge: Cambridge University Press.

Crossland, Z. 2014b. Anthropocene: Locating Agency, Imagining the Future. *Journal of Contemporary Archaeology* 1: 123–8.

Crossland, Z. 2018. Forensic Afterlives. *Signs and Society* 6: 622–47.

Crossland, Z. 2021. 'Contextual Archaeology' Revisited: Reflections on Archaeology, Assemblages and Semiotics. In M.J. Boyd and C.P. Doonan, eds., *Far from Equilibrium: An Archaeology of Energy, Life and Humanity.* Pp. 85–102. Oxford: Oxbow.

Crumley, C. 1979. Three Locational Models: An Epistemological Assessment for Anthropology and Archaeology. In M. Schiffer, ed., *Advances in Archaeological Method and Theory*, volume 2. Pp. 143–73. New York: Academic Press.

Crumley, C. 2007. Notes on a New Paradigm. In S. Kohring and S. Wynne-Jones, eds., *Socialising Complexity.* Pp. 30–6. Oxford: Oxbow.

Crutzen, P.J. 2006. The "Anthropocene". In E. Ehlers and T. Krafft, eds., *Earth System Science in the Anthropocene.* Berlin: Springer, https://doi.org/10.1007/3-540-26590-2_3.

Crutzen, P.J., and E.F. Stoermer. 2000. The Anthropocene. *Global Change Newsletter* 41: 17–18.

Darvill, T., K. Barrass, L. Drysdale, V. Heaslip, and Y. Staelens, eds. 2019. *Historic Landcapes and Mental Wellbeing.* Oxford: Archaeopress.

Daskalaki, E., C. Anderung, L. Humphrey, and A. Götherström. 2011. Further Developments in Molecular Sex Assignment: A Blind Test of 18th and 19th Century Human Skeletons. *Journal of Archaeological Science* 38: 1326–30.

David, B. 2006. Archaeology and the Dreaming: Toward and Archaeology of Ontology. In I. Lilley, ed., *Archaeology of Oceania: Australia and the Pacific Islands.* Pp. 48–68. Malden, MA: Blackwell.

Davis, H., and Z. Todd. 2017. On the Importance of a Date, or, Decolonizing the Anthropocene. *ACME: An International Journal for Critical Geographies* 16: 761–80.

Dawney, L., O.J.T. Harris, and T.F. Sørensen. 2017. Future Worlds: Anticipatory Archaeology and the Late Human Legacy. *Journal of Contemporary Archaeology* 4: 107–29.

De León, J. 2012. "Better To Be Hot Than Caught": Excavating the Conflicting Roles of Migrant Material Culture. *American Anthropologist* 114: 477–95.

De León, J. 2013. Undocumented Migration, Use-Wear, and the Materiality of Habitual Suffering in the Sonoran Desert. *Journal of Material Culture* 18: 1–32.

De León, J. 2015. *The Land of Open Graves: Living and Dying on the Sonoran Desert Migrant Trail*. Berkeley: University of California Press.

DeLanda, M. 2002. *Intensive Science and Virtual Philosophy*. London: Continuum.

DeLanda, M. 2006. *A New Philosophy of Society: Assemblage Theory and Social Complexity*. London: Continuum.

DeLanda, M. 2016. *Assemblage Theory*. Edinburgh: Edinburgh University Press.

Deleuze, G. 1991. *Bergsonism*. London: Zone Books.

Deleuze, G. 1997. Spinoza and the Three 'Ethics.' In W. Montag and T. Stolze, eds., *The New Spinoza*. Pp. 21–34. Minneapolis: University of Minnesota Press.

Deleuze, G. 2004. *Difference and Repetition*. London: Bloomsbury.

Deleuze, G., and F. Guattari. 2004. *A Thousand Plateaus: Capitalism and Schizophrenia*. London: Continuum.

Deleuze, G., and F. Guattari. 2013. *Anti-Oedipus: Capitalism and Schizophrenia*. London: Bloomsbury.

Deleuze, G., and C. Parnet. 2002. *Dialogues II*. New York: Columbia University Press.

Deloria, P.J. 1999. *Playing Indian*. New Haven: Yale University Press.

Deloria, V. Jr. 1997. *Red Earth, White Lies: Native Americans and the Myth of Scientific Fact*. Golden, CO: Fulcrum Publishing.

Deloria, V. Jr. 2001. American Indian Metaphysics. In V. Deloria Jr. and D.R. Wildcat, eds., *Power and Place: Indian Education in America*. Pp. 1–6. Golden, CO: Fulcrum Publishing.

Deloria, V. Jr. 2012. *The Metaphysics of Modern Existence*. Golden, CO: Fulcrum Publishing.

DeMarrais, E. 2016. Making Pacts and Cooperative Acts: The Archaeology of Coalition and Consensus. *World Archaeology* 48: 1–13.

Demay, L., S. Péan, and M. Patou-Mathis. 2011. Mammoths Used as Food and Building Resources by Neanderthals: Zooarchaeological Study Applied to Layer 4, Molodova I (Ukraine). *Quaternary International* 276–277: 212–26.

Denham, T. 2018. Collective Action, Mutual Aid, and Wetland Agriculture in the Highlands of Papua New Guinea. *Journal of Contemporary Archaeology* 5: 213–302.

Dobecki, T.L., and R.M. Schoch. 1992. Seismic Investigations in the Vicinity of the Great Sphinx of Giza, Egypt. *Geoarchaeology* 7: 527–44.

Dolfini, A., R.J. Crellin, C. Horn, and M. Ucklemann. 2018. Interdisciplinary Approaches to Prehistoric Warfare and Violence: Past, Present and Future. In A. Dolfini, R.J. Crellin, C. Horn, and M. Uckleman, eds., *Prehistoric Warfare and Violence: Quantitative and Qualitative Approaches*. Pp. 1–18. New York: Springer.

Domanska, E. 2014. The New Age of the Anthropocene. *Journal of Contemporary Archaeology* 1: 96–101.

Doronicheva, E.V., L.V. Golovanova, V.B. Doronichev, M.S. Shackley, and A.G. Nedomolkin. 2019. New Data About Exploitation of the Zayukovo (Baksan) Obsidian Source in Northern Caucasus During the Paleolithic. *Journal of Archaeological Science Reports* 23: 157–65.

Dunbar, R.I.M. 1998. The Social Brain Hypothesis. *Evolutionary Anthropology* 6: 178–90.

Earle, T. 1991. Property Rights and the Evolution of Chiefdoms. In T. Earle, ed., *Chiefdoms: Power, Economy, and Ideology*. Pp. 71–99. Cambridge: Cambridge University Press.

Eddisford, D., and C. Morgan. 2018. Single Context Archaeology as Anarchist Praxis. *Journal of Contemporary Archaeology* 5: 213–302.

Edgeworth, M. 2014. Archaeology of the Anthropocene. *Journal of Contemporary Archaeology* 1: 73–7.

El-Kamel Bakari, M. 2015. Sustainability and Contemporary Man-Nature Divide: Aspects of Conflict, Alienation, and Beyond. *Consilience* 13: 195–215.

Engels, F. 1972[1884]. *The Origin of the Family, Private Property, and the State*. New York: International.

Estes, N. 2019. *Our History Is the Future: Standing Rock Versus the Dakota Access Pipeline, and the Long Tradition of Indigenous Resistance*. New York: Verso.

Evans, M., S. Eve, V. Haverkate-Emerson, T. Pollard, E. Steinbeck, and D. Luke. 2019. Waterloo Uncovered: From Discoveries in Conflict Archaeology to Military Veteran Collaboration and Recovery on One of the World's Most Famous Battlefields. In T. Darvill, K. Barracks, L. Drysdale, V. Heaslip, and Y. Staelens, eds., *Historic Landscapes and Mental Well-Being*. Pp. 253–65. Oxford: Archaeopress.

Feder, K.L. 2017. *Frauds, Myths, and Mysteries: Science and Pseudoscience in Archaeology*, 8th ed. New York: McGraw-Hill.

Ferrando, F. 2019. *Philosophical Posthumanism*. London: Bloomsbury.

Flewellen, A.O., J.P. Dunnavant, A. Odewale, A. Jones, T. Wolde-Michael, Z. Crossland, and M. Franklin. 2021. "The Future of Archaeology is Antiracist": Archaeology in the Time of Black Lives Matter. *American Antiquity* 86: 224–43.

Flexner, J.L. 2018. Doing Archaeology in Non-State Space. *Journal of Contemporary Archaeology* 5: 213–18.

Flexner, J.L., and E. Gonzalez-Tenant. 2018. Anarchy and Archaeology: Introduction. *Journal of Contemporary Archaeology* 5: 213–18.

Flexner, J.L., and M. Spriggs. 2015. Mission Sites as Indigenous Heritage in Southern Vanuatu. *Journal of Social Archaeology* 15: 184–209.

Flexner, J.L., E. Willie, and M. Horrocks. 2015. Sustenance and Sustainability: Food Remains and Contact Sites in Vanuatu. In M. Leclerc and J. Flexner, eds., *Archaeologies of Island Melanesia: Current Approaches to Landscapes, Exchange and Practice*. Pp. 135–50. Acton: Australian National University Press.

Ford, H., R. Eldridge, K. Buckley, K. Scott, A. Chavet, A. Cachia, T. Pollard, and M. Evans. 2022. *Waterloo Uncovered Impact Report 2022*, https://waterloouncovered.com/wp-content/uploads/2023/02/Waterloo-Uncovered-2022-Impact-Report.pdf. Accessed June 22, 2023.

Ford, J.A., A.C. Spaulding, and C. Evans. 1954. Spaulding's Review of Ford. *American Anthropologist* 56: 109–14.

Ford, J.A., and J.H. Steward. 1954. On the Concept of Types. *American Anthropologist* 56: 42–57.

Foucault, M. 1977. *Discipline and Punish: The Birth of the Prison*. London: Allen Lane.

Foucault, M. 1978. *A History of Sexuality, Volume 1: The Will to Knowledge*. Harmondsworth: Penguin.

Foucault, M. 1988. Truth, Power, Self: An Interview with Michel Foucault. In L.H. Martin, H. Gutman, and P.H. Hutton, eds., *Technologies of the Self: A Seminar with Michel Foucault*. Pp. 9–15. Amherst: University of Massachusetts Press.

Foucault, M. 2001. *The Order of Things: An Archaeology of the Human Sciences*. London: Routledge.

Fowler, C. 2013a. *The Emergent Past: A Relational Realist Archaeology of Early Bronze Age Mortuary Practices*. Oxford: Oxford University Press.

Fowler, C. 2013b. Dynamic Assemblages, or the Past Is What Endures: Change and the Duration of Relations. In B. Alberti, A.M. Jones, and J. Pollard, eds., *Archaeology After Interpretation: Returning Materials to Archaeological Theory*. Pp. 235–56. Walnut Creek, CA: Left Coast Press.

Fowles, S. 2010. People Without Things. In M. Bille, F. Hastrup, and T.F. Sørensen, eds., *An Anthropology of Absence: Materialisations of Transcendence and Loss*. Pp. 23–41. New York: Springer.

Franklin, M., J.P. Dunnavant, A.O. Flewellen, and A. Odewale. 2020. The Future Is Now: Archaeology and the Eradication of Anti-Blackness. *International Journal of Historical Archaeology* 24: 753–66.

French, K.D. 2022. A Round for All My Friends: Understanding the Economic Impact of Moonshine Production. In J.A. Nyman, K.R. Fogle, and M.C. Beaudry, eds., *The Historical Archaeology of Shadow and Intimate Economies*. Pp. 51–66. Gainesville: University Press of Florida.

Gaard, G. 1997. Toward a Queer Ecofeminism. *Hypatia* 12: 114–37.

Gaard, G. 2014. Indigenous Women, Feminism, and the Environmental Humanities. *Resilience: A Journal of Environmental Humanities* 1: 86–99.

Gabucio, M.J., M.C. Fernández-Laso, and J. Rosell. 2018. Turning a Rock Shelter into a Home. Neanderthal Use of Space in Abric Romaní Levels M and O. *Historical Biology* 30: 743–66.

Gailey, C.W. 1987. *From Kinship to Kingship: Gender Hierarchy and State Formation in the Tongan Islands*. Austin: University of Texas Press.

Gallo, T., and C.N. Cipolla. n.d. Three Little Birds: A Materials-Centered Challenge to Birdstone Typologies. *Norwegian Archaeological Review*, accepted Summer 2023.

Gamble, M., and C. Fowler. 2013. A Re-assessment of Early Bronze Age Human Remains in Tyne and Wear Museums: Results and Implications for Interpreting Early Bronze Age Burials from North-East England and Beyond. *Archaeologia Aeliana* 5: 47–80.

Gammage, B. 2012. *Biggest Estate on Earth: How Aboriginies Made Australia*. Sydney: Allen & Unwin.

Gates, B.T. 1996. A Root of Ecofeminism: Ecoféminisme. *Interdisciplinary Studies of Literature and the Environment* 3: 7–16.

Gauri, K.L., J.J. Sinai, and J.K. Bandyopadhyay. 1995. Geological Weathering and Its Implications on the Age of the Sphinx. *Geoarchaeology* 10: 119–33.

Gell, A. 1998. *Art and Agency: An Anthropological Theory*. Oxford: Clarendon Press.

Geller, P.L. 2005. Skeletal Analysis and Theoretical Complications. *World Archaeology* 37: 597–609.

Gero, J., and M. Conkey, eds. 1991. *Engendering Archaeology*. Oxford: Blackwell.

Gibbons, A. 2019. Why Are Adult Daughters Missing from Ancient German Cemeteries? DNA and Artifacts Reveal Marriage and Inheritance Patterns Among Bronze Age Farmers. *Science.org*, https://www.science.org/content/article/why-are-adult-daughters-missing-ancient-german-cemeteries. Accessed June 22, 2023.

Gibson, A. 2007. A Beaker Veneer? Some Evidence from the Burial Record. In M. Larsson and M. Parker Pearson, eds., *From Stonehenge to the Baltic: Living with Diversity in the Third Millennium BC*. Pp. 47–64. Oxford: BAR International Series.

González-Ruibal, A. 2019. Ethical Issues in Indigenous Archaeology: Problems with Difference and Collaboration. *Canadian Journal of Bioethics* 2: 34–43.

González-Ruibal, A. 2021. Excavating Europe's Last Fascist Monument: The Valley of the Fallen (Spain). *Journal of Social Archaeology* 22: 26–47.

Gonzalez-Tenant, E. 2018. Anarchism, Decolonization, and Collaborative Archaeology. *Journal of Contemporary Archaeology* 5: 213–302.

Gosden, C. 2004. *Archaeology and Colonialism: Cultural Contact from 5000 BC to the Present*. Cambridge: Cambridge University Press.

Gosden, C. 2005. What Do Objects Want? *Journal of Archaeological Method and Theory* 12: 193–211.

Gosden, C., and L. Malafouris. 2015. Process Archaeology (P-Arch). *World Archaeology* 47: 701–17.

Gosden, C., and Y. Marshall. 1999. The Cultural Biography of Objects. *World Archaeology* 31: 169–78.

Gould, D.R., H. Herbster, H.L. Pezzarossi, and S.A. Mrozowki. 2020. *Historical Archaeology and Indigenous Collaboration: Discovering Histories That Have Futures*. Gainesville: University Press of Florida.

Grable, K. 2021. Big Oil Is Fueling the Crisis of Missing and Murdered Indigenous Women. *Greenpeace*, May 5, 2021, https://www.greenpeace.org/usa/justice-for-missing-and-murdered-indigenous-women-will-move-us-closer-to-climate-justice/. Accessed 10 August 2023.

Graeber, D., and D. Wengrow. 2021. *The Dawn of Everything: A New History of Humanity*. New York: Macmillan.

Graves, P.C. 2008. From an Archaeology of Iconoclasm to an Anthropology of the Body: Images, Punishment, and Personhood in England, 1500–1660. *Current Anthropology* 49: 35–48.

Graves-Brown, P. 2014. When Was the Anthropocene? (And why?). *Journal of Contemporary Archaeology* 1: 77–81.

Graves-Brown, P., R. Harrison, and A. Piccini, A., eds. 2013. *The Oxford Handbook of the Archaeology of the Contemporary World*. Oxford: Oxford University Press.

Green, J. 2017. Taking More Account of Indigenous Feminisms: An Introduction. In J. Green, ed., *Making Space for Indigenous Feminisms*. Pp. 1–20. Black Point, Nova Scotia: Fernwood.

Grosz, E.A. 1994. *Volatile Bodies: Toward a Corporeal Feminism*. Bloomington, IN: Indiana University Press.

Groucutt, H.S. 2014. Middle Paleolithic Point Technology, with a Focus on the Site of Tor Faraj (Jordan, MIS 3). *Quaternary International* 350: 205–26.

Growdy, K., and L. Krall. 2013. The Ultrasocial Origin of the Anthropocene. *Ecological Economics* 95: 137–47.

Guattari, F. 1984. *Molecular Revolution: Psychiatry and Politics*. London: Penguin.

Guttmann-Bond, E. 2019. *Reinventing Sustainability: How Archaeology Can Save the Planet*. Oxford: Oxbow.

Haak, W., I. Lazaridis, N. Patterson, N. Rohland, S. Mallick, B. Llamas, G. Brandt, S. Nordenfelt, E. Harney, K. Stewardson, Q. Fu, A. Mittnik, E. Bánffy, C. Economou, M. Francken, S. Friederich, R.G. Pena, F. Hallgren, V. Khartanovich, A. Khokhlov, M. Kunst, P. Kuznetsov, H. Meller, O. Mochalov, V. Moiseyev, N. Nicklisch, S.L. Pichler, R. Risch, M.A. Rojo Guerra, C. Roth, A. Szécsényi-Nagy, J. Wahl, M. Meyer, J. Krause, D. Brown, D. Anthony, A. Cooper, K.W. Alt, and D. Reich. 2015. Massive Migration from the Steppe Was a Source for Indo-European Languages in Europe. *Nature* 522: 207–11.

Hagerman, K. 2018. Transformations in Representations of Gender During the Emergence of the Teotihuacan State: A Regional Case Study of Ceramic Figurines from the Basin of Mexico. *Cambridge Archaeological Journal* 28: 689–711.

Hakenbeck, S. 2019. Genetics, Archaeology and the Far Right: An Unholy Trinity. *World Archaeology* 51: 517–27.

Hamilakis, Y. 2016. Archaeologies of Forced and Undocumented Migration. *Journal of Contemporary Archaeology* 3: 121–39.

Hamilakis, Y., ed. 2018. *The New Nomadic Age: Archaeologies of Forced and Undocumented Migration*. Sheffield: Equinox.

Hamilakis, Y., and A.M. Jones. 2017. Archaeology and Assemblage. *Cambridge Archaeological Journal* 27: 77–84.

Haraway, D. 1988. Situated Knowledges: The Science Question in Feminism and the Privilege of Partial Perspective. *Feminist Studies* 14: 575–99.

Haraway, D. 2015. Anthropocene, Capitalocene, Plantationocene, Chthulucene: Making Kin. *Environmental Humanities* 6: 159–65.

Haraway, D. 2016. *Staying with the Trouble: Making Kin in the Chthulucene*. Durham: Duke University Press.

Harding, S. 1991. *Whose Science? Whose Knowledge? Thinking from Women's Lives*. Ithaca, NY: Cornell University Press.

Harding, S. 2004. *The Feminist Standpoint Theory Reader: Intellectual and Political Controversies*. London: Routledge.

Harris, O.J.T. 2018. More Than Representation: Multiscalar Assemblages and the Deleuzian Challenge to Archaeology. *History of the Human Sciences* 31: 83–104.

Harris, O.J.T. 2021a. *Assembling Past Worlds: Materials, Bodies and Architecture in Neolithic Britain*. London: Routledge.

Harris, O.J.T. 2021b. Archaeology, Process and Time: Beyond History Versus Memory. *World Archaeology* 53: 104–21.

Harris, O.J.T., and C.N. Cipolla. 2017. *Archaeological Theory in the New Millennium*. New York: Routledge.

Harris, O.J.T., and J. Robb. 2012. Multiple Ontologies and the Problem of the Body in History. *American Anthropologist* 114: 669–80.

Harrison, R. 2020. Heritage as Future-Making Practices. In R. Harrison, C. DeSilvey, C. Holtorf, S. MacDonald, N. Bartolini, E. Breithoff, H. Fredheim, A. Lyons, S. May, J. Morgan, and S. Penrose, eds., *Heritage Futures: Comparative Approaches to Natural and Cultural Heritage Practices*. Pp. 20–50. London: UCL Press.

Harrison, R., C. DeSilvey, C. Holtorf, S. MacDonald, N. Bartolini, E. Breithoff, H. Fredheim, A. Lyons, S. May, J. Morgan, and S. Penrose, eds. 2020. *Heritage Futures: Comparative Approaches to Natural and Cultural Heritage Practices*. London: UCL Press.

Harrison, R., and J. Schofield. 2010. *After Modernity: Archaeological Approaches to the Contemporary Past*. Oxford: Oxford University Press.

Hayes, K.H. 2013. *Slavery Before Race: Europeans, Africans, and Indians at Long Island's Sylvester Plantation, 1651–1884*. New York: New York University Press.

Henry, A.G., A.S. Brooks, and D.R. Piperno. 2014. Plant Foods and the Dietary Ecology of Neanderthals and Early Modern Humans. *Journal of Human Evolution* 69: 44–54.

Hermann, R., R.J. Crellin, A. Dolfini, Q. Wang, and M. Uckelmann. 2020. Bronze Age Swordsmanship: New Insights from Experiments and Wear Analysis. *Journal of Archaeological Method and Theory* 27: 1040–83.

Hicks, D. 2021. *The Brutish Museums: The Benin Bronzes, Colonial Violence and Cultural Restitution*. London: Pluto Press.

Hicks, D., and S. Mallet. 2019. *Lande: The Calais 'Jungle' and Beyond*. Bristol: Bristol University Press.

Hiscock, P., and P. Faulkner. 2006. Dating the Dreaming? Creation Myths and Rituals for Mounds Along the Northern Australian Coastline. *Cambridge Archaeological Journal* 16: 209–22.

Hobbes, T. 1996[1651]. *Leviathan*. Cambridge: Cambridge University Press.

Hodder, I. 1999. *The Archaeological Process*. Oxford: Blackwell.

Hofmann, D. 2020. Not Going Anywhere? Migration as a Social Practice in the Early Neolithic Linearbandkeramik. *Quaternary International* 560–561: 228–39.

Holbraad, M. 2007. The Power of Powder: Multiplicity and Motion in the Divinatory Cosmology of Cuban Ifá. In A. Henare, M. Holbraad, and S. Wastell, eds., *Thinking Through Things: Theorising Artefacts Ethnographically*. Pp. 42–56. London: Routledge.

Holbraad, M., and M.A. Pedersen. 2017. *The Ontological Turn: An Anthropological Exposition*. Cambridge: Cambridge University Press.

Holtorf, C. 2005. *From Stonehenge to Las Vegas: Archaeology as Popular Culture*. Lanham, MD: AltaMira Press.

Holtorf, C. 2009. *Archaeology Is a Brand! The Meaning of Archaeology in Contemporary Popular Culture*. London: Routledge.

Holtorf, C. 2019. Cultural Heritage, Nuclear Waste and the Future: What's in It for Us? In J. Decker, ed., *Bewaren of Weggooien*? Middelburg: Zeeuwse Ankers and COBRA, 11.01–11.17.

Holtorf, C., and A. Höberg. 2014. Communicating with Future Generations: What Are the Benefits of Preserving Cultural Heritage? Nuclear Power and Beyond. *European Journal of Postclassical Archaeologies* 4: 343–58.

Holtorf, C., and A. Höberg. 2015. Archaeology and the Future: Managing Nuclear Waste as a Living Heritage. In *Radioactive Waste Management and Constructing Memory for Future Generations, Proceedings of the International Conference and Debate*. Pp. 97–101. Paris: OECD Nuclear Energy Agency.

Hornberg, A. 2021. Objects Don't Have Desires: Towards an Anthropology of Technology Beyond Anthropomorphism. *American Anthropologist* 123: 754–76.

Howell, I., L. Blackmore, J. Cotton, and M. Henderson. 2019. *A Bronze Age Barrow Cemetery at Andover Airfield, Penton Mewsey, Near Weyhill, Hampshire: Excavations 2007–2010*. Dorset: MOLA Archaeology Series.

Hunt, E. 2017. Trump's Inauguration Crowd: Sean Spicer's Claim Versus the Evidence. *The Guardian*, January 11, 2017, https://www.theguardian.com/us-news/2017/jan/22/trump-inauguration-crowd-sean-spicers-claims-versus-the-evidence. Accessed June 22, 2023.

Immel, A., F. Pierini, C. Rinne, J. Meadows, R. Barquera, A. Szolek, J. Susat, L. Böhme, J. Dose, J. Bonczarowska, C. Drummer, K. Fuchs, D. Ellinghaus, J.C. Kässens, M. Furholt, O. Kohlbacher, S. Schade-Lindig, A. Franke, S. Schreiber, J. Krause, J. Müller, T.L. Lenz, A. Nebel, and B. Krause-Kyora. 2021. Genome-Wide Study of a Neolithic Wartberg Grave Community Reveals Distinct HLA Variation and Hunter-Gatherer Ancestry. *Communications Biology* 4(113), https://doi.org/10.1038/s42003-020-01627-4.

Ingold, T. 2007. Materials Against Materiality. *Archaeological Dialogues* 14: 1–16.

Ingstad, H., and A.S. Ingstad. 2000. *The Viking Discovery of America: The Excavation of a Norse Settlement in L'Anse aux Meadows, Newfoundland*. St. John's, NF: Breakwater.

Inskip S., C.L. Scheib, A.W. Wohns, X. Ge, T. Kivisild, and J. Robb. 2019. Evaluating Macroscopic Sex Estimation Methods Using Genetically Sexed Archaeological Material: The Medieval Skeletal Collection from St. John's Divinity School, Cambridge. *American Journal of Physical Anthropology* 168(2): 340–51.

Intergovernmental Panel on Climate Change. 2023. *AR6 Synthesis Report Climate Change 2023*, https://www.ipcc.ch/report/ar6/syr/. Accessed June 22, 2023.

Irigaray, L. 1985. *This Sex Which Is Not One*. Ithaca, NY: Cornell University Press.

Isbell, W.H., and A. Korpisaari. 2015. Bodies of Evidence: Mortuary Archaeology and the Wari-Tiwanaku Paradox. In P. Eeckhout and L.S. Owens, eds., *Funerary Practices and Models in the Ancient Andes: The Return of the Living Dead*. Pp. 137–57. Cambridge: Cambridge University Press.

Jameson, F. 1994. *The Seeds of Time*. New York: Columbia University Press.

Jamieson, R. 2018. A Bullet for Señor Cobos: Anarchy in the Galapagos. *Journal of Contemporary Archaeology* 5: 213–302.

Janusek, J.W. 2004a. *Identity and Power in the Ancient Andes*. New York: Routledge.

Janusek, J.W. 2004b. Tiwanaku and Its Precursors: Recent Research and Emerging Perspectives. *Journal of Archaeological Research* 12: 121–83.

Janusek, J.W. 2005. Residential Diversity and the Rise of Complexity in Tiwanaku. In C. Stanish, A.B. Cohen, and M.S. Aldenderfer, eds., *Advances in Titicaca Basin Archaeology 1*. Pp. 143–71. Los Angeles: Cotsen Institute.

Janusek, J.W. 2006. The Changing 'Nature' of Tiwanaku Religion and the Rise of an Andean State. *World Archaeology* 38: 469–92.

Janusek, J.W. 2008. *Ancient Tiwanaku*. Cambridge: Cambridge University Press.

Janusek, J.W. 2015. Of Monoliths and Men: Human-Lithic Encounters and the Production of an Animistic Ecology at Khonko Wankane. In T.L. Bray, ed., *Explorations of the Sacred in Pre-Columbian Andes*. Pp. 335–65. Denver: University of Press of Colorado.

Janusek, J.W. 2020. Assembling Tiwanaku: Water and Stone, Humans and Monoliths. In S.M. Alt and T.R. Pauketat, eds., *New Materialisms, Ancient Urbanisms*. Pp. 94–129. London: Routledge.

Jelinski, D.E. 2005. There Is No Mother Nature: There Is No Balance of Nature: Culture, Ecology and Conservation. *Human Ecology* 33: 271–88.

Jennings, J., and T.K. Earle. 2016. Urbanization, State Formation, and Cooperation: A Reappraisal. *Current Anthropology* 57: 474–93.

Jervis, B. 2018. *Assemblage Thought and Archaeology*. London: Routledge.

Johnson, A.R. 2015. The Paleo Diet and American Weight Loss Utopia 1975–2014. *Utopian Studies* 26: 101–24, https://doi.org/10.5325/utopianstudies.26.1.0101.

Johnson, M. 1996. *An Archaeology of Capitalism*. Oxford: Blackwell.

Johnson, M. 2020. *Archaeological Theory: An Introduction*. Malden, MA: Wiley-Blackwell.

Jones, A.M. 2012. *Prehistoric Materialities: Becoming Material in Prehistoric Britain and Ireland*. Oxford: Oxford University Press.

Jones, S. 1980. Institutions of Violence. In J. Cherfas and R. Lewin, eds., *Not Work Alone: A Cross-Cultural View of Activities Superfluous to Survival*. Pp. 98–111. London: Temple Smith.

Joyce, R.A. 2001. *Gender and Power in Prehispanic Mesoamerica*. Austin: University of Texas Press.

Joyce, R.A. 2020. *The Future of Nuclear Waste: What Art and Archaeology Can Tell Us About Securing the World's Most Hazardous Material*. Oxford: Oxford University Press.

Keating, T.P., and A. Storm. 2023. Nuclear Memory: Archival, Aesthetic, Speculative. *Progress in Environmental Geography*, https://doi.org/10.1177/27539687231174242. Accessed June 22, 2023.

Keeley, L.H. 1996. *War Before Civilization*. Oxford: Oxford University Press.

Kelly, J. 2014. The Anthropocene and Transdisciplinarity. *Journal of Contemporary Archaeology* 1: 91–6.

Kolata, A.L. 1993. *The Tiwanaku: Portrait of an Andean Civilization*. Malden, MA: Wiley-Blackwell.

Kolata, A.L. 2003. Tiwanaku Ceremonial Architecture and Urban Organization. In A.L. Kolata, ed., *Tiwanaku and Its Hinterland: Archaeology and Paleoecology of an Andean civilization*, volume 2. Pp. 175–201. Washington, DC: Smithsonian Institution Press.

Kiddey, R. 2017. *Homeless Heritage: Collaborative Social Archaeology as Therapeutic Practice*. Oxford: Oxford University Press.

Kiddey, R. 2018. From the Ground Up: Cultural Heritage Practices as Tools for Empowerment in the Homeless Heritage Project. *International Journal of Heritage Studies* 24: 694–708.

Kiddey, R. 2019. Reluctant Refuge. An Activist Archaeological Approach to Alternative Refugee Shelter in Athens. *Journal of Refugee Studies* 33: 599–621.

Kiddey, R. 2020. I'll Tell You What I Want, What I Really, Really Want! Open Archaeology That Is Collaborative, Participatory, Public, and Feminist. *Norwegian Archaeological Review* 53: 23–40.

Kiddey, R., and J. Schofield. 2009. Homeless Archaeology. *The Big Issue* 874: 14–15.

Kiddey, R., and J. Schofield. 2010. Digging for (Invisible) People. *British Archaeology* 113(July/August): 18–23.

Kiddey, R., and J. Schofield. 2011. Embrace the Margins: Adventures in Archaeology and Homelessness. *Public Archaeology* 10: 4–22.

Kristiansen, K. 2014. Towards a New Paradigm? The Third Science Revolution and its Possible Consequences in Archaeology. *Current Swedish Archaeology* 22: 11–34.

Last, J. 2013. Longhouse Lifestyles in the Central European Neolithic. In C. Fowler, J. Harding, and D. Hofmann, eds., *The Oxford Handbook of Neolithic Europe*. Pp. 273–89. Oxford: Oxford University Press.

Latour, B. 1993. *We Have Never Been Modern*. Cambridge, MA: Harvard University Press.

Latour, B. 1999. *Pandora's Hope: Essays on the Reality of Science Studies*. Cambridge, MA: Harvard University Press.

Latour, B. 2005. *Assembling the Social: An Introduction to Actor Network Theory*. Oxford: Oxford University Press.

Latour, B. 2013. *An Enquiry into Modes of Existence: An Anthropology of the Moderns*. Cambridge, MA: Harvard University Press.

Lawson, A. 2000. *Potterne 1982–5: Animal Husbandry in Later Prehistoric Wiltshire, Wessex Archaeology Report No. 17*. Salisbury: The Trust for Wessex Archaeology.

Ledger, P., L. Girdland-Flink, and V. Forbes. 2019. New Horizons at L'Anse aux Meadows. *PNAS* 116: 15341–3.

Lekakis, S. 2019. The Archaeology of In-Between Places: Finds Under the Ilissos River Bridge in Athens. *Journal of Greek Media & Culture* 5: 151–84.

Leone, M.P. 1988. The Georgian Order as the Order of Merchant Capitalism in Annapolis, Maryland. In M.P. Leone and P.B. Potter Jr., eds., *The Recovery of Meaning: Historical Archaeology in the Eastern United States*. Pp. 235–62. Washington, DC: Smithsonian Institution Press.

Leone, M.P. 1995. A Historical Archaeology of Capitalism. *American Anthropologist* 97: 251–68.

Leone, M.P. 2010. *Critical Historical Archaeology*. Walnut Creek, CA: Left Coast Press.

Lepofsky, D., C.G. Armstrong, S. Greening, J. Jackley, J. Carpenter, B. Gurensey, D. Matthews, and N.J. Turner. 2017. Historical Ecology of Cultural Keystone Places of the Northwest Coast. *American Anthropologist* 119: 448–63.

Lett, E., E.N. Asabor, R. Corbin, and D. Boatright. 2021. Racial Inequity in Fatal US Police Shootings, 2015–2020. *Journal of Epidemiological Community Health* 75: 394–7.

Lewonton, R.C. 1972. The Apportionment of Human Diversity. In T. Dobzhansky, M.K. Hecht, and W.C. Steere, eds., *Evolutionary Biology*. Pp. 381–98. New York: Springer. doi. org/10.1007/978-1-4684-9063-3_14.

Lightfoot, K.G. 2013. Rethinking the Archaeology of Human/Environmental Interactions in Deep Time History. In P.R. Schmidt and S.A. Mrozowski, eds., *The Death of Prehistory*. Pp. 183–200. Oxford: Oxford University Press.

Lipson, M., A. Szécsényi-Nagy, S. Mallick, A. Pósa, B. Stégmár, V. Keerl, N. Rohland, K. Stewardson, M. Ferry, M. Michel, J. Oppenheirmer, N. Broomandkhosbackt, E. Harney, S. Nordenfelt, B. Llamas, B.G. Mende, K. Köhler, K. Oross, T. Marton, A. Osztás, J. Jakucs, T. Paluch, F. Horváth, P. Csengeri, J. Koós, K. Sebok, A. Anders, P. Raczky, J. Regenye, J.P. Barna, S. Fábian, G. Serlegi, Z. Toldi, E.G. Nagy, J. Dani, E. Molnár, G. Pálfi, L. Márk, B. Melegh, Z. Bánfai, L. Domboróczki, J. Fernández-Eraso, J.A. Mujika-Alustiza, C.A. Fernández, J.J. Echevarría, R. Bollongio, J. Orschiedt, K. Shierhold, H. Meller, A. Cooper, J. Burger, E. Bánffy, K.W. Alt, C. Lalueza-Fox, W. Haak, and D. Reich. 2017. Parallel Paleogenomic Transects Reveal Complex Genetic History of Early European Farmers. *Nature* 551: 368–72.

Little, B.J., and L.J. Zimmerman. 2010. In the Public Interest: Creating a More Activist, Civically Engaged Archaeology. In W. Ashmore, D. Lippert, and B. Mills, eds., *Voices in American Archaeology*. Pp. 131–59. Washington, DC: Society for American Archaeology.

Locker, A. 2000. Animal Bone. In A. Lawson, ed., *Potterne 1982–5: Animal Husbandry in Later Prehistoric Wiltshire, Wessex Archaeology Report No. 17*. Pp. 101–19. Salisbury: The Trust for Wessex Archaeology.

Lorimer, J. 2015. *Wildlife in the Anthropocene: Conservation After Nature*. Minneapolis: University of Minnesota Press.

Lucas, G. 2021. *Making Time: The Archaeology of Time Revisited*. London: Routledge.

Lucas, G. 2023. *Archaeological Situations: Archaeological Theory from the Inside Out*. London: Routledge.

Ludlow Collective. 2001. Archaeology at the Colorado Coal Field War, 1913–1914. In V. Buchli and G. Lucas, eds., *Archaeologies of the Contemporary Past*. Pp. 94–107. New York: Routledge.

Luiz, J. 2022. Clandestine, Ephemeral, Anonymous: Myths and Realities of the Intimate Economy of a Nineteenth-Century Boston Brothel. In J.A. Nyman, K.R. Fogle, and M.C. Beaudry, eds., *The Historical Archaeology of Shadow and Intimate Economies*. Pp. 214–38. Gainesville: University Press of Florida.

Lydon, J., and U.Z. Rizvi, eds. 2010. *Handbook of Postcolonial Archaeology*. New York: Routledge.

Maat, G., R.W. Mastwijk, and E.A. Van der Velde. 1997. On the Reliability of Non-Metrical Morphological Sex Determination of the Skull Compared with that of the Pelvis in the Low Countries. *International Journal of Osteoarchaeology* 7: 575–80.

MacLaughlin, S.M., and M.F. Bruce. 1990. The Accuracy of Sex Identification in European Skeletal Remains Using the Phenice Characters. *Journal of Forensic Science* 35: 1384–92.

Madgwick, R., J. Mulville, and R. Stevens. 2012. Diversity in Foddering Strategy and Herd Management in Late Bronze Age Britain: An Isotopic Investigation of Pigs and Other Fauna from Two Midden Sites. *Environmental Archaeology* 17: 126–40.

Magnani, M., A. Guttorm, and N. Magnani. 2018. Three-Dimensional, Community-Based Heritage Management of Indigenous Museum Collections: Archaeological Ethnography, Revitalization, and Repatriation at the Sámi Museum Siida. *Journal of Cultural Heritage* 31: 162–9.

Malm, A. 2019. *The Progress of this Storm: Nature and Society in a Warming World*. London: Verso.

Matthews, C.N. 2010. *The Archaeology of American Capitalism*. Gainesville: University of Florida Press.

Mauss, M. 1990. *The Gift: The Form and Reason for Exchange in Archaic Societies*. New York: W.W. Norton and Company.

May, S. 2019. Heritage, Endangerment and Participation: Alternative Futures in the Lake District. *International Journal of Heritage Studies* 26: 71–86.

McAtackney, L. 2014. *An Archaeology of the Troubles: The Dark Heritage of Long Key/ Maze*. Oxford: Oxford University Press.

McAtackney, L., and R. McGuire, eds. 2020. *Walling In and Walling Out: Why Are We Building New Barriers to Divide Us?* Santa Fe: SAR Press.

McCobb, L., D. Briggs, W. Carruthers, and R. Evershed. 2003. Phosphatisation of Seeds and Toots in a Late Bronze Age Deposit at Potterne, Wiltshire, UK. *Journal of Archaeological Science* 30: 1269–81.

McGhee, R. 2008. Aboriginalism and the Problems of Indigenous Archaeology. *American Antiquity* 73: 579–97.

McGovern, T.H. 1990. Archaeology of the Norse Atlantic. *Annual Review of Anthropology* 19: 331–51.

McGuire, R.H. 1992. *A Marxist Archaeology*. Clinton Corners, NY: Percheron Press.

McGuire, R.H. 2006. Marxism and Capitalism in Historical Archaeology. In D. Hicks and M.C. Beaudry, eds., *The Cambridge Companion to Historical Archaeology*. Pp. 123–42. Cambridge: Cambridge University Press.

McGuire, R.H. 2008. *Archaeology as Political Action*. Berkeley: University of California Press.

McGuire, R.H. 2013. Steel Walls and Picket Fences: Rematerializing the U.S.—Mexican Border in Ambos Nogales. *American Anthropologist* 115: 466–80.

McGuire, R.H. 2018. Bearing Witness on the US-Mexico Border. *American Anthropologist* 120: 541–2.

McGuire, R.H., and P. Reckner. 2002. The Unromantic West: Labor, Capital, and Struggle. *Historical Archaeology* 36: 44–58.

McGuire, R.H., and R. Van Dyke. 2019. Crossing la Línea: Bodily Encounters with the U.S.-México Border in Ambos Nogales. In T. Sheridan and R. McGuire, eds., *The Border and its Bodies: The Embodiment of the Risk along the U.S.-México Line*. Pp. 41–70. Tucson: University of Arizona Press.

Mears, D.P., J.C. Cochran, W.D. Bales, and A.S. Bhati. 2016. Recidivism and Time Served in Prison. *The Journal of Criminal Law and Criminology* 106: 83–124.

Mirazón Lahr, M., R. Rivera, R. Power, A. Mounier, B. Copsey, F. Crivellaro, J. Edung, J. Maillo Fernandez, C. Kiarie, J. Lawrence, A. Leakey, E. Mbua, H. Miller, A. Muigai, D. Mukhongo, A. Van Baelen, R. Wood, J-L Schwenninger, R. Grün, R., H. Achyuthan, A. Wilshaw, and R. Foley. 2016. Inter-Group Violence Among Early Holocene Hunter-Gatherers of West Turkana, Kenya. *Nature* 529: 394–8.

Missing Migrant Project. 2023. *Migration Within the Mediterranean*, https://missingmigrants.iom.int/region/mediterranean. Accessed August 12, 2023.

Mitchell, P. 2008. Practicing Archaeology at a Time of Climatic Catastrophe. *Antiquity* 82: 1093–103.

Mittnik, A., K. Massy, C. Knipper, F. Wittenborn, R. Friedrich, S. Pfrengle, M. Burni, N. Carlichi-Witjes, H. Deeg, A. Furtwängler, M. Harbeck, K. Von Heyking, C. Kociumaka, S, Lindauer, S. Metz, A. Staskiewics, A. Thiel, J. Wahl, W. Haak, E. Pernicka, S. Schiffels, P.W. Stockhammer, and J. Krause. 2019. Kinship-Based Social Inequality in Bronze Age Europe. *Science* 366(6466): 731–4. doi: 10.1126/science.aax6219.

Mol, E. 2023. New Materialism and Posthumanism in Roman Archaeology: When Objects Speak for Others. *Cambridge Archaeological Journal*. doi: 10.1017/S0959774323000124. Accessed June 24, 2023.

Montoya, J. 2001. Terracotta Figurines from the Pyramid of the Moon at Teotihuacan, Mexico. *Foundation for the Advancement of Mesoamerican Studies, Inc. (FAMSI) Report*, http://www.famsi.org/reports/98060/index.html. Accessed June 23, 2023.

Moshenska, G., and S. Shelly. 2020. Notes for an Archaeology of Discarded Drug Paraphernalia. *Archaeology International* 23: 104–21.

Mrozowski, S.A. 2006a. Environments of History: Biological Dimensions of Historical Archaeology. In M. Hall and S.W. Silliman, eds., *Historical Archaeology*. Pp. 23–41. Malden, MA: Blackwell.

Mrozowski, S.A. 2006b, *The Archaeology of Class in Urban America*. Cambridge: Cambridge University Press.

Nanoglou, S. 2008. Representation of Humans and Animals in Greece and the Balkans During the Early Neolithic. *Cambridge Archaeological Journal* 18: 1–13.

Needham, S., J. Kenny, G. Cole, J. Montgomery, M. Jay, M. Davis, and P. Marshall. 2017. Death by Combat at the Dawn of the Bronze Age? Profiling the Dagger-Accompanied Burial from Racton, West Sussex. *The Antiquaries Journal* 97: 65–117.

Nilsson Stutz, L. 2018. A Future for Archaeology: In Defense of an Intellectually Engaged, Collaborative and Confident archaeology. *Norwegian Archaeological Review* 51: 48–56.

Nugent, R. 2019. Emotion and the Senses in Archaeology. In R. Skeates and J. Day, eds., *The Routledge Handbook of Sensory Archaeology*. Pp. 109–29. London: Routledge.

O'Dell, Y.V., and O.J.T. Harris. 2022. What Can a [Feminist] Body Do? Immanent and Emergent Capacities of Bodies at Chinchorro and Wor Barrow. *Cambridge Archaeological Journal* 32: 295–303.

Olalde, I., S. Brace, M.E. Allentoft, et al. 2018. The Beaker Phenomenon and the Genomic Transformation of Northwest Europe. *Nature* 555: 190.

Oliver, J. 2007. Beyond the Water's Edge: Towards a Social Archaeology of Landscape on the Northwest Coast. *Canadian Journal of Archaeology* 31: 1–27.

Olsen, B., M. Shanks, T. Webmoor, and C. Witmore. 2012. *Archaeology: The Discipline of Things*. Berkeley: University of California Press.

Osgood, R. 2023. *Broken Pots Mending Lives: The Archaeology of Operation Nightingale*. Oxford: Oxbow.

Otterbein, K.F. 1997. The Origins of War. *Critical Review* 11: 251–77.

Otterbein, K.F. 2004. *How War Began*. College Station: Texas A&M University Press.

Panich, L.M., and S.L. Gonzalez, eds. 2021. *The Routledge Handbook of the Archaeology of Indigenous-Colonial Interaction in the Americas*. New York: Routledge.

Parker Pearson, M. 2012. *Stonehenge: Exploring the Greatest Stone Age Mystery*. New York: Simon and Schuster.

Pauketat, T. 2007. *Chiefdoms and Other Archaeological Delusions*. Walnut Creek, CA: AltaMira Press.

Pétursdóttir, Þ. 2017. Climate Change? Archaeology and Anthropocene. *Archaeological Dialogues* 24: 175–205.

Pétursdóttir, Þ. 2020. Anticipated Futures? Knowing the Heritage of Drift Matter. *International Journal of Heritage Studies* 26: 87–103.

Pétursdóttir, Þ., and B. Olsen. 2018. Theory Adrift: The Matter of Archaeological Theorizing. *Journal of Social Archaeology* 18: 97–117.

Porr, M. 2018. Country and Relational Ontology in the Kimberley Northwest Australia: Implications for Understanding and Representing Archaeological Evidence. *Cambridge Archaeological Journal* 28: 395–409.

Posnansky, A. 1945. *Tihuanacu: The Cradle of American Man*. New York: J.J. Augustin.

Preucel, R.W. 2006. *Archaeological Semiotics*. Malden, MA: Blackwell.

Preucel, R.W., and A.A. Bauer. 2001. Archaeological Pragmatics. *Norwegian Archaeological Review* 34: 85–96.

Preucel, R.W., and S.A. Mrozowski, eds. 2010. *Contemporary Archaeology in Theory: The New Pragmatism*. Malden, MA: Wiley-Blackwell.

Puar, J. 2017. *Terrorist Assemblages: Homonationalism in Queer Times*. Durham, NC: Duke University Press.

Questions Worth Asking Symposium. 2023. Advocating for Archaeology's New Purpose. *Sapiens*, https://www.sapiens.org/archaeology/archaeological-reclamation/?fbclid=IwAR00cWvIMkYmUyRtU2baWymP7lMUlFGJdh0CvII9f74ZWsafRDEt-2pHakw. Accessed June 15, 2023.

Rathbone, S. 2017. Anarchist Literature and the Development of Anarchist Counter-Archaeologies. *World Archaeology* 49: 291–305.

Reader, C.D. 2000. A Geomorphological Study of the Giza Necropolis, with Implications for the Development of the Site. *Archaeometry* 43: 149–65.

Reed, K., and P. Ryan. 2019. Lessons from the Past and the Future of Food. *World Archaeology* 51: 1–16.

Reilly, M.C. 2019. Futurity, Time and Archaeology. *Journal of Contemporary Archaeology* 6(1): 1–15.

Rein, L. 2017. Here Are the Photos That Show Obama's Inauguration Crowd Was Bigger Than Trump's. *Washington Post*, March 7, 2017, https://www.washingtonpost.com/news/powerpost/wp/2017/03/06/here-are-the-photos-that-show-obamas-inauguration-crowd-was-bigger-than-trumps/. Accessed June 23, 2023.

Renfrew, C. 1973a. Monuments, Mobilization and Social Organization in Neolithic Wessex. In C. Renfrew, ed., *The Explanation of Cultural Change: Models in Prehistory*. Pp. 539–58. London: Duckworth.

Renfrew, C. 1973b. *Before Civilization: The Radiocarbon Revolution and Prehistoric Europe*. New York: A.A. Knoff.

Ribeiro, A. 2016a. Against Object Agency. A Counterreaction to Sørensen's 'Hammers and nails.' *Archaeological Dialogues* 23: 229–35.

Ribeiro, A. 2016b. Archaeology Will Be Just Fine. *Archaeological Dialogues* 23: 146–51.

Ribeiro, A. 2022. *Archaeology and Intentionality: Understanding Ethics and Freedom in Past and Present Societies*. London: Routledge.

Rizvi, U.Z. 2019. Archaeological Encounters: The Role of the Speculative in Decolonial Archaeology. *Journal of Contemporary Archaeology* 6: 154–67.

Robb, J.E., and O.J.T. Harris. 2018. Becoming Gendered in European Prehistory: Was Neolithic Gender Fundamentally Different? *American Antiquity* 83: 128–47.

Roberts, P., A. Buhrich, V. Caetano-Andrade, R. Cosgrove, A. Fairbairn, S.A. Florin, N. Vanwezer, N. Boivin, B. Hunter, D. Mosquito, G. Turpin, and Å Ferrier. 2021. Reimagining the Relationship Between Gondwanan Forests and Aboriginal Land Management in Australia's "Wet Tropics." *iScience* 24: 102190.

Rockman, M., and C. Hritz. 2020. Expanding Use of Archaeology in Climate Change Response by Changing Its Social Environment. *PNAS* 117: 8295–305.

Roddick, A.P., and J.W. Janusek. 2018. Moving Between Homes: Landscape, Mobility, and Political Action in the Titicaca Basin. In J. Jennings and E.R. Swenson, eds., *Powerful Places in the Ancient Andes*. Pp. 287–322. Albuquerque: University of New Mexico Press.

Rolland, N., and H.L. Dibble. 1990. A New Synthesis of Middle Paleolithic Variability. *American Antiquity* 55: 480–99.

Rorty, R. 1990. *Objectivity, Relativism, and Truth*. Cambridge: Cambridge University Press.

Rose, D.B. 2004. *Reports from a Wild Country. Ethics for Decolonization*. Sydney: University of New South Wales.

Rousseau, J.J. 1984 [1755]. *A Discourse on Inequality*. Translated by M. Cranston. London: Penguin Books.

Rowley-Conwy, P. 2007. *From Genesis to Prehistory. The Archaeological Three Age System and Its Contested Reception in Denmark, Britain, and Ireland*. Oxford: Oxford University Press.

Rowley-Conwy, P. n.d. Mesolithic Landscapes and Niche Construction: A Great Capability for Misunderstanding. In L. Nilsson Stutz, R. Peyroteo Stjerna, and M. Tõrv, eds., *The Oxford Handbook of Mesolithic Europe*. Oxford: Oxford University Press.

Ruddiman, W.F. 2003. The Anthropogenic Greenhouse Era Began Thousands of Years Ago. *Climatic Change* 61: 261–93.

Sabloff, J.A. 2008. *Archaeology Matters: Action Archaeology in the Modern World*. New York: Routledge.

Sahlins, M., and Service, E. 1960. *Evolution and Culture*. Ann Arbor: University of Michigan Press.

Saitta, D. 2007. *The Archaeology of Collective Action*. Gainesville: University Press of Florida.

Scerri, E.M.L., and M. Will. 2023. The Revolution That Still Isn't: The Origins of Behavioral Complexity in *Homo sapiens. Journal of Human Evolution* 179: 103358.

Schulte to Bühne, H., N. Pettorelli, and M. Hoffmann. 2022. The Policy Consequences of Defining Rewilding. *Ambio* 51: 93–102.

Scott, S. 2001. *The Corpus of Terracotta Figurines from Sigvald Linné's Excavations at Teotihuacan, Mexico (1932 & 1934–1935) and Comparative Material*. Stockholm: The National Museum of Ethnography.

Sear, D.A., M.S. Allen, J.D. Hassall, A.E. Maloney, P.G. Langdon, A.E. Morrison, A.C.G. Henderson, et al. 2020. Human Settlement of East Polynesia Earlier, Incremental, and Coincident with Prolonged South Pacific Drought. *Proceedings of the National Academy of Sciences* 117: 8813–19.

Shackel, P. 1994. Interdisciplinary Approaches to the Meanings and Uses of Material Goods in Lower Town Harpers Ferry. *Historical Archaeology* 28: 3–15.

Shackel, P. 2000. Craft to Wage Labor: Agency and Resistance in American Industrial Archaeology. In M.A. Dobres and J. Robb, eds., *Agency and Archaeology*. Pp. 232–46. New York: Routledge.

Shanks, M., and C. Tilley. 1982. Ideology, Symbolic Power and Ritual Communication: A Reinterpretation of Neolithic Mortuary Practices. In I. Hodder, ed., *Symbolic and Structural Archaeology*. Pp. 129–54. Cambridge: Cambridge University Press.

Shanks, M., and C. Tilley. 1987a. *Re-Constructing Archaeology: Theory and Practice*. London: Routledge.

Shanks, M., and C. Tilley. 1987b. *Social Theory and Archaeology*. Oxford: Polity Press.

Simonetti, C., and M. Edgeworth. 2022. *Concrete: A Stratigraphic Marker for the Anthropocene*, https://www.anthropocene-curriculum.org/contribution/concrete-a-stratigraphic-marker-for-the-anthropocene. Accessed June 23, 2023.

Singleton, C.E. 2017. Encountering Home: A Contemporary Archaeology of Homelessness. In L. McAtackney and K. Ryzewski, eds., *Contemporary Archaeology and the City: Creativity, Ruination, and Political Action*. Pp. 229–43. Oxford: Oxford University Press.

Singleton, C.E. 2021. '*Vague Dwelling: An Archaeology of The Pelham Bay Park Homeless Encampment.*' Unpublished PhD Dissertation, Anthropology Department, Columbia University.

Singleton, T.A., ed. 1999. "*I, Too, Am America:*" *Archaeological Studies of African American Life*. Charlottesville: University of Virginia Press.

Singleton, T.A. 2006. *Before the Revolution: Archaeology and the African Diaspora on the Atlantic Seaboard*. In T. Pauketat and D. DiPaolo Loren, eds., *North American Archaeology*. Pp. 319–36. Malden, MA: Blackwell.

Skak-Nielsen, N.V. 2009. Flint and Metal Daggers in Scandinavia and Other Parts of Europe. A Re-Interpretation of Their Function in the Late Neolithic and Early Copper and Bronze Age. *Antiquity* 83: 349–58.

Skoglund, P., J. Storå, A. Götherström, and M. Jakobsson. 2013. Accurate Sex Identification of Ancient Human Remains Using DNA Shotgun Sequencing. *Journal of Archaeological Science* 40: 4477–82.

Slon, V., F. Mafessoni, B. Vernot, C. de Filippo, S. Grote, B. Viola, M. Hajdinjak, S. Peyrégne, S. Nagel, S. Brown, K. Douka, T. Higham, M.B. Kozlikin, M.V. Shunkov, A.P. Derevianko, J. Kelso, M. Meyer, K. Prüfer, and S. Pääbo. 2018. The Genome of the Offspring of a Neanderthal Mother and a Denisovan Father. *Nature* 561: 113–16.

Smith, L.T. 2006. *Uses of Heritage*. London: Routledge.

Smith, L.T. 2012. *Decolonizing Methodologies: Research and Indigenous Peoples*. London: Zed Books.

Smith, R.Z., C. Tammaro, and C.N. Cipolla. 2016. *Remembering Ancient Ceramic Traditions*. Royal Ontario Museum Blog Post, https://www.rom.on.ca/en/blog/remembering-ancient-pottery-traditions. Accessed June 15, 2013.

Sofaer, J. 2006. *The Body as Material Culture: A Theoretical Osteoarcheology*. Cambridge: Cambridge University Press.

Spector, J. 1993. *What This Awl Means: Feminist Archaeology at a Wahpeton Dakota Village*. St. Paul, MN: Minnesota Historical Society Press.

Spikins, P., B. Wright, and D. Hodgson. 2016. Are There Alternative Adaptive Strategies to Human Pro-Sociality? The Role of Collaborative Morality in the Emergence of Personality Variation and Autistic Traits. *Time and Mind* 9: 289–313.

Spinapolice, E. 2020. Lithic Variability and Cultures in the East African Middle Stone Age. In H.S. Groucutt, ed., *Culture History and Convergent Evolution*. Pp. 87–102. New York: Springer.

Squier, E.G., and E.H. Davis. 1848. *Ancient Monuments of the Mississippi Valley*. Washington, DC: Smithsonian Institute.

Starblanket, G. 2017. Being Indigenous Feminists: Resurgences Against Contemporary Patriarchy. In J. Green, ed., *Making Space for Indigenous Feminisms*. Pp. 21–41. Black Point, Nova Scotia: Fernwood.

Steeves, P.F.C. 2015. Decolonizing the Past and Present of the Western Hemisphere (The Americas). *Archaeologies* 11: 42–69.

Steeves, P.F.C. 2021. *The Indigenous Paleolithic of the Western Hemisphere*. Lincoln, NE: University of Nebraska Press.

Steinburg, J.M., D.J. Bolender, and B.N. Damiata. 2018. Getting It Wrong for All the Right Reasons: Developing an Approach to Systematic Settlement Survey for Viking Age Iceland. In S.W. Silliman, ed., *Engaging Archaeology: 25 Case Studies in Research Practice*. Pp. 31–40. Malden, MA: Wiley.

Sterling, K. 2015. Black Feminist Theory in Prehistory. *Archaeologies* 11: 93–120.

Stewart, H.E., I. Ostericher, C. Cokee, and J. De León. 2016. Surveilling Surveillance: Counter-Mapping Undocumented Migration in the USA-Mexico Borderlands. *Journal of Contemporary Archaeology* 3: 159–74.

Stottman, M.J. 2010. *Archaeologists as Activists: Can Archaeologists Change the World?* Tuscaloosa: University of Alabama Press.

Stratton, S. 2016. "Seek and You Shall Find." How the Analysis of Gendered Patterns in Archaeology Can Create False Binaries: A Case Study from Durankulak. *Journal of Archaeological Method and Theory* 23: 854–69.

Supernant, K., J.E. Baxter, N. Lyons, and S. Atalay, eds. 2020. *Archaeologies of the Heart*. New York: Springer.

Swenson, E. 2018. Trace, Revelation, and Interpretant in Archaeological Research: The Graffiti of Huaca Colorada, Peru. *Signs and Society* 6: 349–78.

Tallbear, K. 2011. SACNAS: Beyond "Diversity and Inclusion," Making Science More Multicultural and Democratic. *Blog Post*, https://indigenoussts.com/sacnas-beyond-diversity-and-inclusion-making-science-more-multicultural-and-democratic/. Accessed June 6, 2023.

Tallbear, K. 2013. *Native American DNA: Tribal Belonging and the False Promise of Genetic Science*. Minneapolis: University of Minnesota Press.

Tallbear, K. 2014. Standing With and Speaking as Faith: A Feminist-Indigenous Approach to Inquiry. *Journal of Research Practice* 10(Article N17), http://jrp.icaap.org/index.php/jrp/article/view/405/371. Accessed June 23, 2023.

Tallbear, K. 2017. Beyond the Life/Not-Life Binary: A Feminist-Indigenous Reading of Cryopreservation, Interspecies Thinking, and the New Materialisms. In J. Radin and E. Kowal, eds., *Cryopolitics: Frozen Life in a Melting World*. Pp. 179–202. Cambridge, MA: MIT Press.

Thomas, C. 1894. *Report on the Mound Explorations of the Bureau of Ethnology*. Washington, DC: Bureau of American Ethnology.

Thomas, J. 2002. Taking Power Seriously. In M. O'Donovan, ed., *The Dynamics of Power*. Pp. 35–50. Carbondale, IL: Southern Illinois University Press.

Thomas, J. 2004. *Archaeology and Modernity*. London: Routledge.

Thomas, J. 2015. The Future of Archaeological Theory. *Antiquity* 89: 1287–96.

Thompson, E.L. 2022. *Smashing Statues: The Rise and Fall of America's Public Monuments*. New York: Norton.

Todd, Z. 2016. An Indigenous Feminist's Take on The Ontological Turn: 'Ontology' Is Just Another Word for Colonialism. *Journal of Historical Sociology* 29: 4–22.

Trigger, B.G. 1984. Alternative Archaeologies: Nationalist, Colonialist, Imperialist. *Man* 19: 355–70.

Trigger, B.G. 2006. *A History of Archaeological Thought*, 2nd ed. Cambridge: Cambridge University Press.

Tsing, A.L. 2015. *The Mushroom at the End of the World: On the Possibility of Life in Capitalist Ruins*. Princeton: Princeton University Press.

Tsoraki, C., H. Barton, R.J. Crellin, and O.J.T. Harris. 2020. Making Marks Meaningful: New Materialism and the Microwear Assemblage. *World Archaeology* 52: 484–502.

Tsoraki, C., H. Barton, R.J. Crellin, and O.J.T. Harris. 2023. From Typology and Biography to Multiplicity: Bracers as "Process Objects". *Cambridge Archaeological Journal* Online first. doi: 10.1017/S0959774323000094.

Tuck, E., and K.W. Yang. 2012. Decolonization Is Not a Metaphor. *Decolonization: Indigeneity, Education & Society* 1: 1–40.

Tully, J. 2008. *Public Philosophy in a New Key: Democracy and Civic Freedom.* Cambridge: Cambridge University Press.

Tyrikos-Ergas, G. 2016. Orange Life Jackets: Materiality and Narration in Lesvos, One Year After the Eruption of the "Refugee Crisis." *Journal of Contemporary Archaeology* 3: 227–32.

Ubelaker, D.H., and C.M. DeGaglia. 2017. Population Variation in Skeletal Sexual Dimorphism. *Forensic Science International* 407: e1–e407.

UN Women. 2021. *Prevalence and Reporting of Sexual Harassment in UK Public Spaces: A Report by the APPG for UN Women*, https://www.unwomenuk.org/appg-unwomen. Accessed June 23, 2023.

US Border Patrol. 1994. Border Patrol Strategic Plan 1994 and Beyond. *Homeland Security National Strategy.* Accessed June 23, 2023.

Vaillant, G.C. 1931. *Excavations at Ticoman.* New York: American Museum of Natural History.

Valado, M.T. 2006. *Factors Influencing Homeless People's Perception and Use of Space.* Unpublished Doctoral Dissertation, Anthropology Department, Tucson, University of Arizona.

Van Dyke, R.M., ed. 2015. *Practicing Materiality.* Tucson: University of Arizona Press.

Van Dyke, R.M. 2021. Ethics, Not Objects. *Cambridge Archaeological Journal* 31: 487–93.

Van Heerden, C.G., and A. Eloff, eds. 2019. *Deleuze and Anarchism.* Edinburgh: Edinburgh University Press.

Vandkilde, H. 2013. Warfare in Northern European Bronze Age Societies: Twentieth-Century Presentations and Recent Archaeological Research Inquiries. In S. Ralph, ed., *The Archaeology of Violence: Interdisciplinary Approaches.* Pp. 37–62. New York: State University of New York Press.

Vaquero, M., J. Vallverdú, J. Rosell, I. Pastó, and E. Allué. 2001. Neandertal Behavior at the Middle Palaeolithic Site of Abric Romaní, Capellades, Spain. *Journal of Field Archaeology* 28: 93–114.

Viveiros de Castro, E. 1998. Cosmological Deixis and Amerindian Perspectivism. *Journal of the Royal Anthropological Institute* 4: 469–88.

Viveiros de Castro, E. 2014. *Cannibal Metaphysics.* Minneapolis: University of Minnesota Press.

Vizenor, G.R. 1994. *Manifest Manners: Postindian Warriors of Survivance.* Middletown, CT: Wesleyan University Press.

Voss, B. 2008. Gender, Race and Labor in the Archaeology of the Spanish Colonial Americas. *Current Anthropology* 49: 861–93.

Vranich, A. 2004. The Development of the Ritual Core of Tiwanaku. In M. Young-Sánchez, ed., *Tiwanaku.* Pp. 11–34. Denver: Denver Museum of Art.

Walker, P.L. 2005. Greater Sciatic Notch Morphology: Sex, Age, and Population Differences. *American Journal of Physical Anthropology* 127: 385–91.

Wallace, B. 2003. The Norse in Newfoundland: L'Anse aux Meadows and Vinland. *Newfoundland and Labrador Studies* 19: 5–43.

Wallace, T., K. Yourish, and T. Griggs. 2017. Trump's Inauguration vs. Obama's: Comparing the Crowds. *The New York Times*, January 20, 2017, https://www.nytimes.com/interactive/2017/01/20/us/politics/trump-inauguration-crowd.html. Accessed June 23, 2023.

Watson, P.J., S.A. LeBlanc, and C.L. Redman. 1974. The Covering Law Model in Archaeology: Practical Uses and Formal Interpretations. *World Archaeology* 6: 125–32.

Watts, C.M. 2008. On Mediation and Material Agency in the Peircean Semiotic. In C. Knappett and L. Malafouris, eds., *Material Agency: Toward a Non-Anthropocentric Approach*. Pp. 187–207. New York: Springer.

Watts, V. 2013. Indigenous Place-Thought & Agency Amongst Humans and Non-Humans (First Woman and Sky Woman Go on a European World Tour!). *Decolonization: Indigeneity, Education & Society* 2: 20–34.

Webmoor, T., and C.L. Witmore. 2008. Things are Us! A Commentary on Human/Things Relations Under the Banner of a "Social Archaeology." *Norwegian Archaeological Review* 41: 53–70.

White, T.D., and P.A. Folkens. 2005. *The Human Bone Manual*. London: Elsevier Academic Press.

Whittle, A. 1996. *Europe in the Neolithic: The Creation of New Worlds*. Cambridge: Cambridge University Press.

Whittle, A. 2003. *The Archaeology of People: Dimensions of Neolithic Life*. London: Routledge.

Whittle, A., A. Bayliss, and M. Wysocki. 2007. Once in a Lifetime: The Date of the Wayland's Smithy Long Barrow. *Cambridge Archaeological Journal* 17: 103–21.

Wilkinson, D. 2017. Is There Such a Thing as Animism? *Journal of the American Academy of Religion* 85: 289–311.

Wilkinson, T.A.H. 2000. Comment on C. D. Reader, 'A Geomorphological Study of Giza, Necropolis, with Implications for the Development of the Site. *Archaeometry* 43: 161–3.

Will, M., A.W. Kandel, and N.J. Conard. 2019. Midden or Molehill: The Role of Coastal Adaptations for Human Evolution and Dispersal. *Journal of World Prehistory* 32: 33–72.

Wilson, J.P., K. Hugenberg, and N.O. Rule. 2017. Racial Bias in Judgements of Physical Size and Formidability: From Size to Threat. *Journal of Personality and Social Psychology* 113: 59–80.

Wilson, S. 2020. *Research is Ceremony: Indigenous Research Methods*. Black Point, Nova Scotia: Fernwood Publishing.

Winterton, S. 2014. From the Army Medical Centre to Operation Nightingale: My Entry into Archaeology. *Journal of Community Archaeology and Heritage* 1: 245–7.

Witmore, C. 2019. Hypanthropos: On Apprehending and Approaching That Which Is in Excess of Monstrosity, with Special Consideration Given to the Photography of Edward Burtynsky. *Journal of Contemporary Archaeology* 6: 136–53.

Wolf, E.R. 2010. *Europe and the People Without History*, 2nd ed. Berkeley: University of California Press.

Wollentz, G., S. May, C. Holtorf, and A. Höberg. 2020. Toxic Heritage: Uncertain and Unsafe. In R. Harrison, C. DeSilvey, C. Holtorf, S. MacDonald, N. Bartolini, E. Breithoff, H. Fredheim, A. Lyons, S. May, J. Morgan, and S. Penrose, eds., *Heritage Futures: Comparative Approaches to Natural and Cultural Heritage Practices*. Pp. 294–312. London: UCL Press.

World Food Programme. n.d. *Ending Hunger*, https://www.wfp.org/ending-hunger. Accessed June 23, 2023.

Wurst, L. 2019. Should Archaeology Have a Future? *Journal of Contemporary Archaeology* 6: 168–81.

Wylie, A. 2012. Feminist Philosophy of Science: Standpoint Matters. *Proceedings and Addresses of the American Philosophical Association* 86: 47–76.

Wylie, A. 2020. Radiocarbon Dating in Archaeology: Triangulation and Traceability. In S. Leonelli and N. Tempini, eds., *Data Journeys in the Sciences*. Pp. 285–301. New York: Springer.

Young-Sánchez, M., ed. 2004. *Tiwanaku: Ancestors of the Inca*. Denver: Denver Art Museum.

Yusoff, K. 2018. *A Billion Black Anthropocenes or None*. Minneapolis: University of Minnesota Press.

Zalasiewicz, J., M. William, C.N. Water, A.D. Barnosky, and P. Haff. 2014. The Technofossil Record of Humans. *The Anthropocene Review* 1: 34–43.

Zimmerman, L.J., C. Singleton, and J. Welch. 2010. Activism and Creating a Translational Archaeology of Homelessness. *World Archaeology* 42: 443–54.

Index

Note: Page numbers in *italics* indicate a figure.

#noDAPL *see* Dakota Access Pipeline

academia 3, 174–6
Acebo, Nathan 72, 82–5, 168
activist archaeology 8, 177–8
actual, 80–2, 84–7, 168; *see also* virtual
aDNA 8, 24, 26, 73, 114–15, 123–4, 138
affect 149, 155–7, 160–1, 170
agency 28, 53, 66–7, 86, 148, 157
Ahay:da 78–80, 86–7, 174
alterity, radical 133–7, 142–3, 170;
    see also difference
anarchist archaeology 9, 54, 55–6,
    60–2, 68, 123
Anthropocene 14, 147–64, 170
anthropocentrism 10–11, 14, 32, 60–2,
    163, 173–7
antiquarians 89
anti-racist 10, 12, 13
archaeological data 5, 11, 60, 96, 102–4,
    109, 114–15, 117, 124, 142, 149,
    169, 178
archaeological record 58, 73, 84, *112*, 113,
    117, 138–9, 156, 165
archaeological theory, 1–16, 18, 58, 71, 92,
    93, 177
archaeology of the contemporary world
    8–9, 18, 30–2, 49
assemblage theory 28–31, 33, 75, 102, 166
Australia 19, 128–30, 136, 139, *148*,
    150, 174
authority 53–4, 62, 68, 84, 112, 127
autism 91, 98, 104

Barad, Karen 5
Black Feminism 5, 129, 137–9, 142, 170
blame 30–2, 61, 71–2, 76, 86, 118, 157

BLM 72, 77, 80
Braidotti, Rosi, 54, 133, 153–4, 157, 169,
    177, 179
Bronze Age 8, 18, 52, 55, 64–7, 68, 74,
    109, 111, 113, 124, 157, 167–8
burial practices 58, 64–7, *65*, 100, 109,
    112–16, 129, 167

capitalism 1, 3, 5, 7–8, 30, 31, 35–52, 56,
    82, 94, 127, 130, 150, 153, 162,
    167, 172–3
care 4, 87, 99, 132–3, 139, 149, 158, 161,
    171, 177–9
classification 36, 92–3, 94–5, 96, 169
climate crisis 7, 10, 11, 12, 14, 61,
    147–64, 173
collaboration 5, 14, 28, 47, 99, 127–46,
    166–7, 170, 174
colonialism 1–2, 4, 8, 19–21, 25, 32, 38,
    55, 83–4, 94, 127, 130–1, 154–5,
    168, 175
conflict archaeology 72–4, 81
Crossland, Zoë, 118–20, 163, 169
cultural evolution 23, 58, 64, 89, 94–5, 138
culture history 73

Dakota Access Pipeline 1–4, *2*, 174, 176–7
decolonization 3–4, 132
De León, Jason 18, 30–2, 144, 166, 173–7
Deleuze, Gilles 11, 29, 42–4, 49, 50, 60–1,
    81, 97, 133, 150–1, 168, 177, 178
Deloria Jr., Vine, 176
desire 35, 38, 41–9, 61–2, 95, 167
difference: cultural 134; negative (as lack)
    27, 75, 94; ontological 10, 127–46;
    positive 28, 33, 49, 89–108,
    127–46; radical, 127–46

DNA, 24, 73, 74, 128–9, 131–2, 137–9;
    see also aDNA
The Dreaming 130–1, 134, 136
dualisms 10, 62, 76, 92, 132, 148, 152,
    153–4, 156–7

Earth 111, 128, 134, 141, 147–8, 153,
    169, 179
emergence 11, 33, 44, 82, 117, 147
Estes, Nick, 1–4
Eurocentrism 26, 139, 154
expertise 109–12, 132, 176
explanation 58, 60, 85, 86–7, 89, 117, 122,
    123, 157

fake news 109–12, 127–9
feminism 5, 9, 10, 12, 13, 54, 75, 96, 112,
    114, 115, 169; in archaeology
    130; Black Feminism 5, 129,
    137–9, 142, 170; ecofeminism
    10, 149, 152–5, 156, 157, 162,
    170; Indigenous 128, 154–5, 156;
    posthuman 28, 97, 133, 165, 172
Ferrando, Francesca 154
figurines 99–104
firestorms 156
flow, 35–52
Floyd, George 77, 80, 174
forensics 30, 118–20
Foucault, Michel 115, 123, 131, 171
fur trade 37–8, 39, 43
future-oriented archaeologies 4–9, 38, 45,
    63, 156
futurity, 147–64

gender 5, 12, 18, 21, 43, 62, 98–104, 105,
    115–16, 124, 154, 174
Graeber, David, 9, 55–6, 74
Guattari, Félix, 11, 29, 42–4, 49, 50,
    60–1, 178

Haraway, Donna 5, 114, 132, 158, 169
hegemony 5, 15
heritage 8, 19, 21, 48, 49, 77, 129, 158,
    167, 170, 174
heterarchy 54–6, 58, 60–1, 68
hierarchy 18, 26–30, 39, 41, 53, 55–6, 58,
    60–1, 63–4, 67–8, 75–6, 94, 95,
    105, 132, 142, 153, 172, 177
historical archaeology 20–1, 37–41, 49–50
homelessness 12, 14, 35–52, 71, 128,
    166–7, 171, 172, 173, 178
human evolution 73, 91, 94, 98–9,
    104–5, 158

human exceptionalism 29, 175
humanism 18, 26–8, 75, 87, 133, 154,
    171–2
humanist Man 26–8, 33, 45, 48–50, 53–4,
    72, 75–6, 87, 94–5, 98, 104, 153,
    160–3, 166–7, 169, 171–3, 174
hylomorphism 92

iconoclasm 76–8, 77, 80
identity 28, 74, 96–7, 102–3, 172
ideology 37–41, 43–4, 48–9, 167
Indigenous critiques 10, 127–8, 131–3,
    154–6, 174–7
Indigenous knowledges 38, 85, 129–36,
    139–44, 153–4, 169–70,
    174, 176–7
Isle of Man 109, 112–16, 117, 151

Kiddey, Rachael 30, 46–50, 128,
    166–7, 179

L'Anse aux Meadows 22–3
Latour, Bruno 5, 38, 76, 86, 106, 129
leadership 14, 53–70, 84, 167–8, 178
Linearbandkeramik (LBK) 23–6, 24,
    28, 32–3
longhouse 23–6, 28, 33

Marxism 8, 39–41, 42, 49, 56, 60, 106, 167
materialism see Marxism; new materialism
migration 8, 13, 14, 17–34, 128, 171, 173
missing and murdered Indigenous woman
    and girls 154–5, 173
missions 20–1, 33, 84, 154
more-than-human, 17–34, 67, 71, 74–80,
    166, 173–7
mounds 64, 66–7
movement 13–14, 17–34, 43, 157, 166
multiplicity 12, 109–10, 137–44, 170, 177
museums 4, 72, 78–80, 89, 90, 120, 122,
    174, 176

nature 1, 7, 10, 19, 35, 37, 117, 139–42,
    147–64, 170, 177
neanderthal 95, 137–9, 142
Neolithic 8, 53, 64, 89, 93, 159
NeoMarxism see Marxism
new animism 129, 133–7
new archaeology see processual
    archaeology
new materialism 11, 28–9, 60–1, 71, 154,
    165, 176–7
non-humans 5, 11, 13, 14, 18, 25, 26–33,
    43, 49, 54–5, 60–3, 66–8, 71–68,

136, 150, 157, 158, 160, 163, 165–8, 172, 173–9
normative 43, 91–3
Norse 21–3, *22*, 25–6, 28, 32, 33
nuclear waste 157–62; *see also* waste

objectivity 92, 111–16, 125, 127, 129, 131, 132, 169
oil pipelines 1–4, 153, 155, 175–6
ontological turn 10, 63, 133–7, 142–3, 170
ontology 10, 61, 128–9, 132, 172

Paleolithic 13, 105, 129, 137–9
past for the present 7, 149–52
police 1, 3, 80–2, 109, 124, 167, 168, 177
politics 1–6, 7, 13, 17, 18, 24, 30, 42, 44, 47, 48, 53–70, 71, 73–7, 84, 98, 109, 116, 125, 129, 147, 173, 177
positionality 3, 4, 5, 9, 12–13, 94, 98, 109, 114–16, 120, 124–5, 128–30, 132, 162, 169, 174, 177
positivism 113
post-anthropocentrism 10–11, 28–9, 60, 72, 155, 157, 166, 168, 173–7
posthumanism 5, 9–12, 15, 28–9, 33, 60, 62, 72, 97, 128, 133, 149–50, 153–5, 160, 165–6, 171–3; critiques of 11, 85–6
postprocessual 92, 115
potentia 54, 60–2, 65–6, 68, 167–8, 179
potestas 54, 60–2, 65–6, 68, 167–8, 179
power 5, 14, 18, 25, 38–9, 40–1, 53–70, 71, 74, 84–5, 97, 104, 111–13, 116, 123, 129, 131, 143, 154, 159, 167–8, 172–3, 176, 178, 179
pragmatism 8
praxis 36, 40–1
prefiguration 60, 68, 155
processual archaeology 4, 91, 113
Protestant Reformation 76–7
pseudo-science 110, 121
Puhú 72, 82–5, *83*, 168
purification 38

race 5, 39, 94–6, 105
racism 5, 17, 27, 72, 77–8, 80, 82, 94–5, 138, 173
relational archaeologies 9–11, 28–33, 49, 54, 68, 71–2, 76, 79–80, 85–6, 97, 109–26, 131, 137, 142–3, 156–7, 166–9, 175
relativism 123, 134, 142–3

repatriation 176
resistance 2–3, 36, 40–1, 60, 78, 80, 82–5, 129, 162
rivers 97, 139, 149, 156

science and technology studies 5
sedentism 19, 22–5
settler colonialism *see* colonialism
sexuality 5, 43, 105
situated knowledge 5, 128, 131–44, 172, 174
Sky Woman, 134–5, *135*
slavery 39–40, 77–8, 94–6, 162, 172
Sonoran Desert 31, 166
Sphinx 120–3, *121*, 159
Standing Rock 1–4, 173–7
standpoint 4–5, 12, 14, 114–15, 137–42, 176–7

Tallbear, Kim 128, 131–3, 176–7
technology 28, 73, 104, 113, 116, 123, 138, 147, 151–2, 155, 156, 159, 160, 162, 170
Teotihuacan 99–105, *100–4*, 168–9
three-age system 89–91
Tiwanaku 55–60, *57*, *59*, 62–4, 66, 68
truth 11–12, 14, 82, 92, 109–26, 127–8, 131, 142–3, 161, 169–70
Turbo Island 47–8, 128, 166–7
typology 14, 89–108

Ukraine 23, 75, 81, 86, 138
Undocumented Migrant Project 30–2, 166
universities 3–4, 29, 42, 109, 174–5

Vanuatu 20–1, *20*, 33
Vikings *see* Norse
violence 1–3, 8, 14, 19, 29, 56–7, 66, 71–68, 132, 138, 143, 153, 155, 157, 168, 171, 173, 174; and human nature 73–4, 85–7
virtual, 80–2, 84–7, 168; *see also* actual
Vitruvian man 27, *27*, 133

waste 9, 149, 157–63, 165, 170–1, 179; *see also* nuclear waste
water is life 1–4, 177–9
wilderness 19, 139–42, 149–52

Zuni 78–80, 86–7, 174